MEN, WOMEN
AND
AUTHORITY

Serving together in the church

Editor: **Brian Edwards**

Series Editor: **Andrew Anderson**

Published in association with FIEC by

DayOnepublications

FACING THE ISSUE is a series of books designed to help Christians to think biblically on a variety of pressing issues that confront evangelicals at the present time. The themes are primarily theological but, as the Bible never teaches doctrine in isolation, all have a keen practical edge to them.

The series began its life in the cut and thrust of discussion in the Theological Committee of the Fellowship of Independent Evangelical Churches whose brief is to monitor and respond to challenges and changes in the world of evangelical theology. The committee, whose members currently are Brian Edwards (chair), Andrew Anderson, Paul Brown, Andrew Bryant, David Field, Stanley Jebb, Hywel Jones and Jonathan Stephen, commissions the writers, discusses their approach with them, and is available for consultation. Though united in our understanding of the gospel, we do not always come to exactly the same conclusions on every detail. So the views put forward by the authors do not necessarily reflect in every respect those of the committee or, for that matter, those of the FIEC or the Publisher.

The series is written with the general reader in mind and the books do not assume a background training in theology. They are, however, written by men of proven ability in grappling with important theological trends. We hope that each book will stimulate thought and action both controlled by the Bible.

Andrew Anderson
Series Editor

MEN, WOMEN
AND
AUTHORITY

Serving together in the church

Chapter 1

Where Are We Today?

Mark Johnston
Born in Northern Ireland Mark completed an honours degree in archaeology and ancient history at Queen's University, Belfast; this was followed by a period of study at Westminster Theological Seminary, Philadelphia, where he received a Master of Divinity degree. After ten years planting and pastoring an Evangelical Presbyterian Church in Ireland Mark was appointed as pastor of Grove Chapel, Camberwell, London in 1994. In March 1995 he chaired a British Evangelical Council Study Conference on 'The Bible and the role of women'. Mark is married to Fiona and they have two children.

Where Are We Today?

The trouble with 'Where are we?'-type questions is that their answers have a built-in 'shelf-life'. Where we are today is all too quickly overtaken by where we will be tomorrow. Nowhere is that more true than in the arena of changing attitudes to the role of women.

The twentieth century has seen a dramatic revolution in attitudes to the place and role of women in society. It began with women being denied the vote and being excluded from many areas of life seen as the domain of men, yet it is ending with virtually all areas of society being accessible to them. Whether it be in the board-room or even the Prime Minister's office, people both accept and expect that women will be there. The norms of society in this area, as well as many others, have been rewritten.

The revolution is far from over. Benefits experienced through women's liberation in Western countries are now regarded as a readily exportable commodity, so we find the battle for women's rights taking on global proportions. International congresses attract delegates from every conceivable kind of regime, coming to lobby for improved rights for women in their countries. Even governments which have had a history of being totalitarian and repressive now find themselves struggling to withstand the female cry for freedom. Like it or not, the women's issue is firmly on the agenda of every major nation of the world.

The church has not been immune to these pressures. The struggle for women's rights in the secular realm throughout this century has been paralleled by its counterpart in the ecclesiastical realm. Thus, if we are to understand fully the issues as they are being faced by Christians today, we need to make some attempt to see how they have been shaped and influenced by the wider sphere of thought. So, before we begin to concentrate on the issues as they have surfaced directly in the church - particularly in the evangelical context - we need to take a step back and consider how other concerns have impinged upon them.

It would be wise to reflect on problems which have been the cause of misunderstanding in the debate even before the issues themselves are properly addressed. We need to look - if only in the broadest terms - at the backdrop of the feminist movement in general and ask to what extent the discussion in the church has been fuelled by the discussion in the world. Taking that a little further, we need to acknowledge the spectrum of opinion that exists within the Christian world. There is certainly a distinction to be made between liberal Christian feminism and the variety which has sought to be more self-consciously biblical in its pronouncements. Then we need to dig deeper again and wrestle with the question of whether 'the women's issue' is only a women's issue, or part of a more complex problem which biblical Christians are facing today. Finally we ought to attempt to look, not just at where we happen to be on the road at this point in time, but where the road itself might be leading. In other words, we cannot avoid considering the consequences which are thrown up by this kind of debate.

From the start we need to be sensitive to issues which have led to misunderstanding and try to see if we can at least appreciate where people on different sides in the debate are coming from.

1. Preliminary Problems

The waters of this particular debate, perhaps more than any other in recent history, have been muddied by conflicting concerns. The very expression, 'The Women's Issue', is confusing because it needs to be qualified by the secondary question, 'Which one?' For one group the women's issue is a matter of political rights, for another it is a domestic concern, for another it revolves around the work-place and for yet another it is a question of sexual identity. Then in the Christian sphere, it becomes an issue of ecclesiastical opportunity. Thus it is inevitable, as we engage in the argument, that we must opt to focus on the particular concerns which we deem to be important. In the case of this book and the particular Christian slant which it has, this means a focus on how the Bible affects our view of women and the roles appropriate to them in different spheres. In practical terms that will mean homing in upon the place of women, not just in society in general, but also in the home and in the church in particular.

Although that sharpens our focus in one sense, in that our agenda is set for us and we are forced to be selective in what is covered in detail, there is still the problem of differing perspectives on the same set of issues. It is very difficult to attempt to resolve them if the different parties involved believe that others do not even understand the issues from the outset.

At a fundamental level, some will find problems with the divide between male and female consciousness. There will be, no doubt, some women who will pick up this book, cast their eye over the contents page and list of contributors, close it and dismiss it because of the predominance of men who have been involved in its writing. They assume that it is impossible for a man to understand the problems they have had to struggle with as women. It is hard to argue with such objections, because a man never can be a woman nor can he understand things from her vantage point, any more than a woman can change places with a man. It does, however, highlight a very real problem which has often caused a significant impasse in this particular discussion.

Nevertheless, this must not be allowed to become an insuperable obstacle to progress. There is no reason, if all sides approach the central concerns in the right spirit, why there cannot be a greater meeting of minds and the mutual exchange of help and encouragement.

All parties who engage in this debate need to do so with passions and tempers in check. It is in its very essence an emotive issue fuelled by a history of male pride and chauvinism and female resentment and indignation that goes as far back as the Garden of Eden. Too often and too easily these discussions have triggered defence mechanisms and aroused passions on both sides which are more interested in the self-preservation of personal interests than the genuine well-being of the race and community to which both sides belong. This has justly arisen from the issue being viewed purely as one of 'rights'. When that is the case, gains for one side become concessions which are painfully extracted from the other. The need is not merely for one side to move towards the other, but for both sides to move forward together.

It should go without saying, then, that everyone needs to become a better listener. Stephen Dray, in an editorial comment on this subject, rightly points out that this debate, perhaps more than any other, has suffered through each side assuming what the other is saying, rather than actually listening.[1] It is imperative that the matters which are addressed are real and not assumed.

We should also give due consideration to our choice and use of labels. Despite their convenience, they can often be clumsy items which fail to do justice to the people they attempt to categorise. The epithet 'feminist' is a case in point: the mere mention of it in some circles conjures up extreme images of women with a radical agenda. The sheer breadth of opinion among those who contend for women's concerns makes it difficult to find one adjective which fairly and consistently embraces them all. Particular concerns, raised from whatever quarter, need to be heard and given a response on their own merits.

There is another vital dimension to approaching these concerns in a truly constructive manner and that is readiness to repent. It is not hard to identify, in the history of male attitudes to the role of women in the church, views and behaviour which have been sinful. Even in the desire to implement an understanding and practice which is biblical, there have been occasions where this goal has been pursued without proper sensitivity, love and respect. It is a simple fact that many evangelical churches contain female casualties of male harshness. Where that is so and as God's Word sheds light on both the right thing to do and the right way to do it, men, especially those in leadership positions, need the grace of repentance towards those women who have been hurt in the name of the gospel.

The need for repentance is not one-sided. If men have had a history in the church of being ungracious towards the women with whom they make up the Body of Christ, so also women have made their own peculiar contribution to deepening the wounds. They too are capable of attitudes, choice of words and actions which are not worthy of people who claim to belong to a redeemed race. Again we need to be reminded that the responses required in this area are not merely horizontal, one side towards the other, but vertical, both sides towards the Lord. In that sense, the way this particular issue is sorted out in the church ought to be radically different from what takes place in a non-Christian setting. In the world, it is indeed a battle: slogans which speak of ultimate male or female supremacy only raise the stakes and accentuate the fact that finally one side will win and the other must lose. In the church, as all must be ready to change where change is required by God, so all must ultimately gain. The resolution of the women's issue must be seen as but another facet of the reformation principle of the church's being both reformed and in constant need of reformation.

The most important problem that needs to be addressed on the very threshold of the debate is that of where we start. What presuppositions do we have? In the purely secular realm it has become a conflict of opinions and theories. There is no ultimate reference point to which both sides may appeal. The playing field is not level, indeed it is shifting all the time. To some extent the debate within the church has been affected by this broader confusion. Arguments have been raised from sociological, biological, psychological and many other quarters and the debate has been reduced to an argument between specialists whose views are never constant anyway.

Without being naive, it ought to be said that evangelicals have at least an advantage in this area. Regardless of which side of the gender-divide they may happen to enter the debate, both sides are on the same ground, in theory at least. For us, we start from an evangelical perspective; that is, a framework of understanding that is controlled by the Evangel - the Word of God. This will require closer inspection and clarification at a later stage, but we ought at least to be able to map out the boundaries of discussion as being defined by the Bible. We will look briefly at feminist thinking which has developed with little or no reference to the Bible before looking more closely at that which is self-consciously scriptural in its approach.

2. Secular Feminism

The instigating force behind the gender revolution in the church has been the gender revolution in society at large. Historically, it has only been as the campaign for women's rights gathered momentum through the movement for women's liberation that corresponding pressures for change began to be applied to the ecclesiastical establishment. In other words the ecclesiastical chicken was hatched from a clutch of secular eggs. In and of itself that need not be seen as a bad thing. It would not be the first time that champions for change from the secular world have displayed more courage in pressing their case than their spiritual counterparts have done. What needs to be borne in mind is that a connection exists between these two elements of feminist concern, hence some thought needs to be given to secular feminism.

Whilst there have been various expressions of the women's movement this century the objectives have essentially been equal opportunities for both sexes. In the early part of the twentieth century the concern was for women to be politically enfranchised. From there the focus shifted to the need for equality in educational opportunity and in the work place. More recently the force of the pressures for change has been seen in the constraints put on the very language that we are allowed to use. Political correctness, which became a watchword for the 1980's, has led to major publishers issuing detailed instructions to their authors over the use of gender-specific language. Such is the extent to which feminist concerns have become a shaping influence upon societies.

In some cases the issue has been pressed far beyond that of straightforward equality. Pressure from within certain political groupings has led to positive discrimination in favour of women in the selection of candidates for election. This has been strikingly evident in the 'new-look' Labour Party of the 1990's in Britain. Although such policy may be motivated by the desire to redress the balance after years of discrimination in favour of men, it does not do justice to the very principle of selection on the basis of merit which women's organisations have for so long championed.

A more sinister element of this over-swing of the pendulum of equal rights has emerged in the realm of sexuality. There exists a significant and vocal fringe within secular feminism which is comprised, not simply of those who espouse and endorse lesbian behaviour for themselves, but who seek to make it a determining characteristic of the pro-women movement.[2] That should in no sense lead to the inference that all who contend for women's rights are sympathetic to lesbianism, but it is an element within the broader feminist movement which has had a profile disproportionate to its size and support.

We need to look, not only at the changes which have taken place in favour of women in society, but also at some of the factors which have contributed to change. Undoubtedly the chief underlying influence is ideological. It was the belief in the essential equality of men and women that spurred on those who campaigned for the vote for women and for fair treatment in the work environment. In its earliest manifestation that conviction was quite unsophisticated, but it has been bolstered by claims from scientists and psychologists in recent years that the only real differences between male and female are biological and no more. Their contention is that any other differences to which people point, such as female suitability for some jobs rather than others, or preferences in toys that girls play with as opposed to boys, are entirely the result of nurture rather than nature. Gender stereotyping is the result of society's imposition of values and expectations rather than being due to differences between male and female innate to the sexes. It is, however, by no means clear that the case is as straightforward as some would like to make it. For every set of assertions made by one group of scientific experts these days, there is another set wheeled out to counter them.[3]

Another significant factor which has led to change in this area has been philosophical, in particular the influence of existentialist philosophy. Attention has been drawn to the writings of Simone de Beauvoir, a prominent French feminist who had close associations with the existentialist philosopher, Jean-Paul Sartre.[4] She contended that man is not determined by his natural endowments, but by what he makes of himself. So women should break free from constraints that are imposed upon them by the society of which they are a part. Such a view, which turns human beings into purely self-determining creatures, coupled with the scientific relativism to which we alluded earlier, provides a fertile breeding ground for the most radical of ideas, feminist or otherwise.

There is another influence which has come to bear on the feminist movement that is from a religious source. As the world religions have often been the vehicle for male domination in different cultures around the world, so a new religion is emerging: one which is oriented towards the worship of a pagan goddess and which is dedicated to bringing an end to all concept of God's being male.[5] Although it can hardly be described as a new religion in itself - not least because it draws upon ancient pagan religions - it is religious and it is aimed at eroding and replacing religious establishments in contemporary cultures. The degree to which the subversion of the biblical view of Christ and God is seen as a deliberate aim of the radical wing of the feminist movement is evident in the work of Mary Daly. She is quite comfortable with a presentation of the aims of the feminist movement as the embodiment of the spirit of Antichrist in its fullest sense.[6] Such self-conscious rejection of the God of the Bible, yet espousal of that which is most manifestly satanic from the Bible, is a striking comment on the sinister agenda being pursued by at least one wing of that movement.

If we stand back and evaluate, at least in a broad sense, the aims and achievements of secular feminism, we have to admit that many areas of its concern have been justified. Many societies have degraded and, indeed, continue to degrade women by treating them as second class citizens. Insofar as feminist pressure has been instrumental in gaining rights and privileges for women to which they are entitled but which had wrongfully been denied, then it is to be commended. Where it needs to be seriously challenged, however, is in the realms of sexuality, positive discrimination and religious innovation in which it has become a law unto itself.

3. Liberal Christianity and Feminist Concerns

The most publicised element of the debate concerning the role of women in the church has been where it focuses on a woman's right to be a minister or a priest. From a media perspective this is understandable. The average individual, not in the habit of attending church regularly, is not interested in the niceties and nuances of ecclesiastical debate. Here, however, is a concrete issue: the equal opportunities principle as it is applied to the church. The argument is simple: if a woman can be a pilot, lawyer or even Prime Minister, why can she not do what men are paid to do as ministers? Hence television cameras and press reporters have concentrated their attention on Synods and Assemblies where this professional question is being addressed.

Watching these high profile debates and listening to the case put by opposing factions, it is striking how little reference is made to the Bible. Instead, we hear the kind of reasoning which has swayed thinking in the secular world being applied in an ostensibly spiritual setting. The protagonists have been more interested in the issue of whether a woman is suitable for the work of the ministry or priesthood than whether or not the Bible actually permits her to do such work.

It has been interesting to note also, particularly in the debate in its Anglican setting, that the concentration has been on the sacerdotal issue of whether it is right for a woman to dispense the sacraments. As such it has focused more on the place of women in the church in the light of tradition, than in the light of Scripture.

Such attitudes are not peculiar to the debate over the role of women in church. For decision-making bodies in many churches and denominations today, the Bible has been reduced to one consideration among many in the shaping of church policy. Even when reference is made to the Bible, it is often viewed in a way which trivialises and relativises its significance. Such is the legacy of liberal Christianity.

The liberal wing of the church has provided a natural setting for debating women's issues and it has produced many male and female theologians who have challenged traditional views and practices and called for change. In their most extreme contributions they have called for and, in some cases achieved, the removal of all male allusions to God from liturgies and even from the Bible itself.[7]

If we probe into the mindset of those who fall into the category of liberal Christian feminism, we discover that their starting-point and methodology is consistent with liberal theology in general. Although they wish to give some credence to the Bible as having some contribution to the shaping of beliefs and practice, it is by no means the only, or even necessarily the main influence.

They all tend to 'play fast and loose' with Scripture.

Some refuse to be bound by the text of Scripture. Like their counterparts in the world of liberal scholarship, they reserve the right to amend the text of Scripture where they see fit. As the variant readings they propose are surveyed, it becomes apparent that they consistently gravitate towards rejection of patriarchy and of any idea of male headship in Scripture. Elizabeth Fiorenza is a prime example of this kind of approach to Scripture. For her, the revelation of Scripture is not in the text itself, but 'in the experience of women struggling for liberation from patriarchy'.[8] Such an approach effectively rewrites the Bible with a feminist bias.

Others refuse to acknowledge the uniqueness of Scripture. For them the Bible becomes but one among many as a source of information and direction. Instead of viewing the Bible as it views itself - as God's unique revelation - they regard it merely as one particular religious tradition which has no more inherent worth or authority than the traditions of other world religions. Still others refuse to accept that there are certain principles arising from Scripture itself which govern the way it is to be interpreted. Thus they constantly view the Bible through the tinted spectacles of feminist concerns.

Although such views and such usage of Scripture are far-removed from the high view of the Bible which has characterised evangelical Christianity, it has been alarming to see how some who wish to be identified as evangelicals are beginning to make room for a more liberal approach to difficult texts.[9] Particularly so when such 'evangelicals' hold teaching positions in Bible Colleges and Theological Seminaries and are shaping a new generation of ministers, missionaries and theologians. This is by no means the best way to handle problematic passages.

The great difficulty with such an approach to the Bible is that it makes the task of understanding and applying the Bible a highly subjective exercise. It brings to Scripture a set of presuppositions which arise out of external concerns (in this instance the concerns of one particular grouping within society) and manipulates its message to fit those concerns. In the end the distinctive message of the Bible is lost in the sea of relativism which contains every other message, ideology, religion or philosophy that this world has encountered. It provides no concrete answers.

4. Feminism in the World of Evangelicals

It is however within the evangelical community that the greatest struggle is taking place over these issues. Out of this context has come a particular brand of feminist thinking which wants to be known as biblical, evangelical and conservative. Those who identify themselves with it genuinely claim to be wrestling with the problems thrown up by feminist ideology in the light of God's Word. Unlike their liberal counterparts, they truly want to express views which conform to a God-given norm. Hence we find that much of their work has concentrated on a re-examination of those parts of the Bible which have historically shaped thinking in the church on the role of women.

Undoubtedly some of this renewed interest in these passages in evangelical circles has been somewhat reactionary in nature. Women who have very obvious intellectual and spiritual gifts, who have perhaps been active in missionary work, or in para-church organisations, have struggled with restrictive and even repressive regimes in local evangelical congregations. Situations where the role of women in practice is little more than tea-maker or cleaner. In some cases where these 'evangelical' practices have been questioned by such women, the response they have received has been sufficiently shallow and ungracious to make them wonder even more about what the Bible really says about the worth and usefulness they have as women.

The debate within evangelicalism has focused mainly on the passages which relate to headship and submission in the church and in the family. In other words, it is not merely a question of whether or not a woman is capable of doing the kind of work required by those who teach or rule in the church, or capable of providing the kind of leadership a family needs. (Female capabilities in both these areas are not really in question.) Rather it is the issue of whether or not there is a God-given order which should shape life in our natural families and in the spiritual family of the church.

It has certainly been a helpful thing to concentrate attention on specific biblical passages in this way. In so doing, the debate is taken away from the subjective realms of differing opinions and brought instead into the more objective realm of straightforward exegesis. It is not just a question of what people think, but of what God says. Of course, that has not been as easy as might be hoped. Significant differences have emerged within the evangelical community over exactly what the Bible is saying about headship and submission, in the home and in the church. A vigorous effort is being made to completely reinterpret passages, such as Ephesians 5:21-33 and 1 Timothy 2:11-15, which had long been seen as giving unquestionable support for male headship in these areas. This major reappraisal of a position which has held sway in churches for centuries has involved a corresponding reinterpretation of other key passages, particularly in the early chapters of Genesis, in order to facilitate a complete shift in the view of how families and churches ought to be run.

In itself, the demand to go back to these passages and reconsider what they are saying, is no bad thing. No one generation of God's people can claim a monopoly on understanding what the Bible is teaching. Even if certain views have been traditionally held in evangelical churches, it is not the element of tradition which gives them force. It is only when it is established that the views, whatever they happen to be, are proven to be biblical that they should shape and mould the lives of God's people.

In a wider vein, a positive repercussion of this internal debate within the evangelical family has been that many churches have seriously addressed the question of what women are to be encouraged to do within their fellowships. They have seen that it is not enough for them as evangelicals to speak only of what the Bible forbids, they need to give equal, if not greater weight to what the Bible commands and encourages. This has led in many instances to full recognition of the considerable gifts which God has given to women and creative and constructive use to be made of them within the boundaries God has established.

There are several key issues which are being addressed in evangelical circles today. There is the issue of women in relation to authority positions within the church, namely those which involve church government and authoritative teaching. Historically, in mainstream evangelical churches, women have been excluded from such positions because of a consensus of opinion on passages which relate to these aspects of church life. The interpretation of these passages has now been vigorously challenged and is under scrutiny in the light of contemporary pressures. The second issue is that of a diaconal ministry for women. It has never been disputed that the New Testament allows for a diaconal role for women - they are frequently recorded as performing ministries of mercy - but is there more to it? The verse which is often translated 'deacons' wives' (1 Timothy 3:11) may also be rendered 'deaconesses'.[10] This has opened up a long-standing debate over whether or not there should be some kind of diaconal office for women in the church. A third major issue which needs serious consideration by every evangelical church in the current feminist climate in society, is that of identifying the many positive things which women are able to do and which the Bible encourages them to do. It is not enough for evangelical church leaders to be negative in their pronouncements and only to say what is off-limits for women in their churches; they must be positive.

No-one would pretend that it is an easy task to make this kind of adjustment to church life. There is always the need to recognise the boundaries which God has set and within which his people are to work. Coupled with this is the need to be sensitive to the different viewpoints represented within churches. Those who are progressive in their thinking ought not to ride rough-shod over those who are more conservative in theirs, any more than those who are traditionally-minded should be intransigent in areas where Scripture allows room for flexibility.

5. The Problem of Interpretation

We have said already that the 'women's issue' is not merely an issue about women and how we are to view them in the light of God's Word; it goes much deeper than that. What is at stake is the way in which the

Bible itself is viewed and used by those who profess to hold to it as the only rule of faith and life. In an extreme sense, the Bible can be a very dangerous book if it is used by people who claim its authority but manipulate its message. The cults provide numerous examples of how unsuspecting individuals can be misled by spiritual leaders who claim to derive their teaching from Scripture. Throughout the history of the church it has been acknowledged that in order to understand the message of the Bible accurately, certain rules of interpretation need to be observed. The technical term for these rules is 'hermeneutics' which simply means the 'principles of interpretation'.

The most fundamental principle is simple and has enjoyed a time-honoured place in the history of the study of the Bible: it is the rule that Scripture interprets Scripture. Passages which are difficult should be studied in the light of passages on the same subject which are more straightforward. There is more to it than that, of course, but those who claim to approach the Bible as evangelicals should do so with the conviction that, because of its divine authorship, it speaks with one voice and so its message is consistent with itself. Thus, even though there will be many more specialist skills that will need to be brought to bear upon the task of interpreting the Bible, we can still expect it to be a straightforward task within certain bounds.

It is becoming apparent that in order to sustain their fresh under-standings of ancient texts, the interpretation of which has been virtually undisputed throughout the history of the church, conservative feminists are having to appeal to principles of interpretation which are relatively new on the scene. Emphases on culture, both of the original setting of the passage and also of the contemporary readership, has led to serious cultural relativism in the way particular passages are handled. This shows itself not only in the treatment of parts of the Bible that deal specifically with women's issues, but also with those that deal with such matters as sexual orientation and conduct, norms of family life and many more besides.

The burning issue facing the evangelical community is that of how to handle the Bible. If the term 'evangelical' is to retain any meaningful currency and cease to be a mere flag of convenience, a renewed consideration of what it requires in terms of interpreting God's Word is needed.

6. Broader Implications

The way in which the evangelical consensus on the women's issue has gone and indeed is going has enormous implications. For those who are evangelicals and belong to denominations which endorse the appointment of women to positions of oversight and instruction in the church, there is increasing pressure to conform or be marginalised. In some cases, a man's view of women's ordination has become the test which determines his acceptance or non-acceptance as a candidate for the ministry. The issue has been given credal proportions which are nothing short of ridiculous. Some Anglicans who hold to an Anglo-Catholic churchmanship have responded to these pressures by leaving the denomination and joining the Roman Catholic Church. Although the basis of their convictions is quite different from those held by evangelicals, the serious question is raised as to whether those who oppose women's ordination have a long-term future in the Church of England.

For those who do not belong to churches where such pressures exist, the problem takes on a different form. It is not enough to say, 'Our church excludes women from leadership and the pulpit'. That in itself does not necessarily mean that 'our church' is biblical in its attitude towards women. All churches need continually to consider whether they are being fair and faithful to all its members in the light of God's Word. That will inevitably mean being willing to change.

The challenge facing evangelical Christians of both sexes today is courageously to face the positive and negative dimensions of what God's Word is teaching and to endeavour to implement them in the life of the church.

Notes

1. Stephen Dray, Evangel, Autumn 1994 p.1
2. S. Dowell and L. Hurcombe, Dispossessed Daughters of Eve: Faith and Feminism, (SPCK) 1987 p.47.
3. For a more detailed analysis of studies done in this area, see, Gregg

Johnson, 'The Biological Basis for Gender-Specific Behaviour', in Recovering Biblical Manhood and Womanhood, J. Piper and W. Grudem (eds.) (Crossway Books; Wheaton, Illinois) 1994 pp.280-293.
4. W. Neuer, Man and Woman in Christian Perspective, Translated by Gordon Wenham (Hodder & Stoughton) 1990 pp.16-18.
5. See, e.g., N. Goldenberg, Changing the Gods, (Beacon: Boston, USA).
6. M. Daly, Beyond God the Father: Towards a Philosophy of Women's Liberation, (Beacon; Boston, USA) 1973, p.96.
7. An Inclusive Language Lectionary: Readings for a Year, (Co-operative Publications Association) 1983, published by National Council of Churches (USA). The issue has been aired in a British context in the debate within the Church of Scotland over Mrs. A. Hepburn's addressing God as 'Dear Mother God...' in 1982 at the annual Women's Guild Rally - such form of address was not condemned.
8. E.S. Fiorenza, 'The Will to Choose or Reject: Continuing our Critical Work' in L.M. Russell (ed.) Feminist Interpretation of the Bible, (Philadelphia; Westminster Press) 1985 p.136.
9. See, e.g., Gordon Fee's suggestion that 1Corinthians 14.34-35 is an interpolation and not authentically Pauline. Gordon Fee, God's Empowering Presence, (Hendrickson Publishers Inc.) 1994 pp. 272-281.
10. NIV Margin.

Gender in the history of the church

Kenneth Brownell

Ken is an American from New England. He graduated from Harvard University and completed a Ph.D in modern British history at St Andrews University in Scotland. Ken studied theology at the London Theological Seminary, lectures for the Prepared for Service training course and is at present pastor of East London Tabernacle Baptist Church. He is married to Alison and they have two children.

Gender in the history of the church

Christian women have exercised diverse and significant ministries throughout the history of the church. In every age women have preached the gospel, taught the Bible, helped the poor, visited the sick, raised children, offered hospitality, written hymns and books, suffered for the faith, administered church affairs and much more. Indeed there is nothing men have done that women have not done. What one makes of some of the ministries women have exercised will largely depend on one' s theological convictions on the role of women in the church. But that women have made a great contribution to the life and witness of the church of Christ cannot be disputed. Sadly this contribution has not always been given the recognition it deserves: church history has largely ignored the ministry of women. In part this is due to the tendency of church history to focus on the key players and institutions, and as women have usually been in the background, they appear on the pages of history books only incidentally. Recently, however, church historians, like other historians, have given more attention to popular religion with the result that we can now see more clearly the contribution women have made to Christ's kingdom. [1]

My purpose in this chapter is simply to give an overview of the ministry of women through the centuries. In the limited space available I can only do that superficially but I trust adequately enough to whet readers' appetites to discover more for themselves. I am especially concerned that women would appreciate and draw inspiration from what their spiritual forebears have accomplished. I will argue that until relatively recently in the mainstream tradition of the church women have not been allowed to lead and teach congregations as presbyters or pastor-teachers. Of course there have been exceptions but, generally speaking this has been the case. Whether this prohibition is biblical or not readers will have to decide for themselves in the light of the arguments found elsewhere in this book. It is possible that the consensus of the church has been wrong and needs correcting. My own position is that the consensus is right and therefore needs to be maintained. But having said that I will also try to show that though women have accomplished much, they have also been unnecessarily restricted in much that they could have done and this does need to be remedied.

The Early Church (100-600)

Even a casual reading of the New Testament reveals that women played an important role in the apostolic church, and this was true of the succeeding centuries. From what evidence we have, women made up a large proportion of the early congregations; indeed the remarkable expansion of Christianity around the Roman Empire and beyond was in part due to the evangelism of women. Such was their influence that the pagan emperor Julian complained to the men of Antioch in 363 that "Every one of you allows his wife to carry out of his house everything to the Galileans'. [2] Married women with children had the advantage of their position in the household with which to promote the Christian faith. Patricius, the pagan father of the great theologian Augustine, was married to a Christian, Monica, and she influenced her son towards the Christian faith. Though Christian wives and mothers did not exercise official ministries as such they made an enormous contribution to the life of the church. Not surprisingly the writings of the early fathers contain many exhortations for women to fulfil their domestic responsibilities. In one of the earliest writings, Clement of Rome commends the way the Corinthians taught the women in the church:

'And to the women you gave instruction that they should do all things with a blameless and seemly and pure conscience, yielding a dutiful affection to their husbands. And you taught them to remain in the rule of obedience and to manage their households with seemliness, in all circumspection.'

Similar statements can be found in many of the church fathers. [3]

It is not surprising, in the light of their number, that women were among those martyred for their faith in the early church. There are many accounts of women courageously going to their deaths for refusing to renounce Christ. One of the most notable was Blandina, a slave, who was martyred with her Christian mistress around the year 177 at Lyon. This is how the early church historian Eusebius records her suffering!

> 'But the entire fury of the crowd, governor and
> soldiers fell upon Sanctus... Maturus... Attalus... and
> upon Blandina, through whom Christ showed that
> things which appear mean and unsightly and despicable
> in the eyes of men are accounted worthy of great glory
> in the sight of God, through love towards Him, a love
> which showed itself in power and did not boast itself in
> appearance. For when we were all afraid, ... Blandina
> was filled with such power that those who by turns kept
> torturing her in every way from dawn till evening were
> worn out and exhausted, and they themselves confessed
> defeat from lack of aught else to do to her .... But the
> blessed woman, like a noble champion, in confession
> regained her strength; and for her, to say "I am a
> Christian, and with us no evil finds a place" was
> refreshment and rest and insensibility to her lot.'

Another famous martyr of this period was Vibia Perpetua, born into a wealthy pagan family, who was executed around 202/3 shortly after giving birth to a child and in spite of the pleas of her father. The blood of faithful Christian women was as much the seed of the church as that of men. [4]

More officially, some women in the early church exercised their ministries in the roles of widows, virgins and deaconesses. There is some debate as to whether widows and virgins were recognised ministries or simply states of life. Either way they were highly esteemed by the early fathers. Widows were mentioned by Paul in 1 Timothy and seemed to have been older widowed women who gave themselves primarily to a ministry of prayer and doing good. Virgins were single women, committed to a celibate life and service to the church, who were particularly esteemed because of the high value that the church gave to chastity. Many of the early fathers had a negative view of women and sexuality and considered a celibate lifestyle, even for those who were married, more holy than normal married life.[5] As monasticism developed in the 4th century this attitude would become institutionalised.

Of more significance in relation to the present debate on women's ministry is the office of deaconess. In the New Testament there is some evidence that there was such an office or role in the apostolic church.[6] There are few references to women deacons or deaconesses in the first two centuries, particularly in the east, but from the 3rd century on they are mentioned often.[7] They seem to have been an ordained or recognised ministry, and their responsibilities included caring for the sick and poor, teaching women believers, helping in the baptisms of women and maintaining order in the women's section of the congregation.

It is difficult to ascertain how widespread was the ministry of deaconesses. What is certain is that the early fathers did not consider deaconesses to be ordained to the presbyterate. For example, the third century *Didaskalia Apostolorum* of the Syrian church which provides instructions about deaconesses also explicitly prohibits women from teaching or presiding over congregations.[8] Though women were very active and influential in the early church, they did not hold the office of presbyter or bishop.

Where women did hold principal positions of leadership in churches was among the heretical sects on the fringe of orthodox Christianity. Indeed the negative attitude towards women of the early fathers seems to have been in part a reaction to the prominent position of women in heretical cults. Women were prominent in the Gnostic cults, and in the Montanist movement which put a strong emphasis on prophecy and counted some women among its most eminent prophets. With Montanus two women named Priscilla and Maximilla formed the original trio of prophets and from the evidence we have it seems that women continued to be attracted to the movement for some time.[9]

The fact that women were restricted from leadership in the early church does not mean that they had no concern for learning and teaching the Scriptures. In the 4th century we find a group of remarkable women noted for their piety and learning. One was Marcella, born around 322 and a friend of the great biblical scholar Jerome. Of her Jerome wrote:

> 'And because my name was then especially esteemed in the study of the Scriptures, she never came without asking something about Scripture, nor did she immediately accept my explanation as satisfactory, but she proposed questions from the opposite viewpoint, not for the sake of being contentious, but so that, by asking, she might learn solutions for points she perceived could be raised in objection. What virtue I found in her, what cleverness, what holiness, what purity. I am afraid to say, unless I exceed what belief finds credible. I will say only this, that whatever in us was gathered by long study and lengthy meditation was almost changed into nature; this she tasted, this she learned, this she possessed'.

Another woman close to Jerome was Paula with whom he read and discussed the Bible. Jerome wrote of her:

> 'If at any passage I was at a loss and frankly confessed that I was ignorant, she by no means wanted to rest content with my reply, but by fresh questions would force me to say which of the many possible meanings seemed to me the most likely'.[10]

Space allows me only to mention other such remarkable women: Melania the elder, her daughter Melania the younger, Olympias and Macrina.

The Mediaeval Period (600-1500)

During the mediaeval period the status of women generally declined: women were commonly considered inferior to men. At the Council of

Macon in 585 the question was actually debated as to whether women had souls. Nevertheless women continued to exercise important ministries in local congregations officially and unofficially. In the earlier part of the period we still hear of deaconesses, but eventually they disappear in the western church. Where some women made a very notable contribution was in evangelism among pagans. For example, Lioba was invited by her cousin Boniface, the 'Apostle of Germany', to help him in his mission. She with five other nuns joined him in 748 and made a significant contribution to the work by establishing a number of convents. Lioba was a gifted administrator, biblical scholar, counsellor and teacher and, while she did not hold a teaching office in the church, many bishops and others would come to her for advice and wisdom.[11]

Lioba was also something of a mystic and was credited with doing a number of miracles. In this she was one of many women in this period given to mystical experience.[12] One of the most prominent mystics was Hildegard of Disebodenberg who claimed to be directed from her infancy by a Divine Light. Many other examples could be given including Julian of Norwich whose *Revelations of Divine Love* is still read. Why women have been linked with mysticism in this and other periods is a matter of debate. Traditionally it has been suggested that women are more instinctively mystical and emotional in religion. Recently it has been suggested that a better explanation lies in the fact that women have had limited opportunities for ministry and therefore have resorted to mystical experience as a way of serving God. In relation to this it is perhaps important to note that in this period women were prominent in the various sectarian groups that arose from time to time. Some of these groups were clearly heretical; but others were generally orthodox but were persecuted because of their opposition to certain practices of the church. Among the latter were the Beguines who were a religious order of lay women in the 12th and 13th centuries committed to doing good and promoting spiritual life. Women were also prominent in the Waldensian, Taborite and Lollard movements that were harbingers of the Reformation.[13]

The one channel for women's ministry that stood out above all others in this period was monasticism. Beginning in the 6th century in the west, convents had spread all over Europe by the 8th century, varying greatly in size, prestige and spiritual life. One of the most unusual features was the double monastery with men's and women's sections, often presided over by an abbess. The great abbeys at Wimborne and Whitby, governed by Tetta and Hilda respectively, are two notable examples. But great and powerful as these abbesses were they were not recognised as priests or presbyters and were always under the jurisdiction of a bishop. By the 8th century this kind of monastery was in decline and nuns were increasingly expected to live in closed convents. In this way the influence of women on the church declined, but nevertheless they were able to exercise such ministries as caring for the poor and sick, teaching, art, music, as well as prayer and study.[14]

The Reformation and Post-Reformation Period (1500-1700)

The early 16th century saw a great awakening of spiritual life in western Europe as the gospel of the justifying grace of God was rediscovered. But great as this awakening was it did not, formally at least, significantly affect the status and ministry of women in the church. The ministry of women was not really an issue at all. However, the Reformation did promote the ministry of women in a number of less direct ways. For one thing it attacked the whole monastic system and raised the dignity of Christian marriage and home life. The home was the real monastery and the place where the holy life was to be lived. This was a strong emphasis in the teaching of Martin Luther; indeed his own wonderfully happy marriage to Katrina von Bora in many ways became the prototype of the Protestant marriage. Katrina herself was no pushover; she held strong opinions, often pricked any tendency to pomposity on her husband's part and ran her own business on the side. Luther spoke of her as the 'preacher', brewer, gardener and, all things else.'[15]

John Calvin and the other reformers held similar views to those of Luther. Women as well as men were heirs together of God's grace and equally one in Christ. The reformers also raised the status of women by their emphasis on education. Nevertheless they held a strong view of the subordination of women to men and did not entertain the possibility of women exercising leadership roles in churches. Commenting on 1 Timothy 2:12, Calvin said that Paul does not take from women 'the charge of instructing their family, but only excludes them from the office of teaching, which God has committed to men only'. For sure there might be exceptional circumstances, but that was not the norm. Referring to Deborah in the Book of Judges, Calvin wrote that 'Extraordinary acts of God do not overturn the ordinary rules of government'. However, Calvin did teach that women could fulfil a diaconal ministry in the church. He understood from Scripture that there were two kinds of deacons; those who administer poor and sick relief and those who care for the poor and sick themselves. Women could exercise the latter ministry and Calvin connected this to the 'widows' mentioned by Paul in 1 Timothy 5.[16]

Among the Anabaptists the situation was much the same. Women played an important role in the radical reformation, as they made up a large part of the congregations and many of them suffered greatly for their beliefs. George H. Williams says, 'Nowhere else in the Reformation Era were women so nearly the peers and companions in the faith, and mates in missionary enterprises and readiness for martyrdom, than among those for whom believers' baptism was an equalizing covenant.'[17] Even so the leaders of the Anabaptists, such as Balshazzar Hubmaier and Menno Simons, upheld the view that women were not to lead and teach mixed congregations.[18]

But even though women did not fulfil leadership roles in the Protestant churches they did play an important role in the movement. Across Europe a number of prominent women sided with the Reformation. Argula von Grumbeck was a widely read Bavarian aristocrat who ably defended Luther's doctrines against Roman Catholic attacks. Listen to her spirited defence:

'When I heard what you had done to Arsacius Seehofer under terror of imprisonment and the stake, my heart trembled and my bones quaked. What have Luther and Melanchthon taught save the word of God? You have condemned them. You have not refuted them ....You

*seek to destroy all Luther's works. In that case you will
have to destroy the New Testament which he has
translated .... Even if Luther should recant, what he has
said will be the word of God.'*

Needless to say Luther thought highly of this woman. He wrote of
her:

*'The Duke of Bavaria rages above measure, killing,
crushing, and persecuting the gospel with all his might.
That most noble woman, Argula von Stauffer, is there
making a valiant fight with great spirit, boldness of
speech and knowledge of Christ. She deserves that all
pray for Christ's victory in her... She is a singular
instrument of Christ'.* [19]

Other allies of the reformers were Jeanne d'Albert, a leading French
Huguenot, and Renee of Ferrara, a confidant of Calvin. Less well
known but equally important were the countless women who confessed
the reformed faith often at great cost to themselves. In the troubled
world of the sixteenth century many women suffered for their faith by
exile, imprisonment, torture, poverty, harassment and death. As is
usually the case in such circumstances the care of families would have
fallen on their shoulders.

Some of the most remarkable women in this period were the wives of
leading reformers. I have already mentioned Katrina von Bora. Another
formidable woman was Katherine Zell, the wife of the Strasbourg
reformer Matthew Zell. She married Zell when he was still a Catholic
priest and was outspoken in defending what she had done. She was
noted for her hospitality and opened the Zell home to many visitors,
including religious refugees who came to the city. She was active in
visiting the sick and teaching other women the Bible; indeed some of her
husband's colleagues seemed to have found her a bit overpowering and
accused her of wanting to be 'Doctor Katrina'. She denied this and that
she ever wanted to mount a pulpit. Katherine Zell also compiled a book
of hymns and songs for the ordinary church people. This is what she
wrote of her efforts:

'When I read these hymns I felt that the writer had the

whole Bible in his heart. This is not just a hymn book but a lesson book of prayer and praise. When so many filthy songs are on the lips of men and women and even children I think it well that folk should with lusty zeal and clear voice sing the songs of salvation. God is glad when the craftsman at his bench, the maid at her sink, the farmer at the plough, the dresser at the vines, the mother at the cradle break forth in hymns of prayer, praise and instruction'.

Of similar ilk to Zell was Wibrandis Rosenblatt, wife of the Berne reformer Oecolampadius, who was part of a circle of other wives of reformers, including Anna Zwingli, Elisabeth Bucer and Agnes Capito.[20]

In England and Scotland there were also many notable women who identified with the Protestant faith, among them Queen Catherine Parr, Lady Jane Grey and Catherine Brandon, the Duchess of Suffolk. The latter was one of several influential women who sought to help reformed preachers. Ann Locke was a supporter and correspondent of the Scottish reformer John Knox. She sought Knox's counsel in regard to her assurance, but also helped to translate Calvin's sermons into English and proof read Knox's short work on the temptations of Christ.[21] This friendship reveals another side to Knox's attitude to women which has usually been considered as very negative due to his intemperate *First Blast against the monstrous regiment of women.* Without such faithful women the work of the reformers would have been much harder.

As on the Continent there were also many ordinary women who supported the reformed cause. Many suffered for their faith. One of the most notable was Anne Askew who was burned at the stake in the reign of Henry VIII at the age of twenty-five. She was cruelly tortured and interrogated about her Protestant convictions, but through it all robustly defended herself and refused to give way to her opponents. Here is part of her interrogation by Christopher Dare, a Roman Catholic theologian:

Dare: Why did you say that you would rather read five

lines in the Bible than hear five masses?
Anne: Because the one does greatly edify me, the other
nothing at all: as St. Paul says, 'If the trump give an
uncertain sound who will prepare himself for battle? . . .
Dare: Do you think that private masses help departed
souls?
Anne: It is great idolatry to believe them of more value
than the death that Christ dies for us.

Later, during the reign of the Catholic Mary Tudor a number of other women were burned at the stake, among them Joyce Lewes, Catherine Hut, Joan Hornes, Elizabeth Thackwell and Joan Waste. The latter was blind and yet had memorised large portions of the New Testament and had refused to attend mass.[22] During the reign of Elizabeth it was noted, usually with dismay, that women made up the majority of the congregations tending towards Puritanism. The Anglican apologist Richard Hooker complained that women tended to gossip what they heard in sermons and thereby disseminate the views of the radical preachers. It was also noted that these women gave generously to support their favourite preachers.[23]

In the 17th century many women were active supporters of the Puritan movement. By and large most women were content to fulfil the traditional role of wife and mother. Puritan preaching exalted marriage and the family: the home was a little church and husband and wife were joined in a covenant of love, joy and affection. Leland Ryken sums up the Puritan view of marriage this way:

'The Puritan doctrine of sex was a watershed in the
cultural history of the west. The Puritans devalued
celibacy, glorified companionate marriage, affirmed
married sex as both necessary and pure, established the
ideal of wedded married love, and exalted the role of
the wife'.[24]

In the mainstream Puritan movement women continued to be prohibited from holding church office. What ministry they exercised was of an informal nature: for example, it was not uncommon for women to meet together in homes to discuss the Sunday sermon.

Outside the mainstream things were different. The 17th century was a turbulent period of social change, and with the breakdown of ecclesiastical authority many new groups and small sects grew up. New churches were formed. Women were active in the early separatist churches and conventicles in London and elsewhere. It was during the Civil War period that the public ministry of women exploded in many of the radical sects. Among the Baptists there was great debate about what women could and could not do.[25] It is interesting to note that eight of the twelve founding members of John Bunyan's church in Bedford were women. Women preachers among Baptists were not unknown.[26] In many congregations women were allowed to pray and prophesy, by which was meant to exhort as led by the Spirit, and also to participate in church meetings and vote for officers. But nevertheless most of the more radical Puritan groups retained the principle that preaching and leadership in churches were restricted to men.

The group that gave women the most freedom to preach and lead was the Society of Friends or Quakers. There were a number of notable women preachers among the early Quakers, the most eminent of whom was Margaret Fell who later married George Fox. Fell was a remarkable woman by any standard who had a powerful influence on the movement; she travelled extensively preaching and organising and for several periods she suffered imprisonment. She also wrote the first book defending female preaching *Women's Speaking justified, proved and allowed of by the Scriptures* – in 1667. Her basic justification for female preaching was that the Spirit had been given both to men and women and according to Joel 2 both could therefore prophesy or preach. But in spite of Fell's effort and example there was resistance even among the Quakers to the preaching and leadership of women.[27]

Before we leave this period we should note what was happening among Roman Catholics. In an effort to counter the impact of the Reformation, the Roman Catholic Church instituted a number of reforms. The main focus of women's ministry continued to be in the monasteries where a number of women made a significant impact on church life, perhaps the most notable being Teresa of Avila. Some of these women were given to mystical experiences, but they also contributed much to education, helping the poor and sick, and to Catholic missions. It was during this period that the cult of Mary grew increasingly popular. One Catholic woman who had a lasting influence on many Protestants was Madame Guyon who wrote and counselled on the spiritual life.[28]

The Eighteenth and Nineteenth Centuries

The beginning of the 18th century was a time of spiritual declension in the Protestant churches. By the 1730s, however, a movement of renewal and revival had begun on the Continent, in Great Britain and in America, in which women were actively involved. In America the great preacher and theologian Jonathan Edwards recorded the experiences of his wife Sarah as well as a number of other women in his congregation in Northampton, Massachusetts.[29] In the Middle Colonies a notable promoter of evangelical renewal in the churches was a lady called Jufvrouw Dinah Hardenbergh who was married successively to two Dutch Reformed pastors, John Freylinghuysen and Jacob Hardenbergh. Dinah was active in gathering women together for Bible study and promoting experiential Calvinism. In her later years she was much sought after by pastors for her counsel.[30] In the Netherlands, from whence Dinah had come, a number of women were involved in the pietist movement as were they in Germany. One of these was Anna Maria van Schurman who was widely respected for her theological insight and concern for spiritual renewal in the churches.[31]

In Britain women were also active in the spiritual awakening. Selina Hastings, the Countess of Huntingdon, exercised a remarkable and unusual ministry. Because of her wealth and social position she had the resources and contacts with which to advance evangelical Christianity. She was a strong Calvinist and supporter of George Whitefield. She sought to place evangelical clergymen in churches and built a number of chapels around England as well as establishing a college for preachers in Trevecca in Wales.[32] The Countess had a friend and counterpart in Scotland in the person of Lady Glenorchy. The majority of women, of course, had much less visible ministries in their homes and local churches. Women along with men sought new life in older churches and helped to establish new ones. Some women used their homes for a ministry of hospitality: one such was the Baptist Martha Wallis in whose home in Kettering some of the early meetings of the Baptist Missionary Society took place.[33] Other women had a more theological inclination. Ann Dutton was a somewhat hyper-Calvinistic Baptist who maintained a wide circle of correspondents that included Philip Doddridge, Howell Harris, George Whitefield and John Wesley. A woman of strongly held and forcefully expressed views, Dutton was a great encourager of evangelical ministers. Whitefield considered her conversation 'as weighty as her letters' and Harris believed that the Lord had given her a gift of 'writing for him'.[34]

All these ministries were informal and unofficial. There was no question of women holding the office of pastor nor even evangelist among Anglicans, the nonconformists or the Calvinistic Methodists. Among the Wesleyan Methodists things were different. John Wesley was early on faced with the fact that some of his preachers were women. Initially Wesley was against the practice but his correspondence reveals that over the years his views changed. He advised women preachers not to cause offence by screaming or bawling, to 'intermix short exhortations with prayer', to 'keep as far from what is called preaching as you can' and not to preach on texts. But the women did preach and in 1771 we find him writing this to Mary Bosanquet:

> 'I think the strength of the cause rests here – on your
> having an extraordinary call. So I am persuaded has
> everyone of our lay preachers . . . The whole work of
> God called Methodism is an extraordinary dispensation
> of his providence. Therefore I do not wonder if several
> things occur therein which do not fall under the
> ordinary rules of discipline. St. Paul's ordinary rule was
> "I permit not a women to speak in the congregation."
> Yet in extraordinary cases he made a few exceptions; at
> Corinth in particular'.[35]

So Wesley allowed women preachers in extraordinary circumstances such as revival. In ordinary circumstances it would seem that he would not permit woman preachers. Nevertheless Wesley's position indicates a significant shift in thinking. It will be no surprise when we come to the later 19th and early 20th centuries that women ministers first appear in significant numbers in Wesleyan, Holiness and Pentecostal groups that trace their ancestry to Wesley.

The 19th century saw an explosion of women's ministries. The century was characterised by the proliferation of voluntary societies for doing every conceivable form of good. One of the most notable figures early in the century was Hannah More, friend of William Wilberforce and of other members of the 'Clapham Sect' of Anglican evangelicals. Hannah More was exceedingly active in writing 'improving' moral and religious literature for the poor and children and in establishing schools. A comparable figure in the United States was Joanna Bethune, who with her husband started the Sunday School movement there. Like all voluntary benevolent societies the Sunday schools depended largely on women for staffing. Indeed the involvement of women was a problem to some men, both because women were teaching the Bible and because they would be exposed to danger. Such objections did not stand for long. By mid-century Christian women were leading societies and movements to promote temperance, evangelise soldiers and sailors, reform prisons, relieve the urban poor, rescue prostitutes and much else. Among the most prominent in Britain were Louisa Daniell who founded the Army Prayer Union and Scripture Readers Society, Josephine Butler who worked among prostitutes and Catherine Marsh who sought to evangelise labourers in London. In 1858 Marsh wrote a book entitled *English Hearts and English Minds* indicting the indifference of the upper classes to the moral and spiritual condition of the poor.[36]

Clearly these societies provided women with a channel for exercising ministries unlike anything that had gone before. But these ministries were not by and large formally part of the church. There were some churches that did use women in their outreach to the poor. The great Scottish preacher Thomas Chalmers had women involved in his pioneering parish visitation scheme at St. John's in Glasgow in the 1820s. But it was the Anglican evangelical William Pennefather who sought to revive in Britain the ancient office of deaconess. Pennefather and his wife started to train deaconesses in 1860, based first at his church in Barnet and later at St. Jude's, Mildmay Park in Stoke Newington. His model was the Deaconess Institution at Kaiserworth in Germany founded by the Lutheran pastor Theodor Fliedner. When Pennefather founded the Mildmay Mission Hospital in 1877 deaconesses were an intrinsic part of the ministry. From then on deaconesses multiplied in the Church of England and later among the nonconformist churches.[37]

In other ways the ministry of women continued to take on new forms in the 19th century, particularly in the United States. The seminal American evangelist Charles Grandison Finney broke new ground in this as he did in other areas and was criticised for the role women played in his meetings, particularly in speaking from the platform. Though Finney himself did not approve of the ordination of women, his ministry marked a change of sentiment that would only come to fruition in the next century. It is not insignificant that the first woman to be ordained to the pastorate was Antoinette Brown, who was ordained in 1853 to the Congregational ministry, having trained at Finney's Oberlin College in Ohio.

As the century went on there were a growing number of women engaged in public preaching and teaching ministries. Some smaller groups such as Free Will Baptists in the United States had for some time allowed women preachers. Though other churches were reluctant or opposed to doing the same there were some eminent itinerant preachers, especially on the holiness and temperance circuits. Among the best known were Phoebe Palmer, Amanda Smith, Jessie Penn Lewis and Frances Willard.[38] The latter was the leading light of the Women's Christian Temperance Union, perhaps the most effective women's organisation in the 19th century. The WCTU was involved in an extensive ministry of evangelism and visitation among prisoners, railwaymen, soldiers and others. Speaking of her army of women Willard said, 'These make an aggregate of several thousands of women who are regularly studying and expounding God's word to the multitude, to say nothing of the army in home and foreign missionary work, and who are engaged in church evangelism.' Willard was a Methodist who also campaigned in that denomination for the ordination of women.[39] A group that combined concern for evangelism, holiness, temperance and social ministry was the Salvation Army. From the beginning William Booth recognised that his 'best men were women'. His own wife Catherine proved a valued partner in ministry and provided a model for other women in the movement.

By far the most significant development in the ministry of women in the 19th century was in foreign missions. Initially women were sent out as the wives of male missionaries. Some women, such as William Carey's wife Dorothy, went out very reluctantly and in her case suffered greatly. It is not surprising that Carey himself advised the Baptist Missionary Society committee to look carefully at the wives of candidates.[40] Other women, such as Adoniram Judson's wife Ann (and subsequent wives Sarah and Emily), went very much as partners with their husband in the work.[41] As the missionary movement expanded women played a crucial role in evangelising the peoples of the world. For example, both Maria and Jennie Taylor, the two wives of Hudson Taylor, played vital roles in the development of the China Inland Mission. In 1878 Jennie Taylor left her sick husband in England and returned to China to organise famine relief work.[42] But the cost to married women missionaries was high: they had to leave their homes and relations and often to be separated from their children during their education, and many died from disease and the effects of harsh climates.

Later in the century the issue of single women going to the mission field arose. In the United States the older societies refused to send single women and therefore a separate women's missionary movement developed for that express purpose. By the end of the century the 'female missionary societies' were one of the most powerful forces in American church life. Though initially not welcomed by missionaries from the other societies, the single women missionaries became an indispensable asset on the field. The older British societies generally allowed single women to go overseas. Together with their married women colleagues they have made a contribution to Christ's kingdom that only eternity will reveal.[43] Space prevents telling of the remarkable ministries of women like Mary Slessor in Calabar (Nigeria), Amy Carmichael in India, Malla Moe in South Africa, Lottie Moon in China, and many, many others. Mary Slessor was convinced that single women such as herself were better suited to reaching une-vangelised peoples because they were less threatening to the male authority structures.[44] For that reason Slessor turned down a proposal of marriage even though this involved great loneliness in later years.

The other area of women's ministry that should be noted in this period is that of hymn-writing. Before the 19th century few women wrote hymns. Our modern hymnary owes much to hymn-writers such as Charlotte Elliott ('Just as I am'), Frances Ridley Havergal ('Take my life'), Fanny Crosby ('To God be the glory'), Elizabeth Clephane ('Beneath the cross of Jesus'), Anna Ross Cousin ('The sands of time') and Mrs. Cecil F. Alexander ('There is a green hill').

The Twentieth Century

In the early years of this century many of the developments from the 19th century continued. The larger denominations did not recognise the ordination of women to pastoral ministry. There was movement on this front however among Holiness and Pentecostal groups. I have mentioned the role of women in the former. One prominent early twentieth century leader in the United States was Alma White of the Pillar of Fire movement. In 1901 the Church of the Nazarene, the largest holiness denomination, allowed women to be ordained, though not without opposition. Perhaps of more long-term significance was the early Pentecostal movement where women had a very significant and formative role. The experience of Agnes Ozman on January 1, 1900 at the Bethel Bible School in Kansas persuaded Charles Fox Parham of the necessity of tongues as evidence of the baptism of the Spirit. Not surprisingly women were as involved as men in the famous Azusa Street meetings in Los Angeles in 1906 that are taken to be the birth of the modern Pentecostal movement. Subsequently other women rose to prominence in the movement. Florence Crawford led the

Apostolic Faith movement and Maria Woodworth-Etter had a nationwide preaching and healing ministry. One of the most colourful and controversial Pentecostal leaders was Aimee Semple MacPherson, the founder of the International Church of the Foursquare Gospel. These women were forerunners of people like Katherine Kuhlmann, Agnes Sanford and Ruth Stapleton Carter. As far as larger Pentecostal denominations were concerned the Assemblies of God was the most open to the ministry of women: it allowed them to do everything, including being ordained, but not to become ruling elders.[45]

Initially the mainline denominations – Baptists, Methodists, Presbyterians, Anglicans, Congregationalists – were reluctant to ordain women to pastoral office. In the different denominations there was a great deal of discussion, but by the 1980s almost all the large church bodies in the west had sanctioned the ordination of women. One of the last major bodies to do so was the Church of England, even though many of her sister churches had already ordained women. Some major church bodies, however, have refused to allow women into pastoral office. These include the Southern Baptist Convention and the Missouri Synod Lutheran Church in the United States. The historic position in regard to women in pastoral office has also been maintained by smaller conservative bodies such as the Presbyterian Church in America, the Fellowship of Independent Evangelical Churches in the United Kingdom and similar groups around the world. Space forbids even a cursory account of how this came about; the issues involved are discussed elsewhere in this book.

The ministry of women has been a subject of much discussion among evangelicals. Until 1970 or so there was a general consensus that women could not be pastor-teachers or ruling elders in churches. But in the 1970s a number of books began to appear, such as Letha Scanzoni and Nancy Hardesty's *All We're Meant to Be* (1974) and Paul K. Jewett's *Man: Male and Female* (1975), advocating a reinterpretation of the passages traditionally used against allowing women to become pastors. Since then others have joined battle from both sides of the issue. Without a doubt this is a matter that deeply divides evangelicals and since it involves our approach to the Bible it is a controversy of great significance. In all this we need to remember the cultural context in which the debate is taking place. The late 20th century has seen the rise of a strong and outspoken feminist movement. For good or bad this affects the climate in which evangelical Christians try to live out their faith. It is impossible for evangelicals to remain untouched by this new ethos.

It is sad that this controversy has obscured the way in which women today are serving Christ in his church and beyond. In the 20th century we have seen an explosion of parachurch organisations seeking to do many things for the kingdom and in a variety of ways women are involved in these. Women are still also at the forefront of world mission: in this century they have risen to senior positions in mission agencies as well as serving on the field. One point not lost in the debate on women's ministry is the discrepancy between what women are allowed to do overseas and what they are allowed to do at home.

Another area of ministry has been the development of body life in local churches. With the mobilisation of the whole congregation women have a wide array of ministries in which to be involved in addition to the traditional ones of ministering to women and teaching children. In many churches the diaconal ministry of women has also been recognised. Larger churches have increasingly developed team ministries in which women make a valuable contribution. A growing number of women are involved in theological research and teaching. Not least has been the role women have played in the proliferation of small groups for prayer and Bible study. In all this the twentieth century has supplied some great models of women who have used their gifts for the advancement of Christ's kingdom. To name a few: Henrietta Mears (who ran an influential Bible class at Hollywood Presbyterian Church); Corrie ten Boom; Helen Roseveare; Jackie Pullinger; Joni Earekson Tada; Edith Schaeffer; Elisabeth Elliot Leitch. There are many others.

But perhaps most significant in the 20th century is the shift of the centre of gravity away from the west to the developing world. The churches planted by western missionaries have come of age and have developed their own patterns of ministry from which we can learn. As in the early church, the church in many developing countries has grown due in no small measure to the evangelism of women. Many of the early missionaries trained and deployed Bible women to assist them. Margaret Burton wrote of these largely unknown and unsung women in her book *Women Workers of the Orient:*

> *'Often she may enter doors which do not yet swing*
> *open for the foreign missionary. She goes from zenana*
> *[part of a house reserved for women] to zenana and*
> *house to house, teaching the women and girls to read,*
> *telling them the story of the Good Tidings . . . Wholly*
> *new ideas and purposes spring up in the homes where*
> *these humble, consecrated workers have patiently*
> *gone'.*[46]

In Africa there were movements dedicated to promoting the welfare of women as well as to preaching the gospel. The 'Red Blouse' movement begun in the 1960s in Zimbabwe and Botswana is one example and the 'Women of Good News' began in the 1970s in Zaire is another. The latter combined Bible study, evangelism, good works, social ministry, family support, etc.[47] The same story can be told of other parts of the world. In Myanmar (Burma), women have long been involved in reaching unevangelised groups. In addition women have been involved in social and educational ministries of various kinds. As for ordination to the pastorate the picture is varied. Aside from any biblical considerations such a ministry would be unacceptable in many cultures, while in other cultures this is not a problem. In Sarawak, the Evangelical Church of Borneo ordains women as pastors and evangelists largely because there is such a great need for workers, as does the Baptist Convention in Myanmar.

Conclusion

What conclusions can we draw from this survey? Let me suggest five.

First, women have not been permitted generally speaking to hold pastoral office, whatever form that has taken. Indeed it is only within the last century, indeed the last few decades, that this has been seriously challenged. The proponents of change need to argue a convincing biblical and theological case to show that the historic position of the church has been wrong and needs to be corrected. If they cannot, then the historic position of the church needs to be maintained – not because of tradition but because of Scripture.

Secondly, throughout the history of the church women have exercised a wealth of ministries other than that of pastor-teacher. Today we need to encourage this. A little imagination will enable us to see the opportunities that abound. Certainly one of the lessons of overseas missions is that women at home can do far more than has been generally allowed or encouraged. With the increasing paganisation of the west, many of the ministries used to reach the lost in traditional recipient countries can be of great benefit at home. In particular we need to ask whether there is any biblical reason for a woman not to be recognised and set apart as an evangelist?

Thirdly, we have to give serious thought to the ministry of single women in our churches. The historic channels of ministry for single women were the convent (not a likely option for an evangelical), the school or the mission field. Single women who don't go overseas need to have their gifts used in our churches, perhaps in a way that those of married women do not.

Fourthly, we should consider opening up the office of deacon to women. In so far as the deacons of a church assist the elders by undertaking practical ministries such as administration, mercy, and maintenance, I cannot see why women cannot hold this office. There is good historical precedent as well as biblical warrant for this.

Fifthly, we need to beware of the impact of culture on our thinking and attitudes. Down the centuries many men have imbibed the misogynist attitudes of their culture: the early church fathers are a notorious example of this. Today some who oppose the ordination of women can react by advocating a view that owes more to cultural conservatism than Scripture. Likewise some of those who promote the ordination of women seem to owe more to the secular feminism than Scripture. None of us is immune to cultural influences, so all of us need to come back again and again to the Word of God. Valuable as it is to look at history and to learn from it, in the end we must look to Scripture alone as our rule.

Notes

1. The most helpful survey of the ministry of women in history from an evangelical perspective is Ruth A. Tucker and Walter Liefield, *Daughters of the Church*, Zondervan Publishing House 1987. I have drawn heavily upon this work in writing this chapter. Tucker and Liefield favour the ordination of women to pastoral ministry and this flavours their interpretation of history, but nevertheless the book is very helpful and fair in its treatment. Another useful older work is Edith Deen, *Great Women of the Faith*, Independent Press 1960. This now out-of-print book consists of a number of historical cameos. There are some surprising entries such as 'Mother Ann' Lee and Mary Baker Eddy, but the book is a good and informative source of information.

2. W. H. C. Frend, *The Rise of Christianity*, Darton, Longman & Todd 1984, p. 561.

3. See for example, Clement's First Letter to the Corinthians 1:1, 6:2; Polycarp's Letter to the Philippians 4; Ignatius's Letter to Polycarp 5 in *The Ante-Nicene Fathers*, Roberts, Donaldson & Crombie (eds.), Edinburgh 1868 [hereafter ANF], vol. I, pp. 8, 71, 261.

4. J. Stevenson (ed.), *A New Eusebius*, SPCK 1960, pp. 2-6, 31-36; Tucker and Liefield, p. 114.

5. See Polycarp's Letter to the Philippians 4, 5; Ignatius's Letter to the Philadelphians 4; Ignatius's Letter to Polycarp 4, 5, ANF, I, pp. 71, 227, 262; Tertullian's De Corona 4; Letter to his Wife 1:1; On Chastity 1, ANF, III, pp. 40, 50, 95; and On Apparel 1:1, ANF, IV, p. 14; Cyprian, Epistle LXI, ANF, V, p. 356; Clement of Alexandria, Two Epistles on Virginity, ANF, VIII, p. 51; Frend, p. 411.

6. See Romans 16:1-2; 1 Timothy 3:11.

7. Tucker and Liefield, pp. 109, 122.

8. The *Didascalia Apostolorum* was later incorporated into the *Apostolic Constitutions*, for which see ANF, XVIII, pp. 96-7, 100; Frend, p. 411.

9. Stevenson, pp. 109, 113-114; Hans Lietzmann, *The Founding of the Church Universal*, Lutterworth Press 1953, pp. 194-99; Jaroslav Pelikan, *The Emergence of the Catholic Tradition (100-600)*, University of Chicago Press 1971, pp. 100-1.

10. As quoted in Tucker and Liefield, p. 118.

11. Deen, p. 324; G. W. Greenway, *St. Boniface,* London 1955, pp. 68, 71.

12. David L. Jeffrey (ed.), *The Law of Love, English Spirituality in the Age of Wyclif,* Wm. B. Eerdmans 1988, pp. 17-20; C. F. Kelly (ed.), *The Book of the Poor in Spirit,* Longman, Green & Co. 1954, p. 6.

13. Margaret Astor, *Lollards and Reformers,* London 1984, pp. 49-75.

14. R. W. Southern, *The Making of the Middle Ages,* Arrow Books 1959, pp. 161ff, 192.

15. Roland Bainton, *Here I Stand,* Lion Publishing 1986, pp. 286-304; Steven Ozment, *Protestants,* Fontana 1992, pp. 152, 159-62.

16. John Calvin on 1 Timothy 2:12 in his *Commentaries on the Epistles of Timothy, Titus and Philemon,* Calvin Translation Society 1856; *Institutes of the Christian Religion,* John T. McNeill (ed.) and Ford L. Battles (trans.), Westminster Press 1960, IV,iii,9, p. 1061. It is not entirely clear whether or not Calvin considered this second kind of deacon an office or an informal ministry.

17. George H. Williams, *The Radical Reformation,* Wiedenfeld & Nicolson 1962, pp. 506-7, also pp. xxx, 96, 184.

18. Claus-Peter Clasen, *Anabaptism,* Cornell University Press 1972, pp. 207, 305.

19. As quoted in Tucker and Liefield, p. 185.

20. Ibid.

21. Patrick Collinson, 'The Role of Women in the English Reformation illustrated by the life of Anne Locke', *Studies in Church History,* Thos. Nelson 1965, pp. 258-272.

22. Tucker and Liefield, p. 190.

23. Richard Greaves, 'The Role of Women in Early English Nonconformity', *Church History* (1983), pp. 300ff.

24. Leland Ryken, *Worldly Saints,* Zondervan Publishing House 1986, p. 53; see also pp. 76-78, 195-96, 263; J. I. Packer, *A Quest for Godliness,* Crossway Books 1990, pp. 259-73.

25. See Greaves, p. 302; Antonia Fraser, *The Weaker Vessel,* Methuen 1985, pp. 274-97; Patrick Collinson, *The Elizabethan Puritan*

Movement, pp. 82, 379; Keith Thomas, 'Women in the Civil War Sects', in Trevor Aston (ed.), *Crisis in Europe 1560-1660,* Basic Books 1965, pp. 317-40.

26. Leon MacBeth, *The Baptist Heritage,* Judson Press 1987, p. 516; Michael Mullett, 'Radical Sects and Dissenting Churches, 1600-1750', in Sheridan Gilley and W. J. Shields (eds.), *A History of Religion in Britain,* Blackwell 1994, pp. 201, 208; Rufus Jones, *Studies in Mystical Religion,* Macmillan & Co. 1909, pp. 419ff. Jones gives an account of Mrs. Attaway, the famous 'she-preacher' of Coleman St. in London.

27. Isabel Ross, *Margaret Fell, Mother of Quakerism,* Longman Green & Co. 1949, pp. 199, 283; see also Fell's entry in the *Dictionary of National Biography,* vol. XVIII, p. 297.

28. Tucker and Liefield, pp. 211-216.

29. Jonathan Edwards, *Works,* Banner of Truth Trust 1974, vol. I, pp. lxii-lxx; Iain Murray, *Jonathan Edwards,* Banner of Truth Trust 1987, pp. 171, 173, 193-9.

30. F. Ernest Stoeffler, *Continental Pietism and Early American Christianity,* Wm. B. Eerdmans 1976, pp. 58-9.

31. F. Ernest Stoeffler, *The Rise of Evangelical Pietism,* E. J. Brill 1965, pp. 142, 168.

32. Sarah Tytler, *The Countess of Huntingdon and Her Circle,* Sir Isaac Pitman & Sons 1907; Elizabeth Catherwood, *Selina Hastings: The English Deborah,* Evangelical Library 1991.

33. Michael A. G. Haykin, *One Heart and One Soul, John Sutcliff of Olney, his friends and his times,* Evangelical Press 1994, pp. 218-20, 223, 224.

34. Haykin, p. 295.

35. John Wesley, *Letters,* Epworth Press 1931, vol. V., p. 257; see also IV, pp. 133, 164; V, p. 130; VIII, p. 190; Henry Rack, *The Reasonable Enthusiast,* Epworth Press 1989, p. 244.

36. Ian Bradley, *The Call to Seriousness,* Jonathan Cape 1976, pp. 43, 48.

37. Kenneth Hylson-Smith, *Evangelicals in the Church of England 1734-1984* T. & T. Clark 1988, p. 152.

38. Tucker and Liefield, p. 251.

39. Ibid., p. 272; see also Frances E. Willard, *My Happy Half Century,* New York 1894.

40. S. Pearce Carey, *William Carey,* Hodder & Stoughton 1922, pp. 107, 109, 126, 145-7, 162, 270.

41. Courtney Anderson, *To the Golden Shore,* Judson Press 1987, pp. 110, 170-78, 196, 231, 417-22, 490-93.

42. Tucker and Liefield, pp. 298, 318.

43. Ibid., p. 300.

44. John Piper and Wayne Grudem (eds.), *Recovering Biblical Manhood and Womanhood,* Crossway 1991, pp. xxi-xxii, 76.

45. Tucker and Liefield, pp. 359-364.

46. Ibid., p. 341.

47. Ibid., p. 338.

Leadership in the Bible

Brian Edwards

Brian gained a Bachelor of Divinity degree from London University in 1963 and after a short period of teaching accepted a call to the pastorate of Hook Evangelical Church, Surrey where he remained for almost thirty years. In 1995 Brian resigned his pastoral leadership in order to become President of the Fellowship of Independent Evangelical Churches. Brian is chairman of the FIEC Theological Committee, lectures for the Prepared for Service and Genesis Project training programmes and has written a number of historical and theological books including Nothing But the Truth, a study of the doctrine of Scripture. He is married to Barbara and they have two sons.

Leadership in the Bible

It is perhaps simplistic to divide all feminists into one of three cate-gories: the radical, the liberal and the evangelical. However, since each relates in some way to the Bible these divisions become a useful tool. In my view radical feminism is ridiculous, liberal feminism is dangerous and evangelical feminism is boring. I had better explain that!

Mary Daly in *Beyond God the Father* re-interprets the story of Eve as a 'fall into freedom' (p.44), and Daly's venom against all things male is worked out in her desire for 'castrating God' from his maleness (p.19), and by ridiculing the 'Christian idolatry of Jesus as the incarnate God' (p.69). She would like us all to return to the great Mother Goddess (p.92) and to recognise that radical feminism is the one cause that can set the world free and create a fully egalitarian, or equal, society. As the cover of her book declares: 'The women's movement... may well be the greatest single hope for survival of spiritual consciousness on this planet'[1] Mary Daly's fury against all things male, her reading of history entirely as the domination of male over female, and her remedy for all the problems of the world as lying in the reliable hands of women is frankly ridiculous. A little overstatement in support of a good cause is one thing, gross distortion is quite another. In her pathological hatred of all things biblical Mary Daly even dismisses the high qualities of Christianity – sacrificial love, the acceptance of suffering, humility and meekness etc. - as 'precisely those (qualities) that keep women subservient' (p.77). When Mary Daly rejects Christ as an 'impossible model' for women and suggests that in Catholicism the nun becomes her model and in Protestantism the minister's wife, one begins to wonder if Daly is living in the same century as the rest of us.

The most positive thing about Mary Daly's approach to Scripture is the fact that, unlike her liberal and evangelical sisters, she does at least acknowledge the clear male leadership role taught throughout the Bible – though for that very reason she hates all that the Bible stands for.

Beyond Mary Daly, Elizabeth Fiorenza attempts a brave theological defence of feminism in her book *In Memory of Her*[2] Fiorenza has no loyalty to the biblical texts as inspired; for her they are at best 'historical formulations within the context of a religious community' (p.xv). Her reconstructed historical model is open to serious objections, giving us a classic example of how easily any of us can re-read and misread first century history to suit our own thesis. For example, whilst concluding that 'the beginnings of the early Christian missionary movement are shrouded in historical darkness' (p.160), Fiorenza boldly asserts that 'Women were engaged in mission and church leadership actively both before Paul and independently of Paul'. She continues: 'Without question they were equal and sometimes even superior to Paul in their work for the gospel' (p.161). It will be hard for most readers to appreciate how something that is 'shrouded in historical darkness' on one page can be declared to be 'without question' on the next! At Mark 3:31-35, Elizabeth Fiorenza illustrates how we can all use an exegetical sledgehammer to crack a hermeneutical nut the kernel of which has never been in doubt among evangelicals – namely, that women are equally disciples in the 'Jesus Movement'. That is not the issue; the issue is whether they were leaders.

Liberal feminists are dangerous just because they exhibit a pseudo-loyalty to Scripture. Bible texts are given weight, but are not taken at face value. Fiorenza dismisses 'biblicist certainty' as based not only on 'an outdated theological understanding of revelation but also on a historicist misunderstanding of what the Bible is all about'. She concludes that history, including therefore the Bible, was not only written by the winners (men), but it was also made by them on the backs of 'women, slaves and the lower classes' (p.79). As an example of this Fiorenza, without a shred of textual evidence, concludes that the 'woman prophet' (p.153) who anointed Jesus with oil was changed by the male-centred gospel writer in Luke 7 to a 'repentant sinner'; the beautiful things said of a similar action by another woman, Mary, seem to be conveniently forgotten (Matthew 26:6-16 and Luke 10:38-42). All through her book Elizabeth Fiorenza assumes that behind the stories of the Bible we can detect the 'androcentric (male-centred) character of our sources'; we must rescue the truth by 'historical imagination'. Bible texts must not be taken as 'descriptive of the actual situation' (p.167-168).

The logic of this way of handling Scripture is actually more dangerous that that of the radical feminist. The radicals are glad of the clear teaching of male leadership in Scripture since it reinforces their dismissal of the entire book. On the other hand the liberals set out to use the authority, not of the Bible we actually read, but of the one we should be reading, the one hidden beneath the male-centred gloss on first century history. Presumably we have been waiting all these years for our liberal feminist theologians to read the Bible to us correctly.

Elaine Storkey is quite right to distance evangelical feminists from the Scriptural hermeneutic of Elizabeth Fiorenza and others who see the Bible as a culturally-bound document of patriarchal polemic.[3] However, even the evangelical cannot avoid slipping into the liberal errors of thinking. Elaine Storkey suggests that 'If divinity has to be identified with maleness not femaleness . . . then no wonder that women are oppressed'[4], and still more alarmingly: 'Even the loving Christ can only see things from the vantage point of being a man. It is this most basic dilemma which Christian feminists face'.[5] Just for a moment Elaine Storkey has forgotten that Christ sees women from the vantage point of their creator. Surely her way out of this dilemma would have been to remind us of the full character of Christ but she only directs us to the nature of God who is neither male nor female (p.126).

I have suggested that the evangelical feminist is boring! The God who created both male and female created the distinctions that make them compatibly different. The word suitable in Genesis 2:18 literally means 'corresponding to him', and conveys the idea of both difference and compatibility. The differences between men and women physically, emotionally and in function, roles and responsibilities is part of the rich diversity of life. Elaine Storkey says that 'From a biblical standpoint there is just one set of characteristics given for both men and women – that is, the fruit of the Spirit: love, joy, peace, faithfulness, gentleness, self control and so on'.[6] But that is very selective. No reference is made to the distinctive characteristics referred to by Paul in 1 Timothy 5:9-10,14 and Titus 2:4-5 for example. To overlook the clear distinctives in the biblical role of men and women is boringly bland. God created exciting differences between the sexes and the one who created them male and female knew how best he would use their differences to limit the tragedies brought about by the Fall.

The problem for the evangelical is not *what* Scripture teaches about the role of men and women in leadership – I believe that has generally been properly determined by evangelicals – but rather, *how* that teaching should be applied. It has to be admitted that often in the history of the church the application has been narrow and overbearing to the point of being clearly unbiblical. However, our danger today is that we swing in the opposite direction, dutifully fall in line with contemporary secular thinking and so find ourselves embarrassed by the plain statements of Scripture.

The weakness of the way too many evangelicals interpret Scripture on this issue (hermeneutics) is ably dealt with by Stephen Rees in chapter 4. He shows that their approach is even more dangerous than that of the liberal feminist. My immediate task is to survey what I believe to be the thrust of Scriptural teaching on the subject of male leadership. I will claim that nothing new has come to my attention that would make me doubt the historical understanding of the teaching of the Bible in general, and Paul in particular, on the relationship of men and women in the church. On the other hand, I have to admit that the track record of some parts of the Christian church on this subject, both in history and contemporary society, is not good. Indeed we have cause to be grateful to the feminist movement for one reason at least: it has forced us to re-examine the biblical texts on this issue. Much work has been done on both sides, and if some of us come away all the more convinced that the male spiritual leadership model is thoroughly biblical it must not be assumed that this is merely because we have allowed tradition to triumph over exegesis. Sometimes the traditional exegesis is the right one.

1. Creation and the Fall

The uniqueness of man and woman in creation, the exclusive relationship of one man and one woman in marriage, and the bond of perfect equality is all found in Genesis 2:20-25 and confirmed by the New Testament in Matt. 19:4-6. That perfect model was shattered by the Fall, and the relationship between man and woman was the first casualty after the breach of their relationship with God. Sin affected every area of their life together: sex, worship, love, suffering, leadership and work. In order to bring divine order out of sin's chaos, God began with the man-woman relationship and imposed this judgement: 'Your desire will be for your husband, and he will rule over you' (Genesis 3:16). That statement is God's response to the anarchy let loose by sin, although according to Paul in 1 Corinthians 11:7-8 and 1 Timothy 2:13 male leadership was God's plan revealed in the order of creation – Adam was formed first, then Eve. The word 'rule' (Hebrew - *mashal*) is unambiguous. It is used in the Old Testament to refer to the sun ruling over the day (Genesis 1:16), to kings ruling over their people (Isaiah 19:4), and to the LORD himself ruling from his throne (Zechariah 6:13). Rulers are frequently warned about the way they use their authority but never about the authority itself.

According to Genesis 2 and 3 man was created first and woman was deceived first. For Paul in 1 Timothy 2:11-15 those two facts are highly significant and form the basis for one aspect of woman's submission. This does not imply that Eve was more responsible for sin than Adam was; elsewhere, in Romans 5:12-19, Paul places the blame fully and fairly upon Adam, but here when he is concerned to explain the origin of woman's submission to man the Apostle looks at the Fall from the perspective of the woman. Whilst Adam brought death upon the entire human race, Eve brought particular judgement upon her own sex: pain in childbirth and submission to male leadership.

The rest of the Old Testament continues the theme of male headship. The line of the Messiah is traced through the man in each family, not through the woman. The tribal leaders chosen by God were patriarchs and then the sons of Israel, not his daughters. The first anointed leaders of the monarchy in Israel were kings, the sacrificial system was operated by male priests and the Word of the LORD for the nation came, with a few rare exceptions, through male prophets. It was the man who led his family in worship and presented the offerings on behalf of his family; this did not de-personalise his wife any more than it did his children, it was a matter of leadership or headship. These are inescapable facts of God's history.

When confronted by the key New Testament passages on the role of women in ministry, Andrew Kirk seeks refuge in the alarming conclusion: 'Radical though the suggestion may seem at first sight, I think we may have to face the possibility that these passages simply are not directly applicable to the church today, at least along the lines of the controversy we have been outlining. It just could be that we are engaged in debating a non-issue'.[7] But having comfortably off-loaded the most embarrassing texts he still cannot avoid the total thrust of Scripture in general and the New Testament in particular. It is not sufficient for the evangelical feminist to dismiss the male leadership role in Scripture as 'just the way things were', or as God accommodating himself to local culture; there were many things in contemporary culture to which the Father and the Son did not accommodate. If male leadership is so wrong then it is at least highly embarrassing that the Christian church has had to wait for the advent of Mary Daly and Elizabeth Fiorenza to give us the instructions that our Creator God failed to issue over two thousand years of biblical revelation!

The new birth no more changes this authority order between man and woman than it changes the authority between slave and master, subject and sovereign. Galatians 3:28 , 'the feminist charter', refers to equality as children of God (v.26) not to equality in society. The Bible never recognises total egalitarianism whether in the home, the church, or in society generally; what it does insist upon, however, is that inequality does not diminish quality. Or to put it another way, submission to authority never implies secondary value. Onesimus was sent back to Philemon 'no longer as a slave, but better than a slave, as a dear brother' (Philemon 16), at the same time this equal quality did not mean that in future he would no longer serve his old master. On the contrary, Onesimus was now useful in a way he never had been before (v.11); he would serve as a slave, but with the dignity of a brother in Christ.

2. Arguments for the leadership of Women

The arguments put forward in favour of the equality of women in leadership/teaching in the Bible include the following:

First. It is noted that women have always been included in the prophetic ministry. Miriam, Deborah, Huldah, and Anna are offered as the only named examples in two thousand years of Bible history. That women had the gift of prophecy in the New Testament is without question (Acts 2:17-18; 21:9; 1 Corinthians 11:5), and, the argument runs, if prophecy as the highest authority is open to women then teaching can hardly be denied to them. But prophetesses were rare in God's Old Testament provision and they were not all considered as leaders. When men ceased to act as leaders during the dark ages of unparalleled spiritual rebellion recorded in the book of Judges, there was the occasional exception to God's male leadership pattern; and Deborah is the single clear exception (Judges 4-5). The exceptions demonstrate that principles are sometimes suspended when the sinfulness of humanity demands it. Compare the provision of divorce 'because your hearts were hard' (Matthew 19:8). Significantly, however, it was the priest who had the main teaching function within the Old Testament (see for example Nehemiah 8:8) and there were no priestesses in the Jewish cultus – unlike many of the surrounding nations. It is evident that the role of expounding and teaching the Word of the Lord in the Old Testament was male.

Secondly. It is argued that there is no stated limitation upon the gifts of the Spirit being distributed among women and some of these gifts include teaching and leadership. *In Men, Women and God,* Faith and Roger Forster struggle to make a clear case for women in leadership in the New Testament. In a moment of incredible special pleading they conclude that Paul's reference to Euodia and Syntyche labouring alongside him in the gospel (Philippians 4:2) is evidence that they were engaged in evangelism and pastoring.[8] Elizabeth Fiorenza is certain that the phrase 'side by side' means 'on a level with himself'.[9] Tell that to the platoon sergeant when his soldiers fight side by side with him! There are a thousand ways they could have been working with Paul in the gospel; the army of men and women who organise publicity, print the tracts, prepare our evangelistic suppers, invite their friends or engage in one-to-one witnessing are all 'labouring alongside' the leaders. Besides, evangelism and pastoring is not necessarily leadership. We need something more substantial than this to demonstrate women in leadership in the New Testament.

The Forsters only make matters worse when they deal with the question of eldership. That there were no women elders in the New Testament is clear, so they can only resort to the observation: 'At some point in the first three centuries of the Christian church there were also women elders, since this office was disbanded by the Council of Laodicea in 363 AD, which proves it was in existence prior to this time.'[10] With an argument as vague as that the case is surely lost! Is it not possible that the Council of Laodicea simply returned wisely to the practice of the New Testament?

The claim that all the New Testament gifts are available to women because no limitation is placed upon them in the gift lists is special pleading. If we take the whole teaching of the New Testament there *are* limitations. What does Paul mean in 1 Timothy 2:12 'I do not permit a woman to teach' if he is not making a limitation to the gift of teaching? An embarrassing verse like that must, of course, be dispensed with in some way; in the next chapter Stephen Rees ably deals with the arguments of those who try to do so. It is evident that there are limitations to the gifts but Paul deals with these not where he lists the gifts but when he deals with authority within the church.

Thirdly. It is claimed that there is evidence of the teaching ministry of women in the New Testament. The dubious examples of Priscilla and Phoebe are offered. In fact it is because Priscilla 'undoubtedly had the gift of teaching' that Faith and Roger Forster suggest that 1 Timothy 2:11-15 must be interpreted another way or else these two women would be 'disobeying Paul'.[11] To build a case for the public preaching and teaching of women from the private and supportive ministry of Priscilla, whatever form it took, is wholly unjustified. But it must forever remain an open question as to how far Priscilla was involved in actually teaching Apollos. That she is linked with her husband need reveal no more than a partnership in which she fully supported her husband's ministry in a variety of ways. That her name precedes that of Aquila in Acts 18:26 and Romans 16:3 may be no more than a nice courtesy on the part of Luke and Paul. Traditionally it has been a British characteristic to put the man's name first but that is not shared by our continental friends. The fragile argument from the ministry of Priscilla is bolstered by the even more fragile suggestion that she may have authored the anonymous letter to the Hebrews. The Forster's claim that Harnack's argument for this is 'well-reasoned'.[12] This reveals a painfully slim understanding of the debate over the authorship of Hebrews. Dr. Donald Guthrie in his definitive *New Testament Introduction* dismisses Priscilla's authorship of Hebrews as the least likely of eight options![13]

The role of Phoebe as 'diakonos' can never be used to prove that she had a teaching ministry. Even if we allow that she was a 'deacon' in the sense of the office recorded in 1 Timothy 3, something that cannot be proved from the words used in Romans 16:1, we have still to show that the office of deacon implied a ministry of teaching – a most unlikely conclusion. Amazingly Elizabeth Fiorenza asserts that the word 'diakonos' referring to Phoebe in Romans 16 shows that she was 'a missionary entrusted with preaching and teaching churches'.[14] It is impossible to draw such a sweeping agenda from that one word which means simply that she 'served' the churches in some way unspecified by Paul.

Fourthly. It is suggested that women took the role of deacon in the first century. This is certainly one way of understanding the 'women' referred to in 1 Timothy 3:11, and the designation of Phoebe in Romans 16:1; more significant is the suggestion that the 'older women' of Titus 2:3 refers to women elders since the word 'presbytidas' is used. However many churches that deny ultimate spiritual leadership to women would have no problem appointing women deacons; we need to define beyond doubt the role and authority of the deacon before we can use 1 Timothy 3:11 in this debate – even assuming that 'gunaikas' refers to deaconesses and not to the deacons' wives. As for the 'older women' of Titus 2:3, the feminine form of 'presbyteros' would be 'presbytera', NOT the word 'presbytidas' which is used here.

Fifthly. It is similarly argued that if 2 John is addressed to an individual, 'the chosen lady' must have been a leader in the church. Also some conclude from Romans 16:7 that there were women apostles: 'Greet Andronicus and Junias . . . They are outstanding among the apostles.' But the identity of the recipient of John's second letter is a matter of debate amongst Bible commentators. There are as many good arguments in favour of the 'chosen lady' being a pseudonym for a church as there are for it being an individual; and even if the recipient is an individual, she may be no more than the wealthy woman in whose home the church met, like Mary, the mother of John Mark. Actual spiritual leadership must be proved, not assumed. With regard to Andronicus and Junia there is an alternative and well established understanding of the reference to Junia and her husband (assuming they are a husband and wife) as having an outstanding reputation among the apostles. In her chapter in *Men, Women and God* Valerie Griffiths refers to the Christian gospel setting women free 'to serve God as full, participating members of the local church, working alongside men in witnessing to the Christian faith' – an excellent claim from which no Christian I am aware of would dissent – but then she adds 'including Junia, a woman apostle'.[15] No reference is made to the slim evidence on which such a claim rests, nor to the more generally accepted alternative understanding of this verse.

It is time we admitted that if Priscilla, Phoebe and Junia are the only evidence that can be offered for women in leadership and teaching in the church, then the case is lost simply because none of them is clearly stated to have had either a leadership or a teaching ministry.

3. Women in the ministry of Christ and the Apostles

Women played a significant and important role during the ministry of Christ but there is no evidence that this was in leadership. It was exclusively men whom he chose for both his inner circle of twelve and for the seventy he sent out to preach (Matthew 10:2-3; Luke 10:1). Ministry to him and his disciples was undertaken by the women (Luke 8:3) but the authority of gospel preaching and leadership within the church was committed exclusively to men. To accuse Christ of simply conforming to his culture overlooks the radical nature of so much of his teaching. He never passively accepted culture or tradition when a fundamental principle of freedom was at stake. Christ frequently clashed with both tradition and culture in order to set people free as for example on the issues of handwashing and Sabbath observance. This was something clearly recognised by the disciples when Christ spoke of the equality of husbands and wives and the limitations to divorce (Matthew 19:1-12). Notice their shocked response: 'If this is the situation between a husband and wife, it is better not to marry.' (v.10).

I find Elizabeth Fiorenza's brave reconstruction of first century society unconvincing and self-defeating. She maintains that we ought to read all first century references to women by both Jews and church leaders as androcentric texts because they do not necessarily reflect the historical reality of the position of women in society, but simply how men saw their role. She points out that what we do not have are first century texts that are written by women about women.[16] But why not, if women were in equal leadership roles within society? I am equally unconvinced by Fiorenza's assertion that 'Women... were leaders in expanding the Jesus Movement in Galilee and in developing a theo-logical argument'[17], and that, 'Without question they were equal and sometimes even superior to Paul in their work for the gospel'.[18] But then, as we have seen, Fiorenza also admits that the historical texts must not be taken 'as descriptive of the actual situation'.[19]

On the contrary, I believe the pattern of male leadership set from the Old Testament and by Christ himself was clearly followed in the life of the early church described in Acts. When a replacement Apostle was required it was necessary to choose 'one of the men' (Acts 1:21), and that pattern continued. That women were involved in gospel work is clear, but the leadership of the churches (elders) and the work of the 'Word' and teaching (1 Timothy 5:17) was male. The references to

Euodia and Syntyche working 'side by side' with Paul (Philippians.4:2-3), to Phoebe 'serving the church at Cenchrea' (Romans 16:1), and to the hard work of Mary, Tryphena and Tryphosa (Romans 16:6,12) tell us a great deal about the vital and significant role of women in the work of the gospel, but nothing about their position as leaders or teachers.

It is a sad comment upon the way evangelical minds have been captured by political correctness that when we describe the actual role of women portrayed in the New Testament we are confronted with a groan of despair or anger. It all appears so traditional and domestic. One of the tragedies of the current debate is that, in a desperate attempt to squeeze women into the role of full teaching and leadership, we have lost sight of the vital and biblical ministry our Lord gave them. This has somehow become everything, and anything else is reduced to nothing.

The Bible contains many stories of the lives of good women but almost all of them, with the rare exception of figures like Deborah the leader and prophetess, and Esther the queen, are noteworthy for their domestic role. This may not be popular but it happens to be a fact. The model wife of Proverbs 31, the mother of Samson (Judges 13), Naomi and Ruth, Hannah the mother of Samuel (1 Samuel 1), the widow of Zarephath (1 Kings 17), the Shunamite who gave hospitality to Elijah (2 Kings 4), Dorcas (Acts 9), Lydia (Acts 16), Priscilla (Acts 18 and Romans 16), and Lois and Eunice (2 Timothy 1) are all examples of godly women who are noted for their care of their homes and children. Paul sends his greetings to both men and women in the churches, commends both for their hard work and loyalty – as he does in Romans 16 – but his instructions for leadership are always for the men alone (Romans 16:17).

More particularly the women in the gospel records provided hospitality for Jesus and his disciples. Four women are especially noted in Mark 15:40-41 as those who had 'cared for his needs'. A verb from the Greek noun 'diakonos' is used here and the literal translation is 'served him'. Some of the same women are referred to in Luke 8:2-3 as those who 'were helping to support them out of their own means'. The same word for serve, diakonos, is used with the added reference to their own 'means', a word which can only apply to their own goods, wealth or property. No teaching or leadership role is suggested for the women in the gospels and it is wishful speculation to imagine otherwise.

Paul follows the same pattern in his letters. The qualification for a destitute widow to be cared for by the church was that she was 'well known for her good deeds, such as bringing up children, showing hospitality, washing the feet of the saints, helping those in trouble and devoting herself to all kinds of good deeds' (1 Timothy 5:10). Younger widows were encouraged to remarry 'to have children, to manage their homes and to give the enemy no opportunity for slander' (v.14). Writing to Titus, the apostle encourages the older women to train the younger women 'to love their husbands and children, to be self controlled and pure, to be busy at home, to be kind and to be subject to their husbands, so that no one will malign the word of God' (Titus 2:5). Not a word is said of teaching and leadership in the church.

Significantly, Paul attributes a major part of Timothy's early spiritual growth to the ministry of his mother and grandmother (2 Timothy 1:5). What greater ministry could these two women have had than to exercise a significant influence in the young life of an outstanding preacher and teacher in the church at Ephesus?

However, this is by no means all that can be said of the role of women in the New Testament. While there is no clear evidence of women engaged in a leadership or teaching role over men, and significant evidence to the contrary, they were equal partners in prayer (Acts 1:14 and 1 Corinthians 11:5), and some prophesied (1 Corinthians 11:5). What is more, the quality of the spiritual lives of many of the women in the New Testament is significant. They are marked out as those with courage to stand at the cross when the men had fled (Matthew 27:55-56), they were first at the tomb and therefore the first to be rewarded with the privilege of meeting the risen Christ (Mark 16:9). They show a discernment and faith that seems to have escaped the men for a long time.

Perhaps the most significant counterbalance to the major domestic role that was clearly theirs is the story of Mary of Bethany. On the three occasions when she appears, her priorities of faith and worship are evident. Luke 10:38-42 reveals Mary in her own home, John 12:1-8 shows Mary as a guest and John 11:1-45 has Mary at the grave of her brother. On each occasion she is treated both by the Lord himself and therefore by the gospel recorder with a commendation and respect that seems to have escaped most feminist commentators in their eagerness to discredit the male-centredness of the New Testament writers. Mark records the words of our Lord that she had done 'a beautiful thing to me' (14:6) and that wherever the gospel is preached throughout the world this story must be told to her credit (14:9). Luke tells us that our Lord commented upon Mary's worship as the 'better thing' and the 'one thing necessary' that would not be taken from her (Luke 10:42); it was partly Mary's adoration and faith that moved our Lord to tears in John 11:35. In the first story of Mary, which is recorded by Matthew, Mark and John, the men are cast in a less than favourable light by contrast, as they are in the similar story of another woman given to us in Luke 7. So much for the male bias of our gospel writers!

Our Lord's response to Mary, one of unqualified commendation and acceptance, reveals the equality of women in worship and discipleship. [20] Jesus healed women, talked with them at length, raised their dead, cared for their children, preached the gospel to them, referred to them in his stories and even told some parables especially for them. Yet when he returned from a night of prayer with his Father he chose only men for the leadership of the church and the heralding of the good news.

In her book *The Role of Women*[21] Elizabeth Catherwood remarks that as a result of feminist publicity, 'no word is more laden with the aura of boredom, lack of ability and character, or even sheer horror, than that of "housewife".' Sadly Elizabeth Catherwood is right. Our feminists have a lot to answer for – the evangelicals among them. A few years ago, the head of a girls' High School was being interviewed on the radio. She lamented that girls had no drive for top management and complained: 'There is no doubt at all that babies and the home knock the fight out of a girl'. What a miserably one-sided and inadequate view of the home-maker. The wife, mother and home-maker is already in top management!

A mother was out shopping with a baby in the pram and two toddlers dragging behind. A young woman approached from the opposite direction: smartly dressed, she had obviously reached the top of her profession. As she came closer, the mother recognised her as an old school friend. 'Hello', the professional greeted, 'and what are you doing in life?'. The weary mother pulled herself upright and responded: 'I'm working in a partnership for social development and I supervise the 'under-five's' department. I also spend a fair bit of my time in the department of health, hygiene and food, and assist in financial control. What do you do?'. 'Oh', gasped the admiring young professional, 'I'm just a model'.

Why is the commendation of Mary's quiet spirit of adoration so consistently overlooked by our feminist writers? Why is the vital role of domestic management and the earliest training of the next generation of Christian leaders, evidenced by Lois and Eunice, so deplored by feminists? Why is there such a feverish search for the non-existent evidence of women in teaching/leadership in the New Testament? Why are Christians who claim a loyalty to the Bible so neglectful of the clear thrust of the biblical emphasis on this subject? Why has hermeneutics been dragged into disarray by special pleading, and fanciful imagination? And why are we so unprepared to accept what the Scriptures so plainly teach?

At the end of a conference during which I had taken part in a debate on this subject, I was asked how I would explain the fact that speakers all claiming to be loyal to the Bible could come to such different conclusions. The problem does not lie in the clarity of the Bible but in the prejudices of our minds. A generation has grown up that has been trained to think that the feminist agenda is the right one and so the clear and beautiful New Testament role distinctions between men and women are rejected and despised. If sufficient voices speak loud enough and long enough, even Christians will fall in line. As Joni Erickson Tada has written in another context: 'Gradually, though no one remembers exactly how it happened, the unthinkable becomes tolerable. And then acceptable. And then legal. And then applaudable'.[22]

Finally

I believe God's plan for his chosen people was for order and leadership in the home and in the community. God established a male leadership. The patriarchs, Moses, Joshua, Samuel, Saul and David were all specifically ordained as leaders by God. We never read of a woman set apart by God for religious or state leadership, and there were no priestesses within Judah, though many among the surrounding nations.

While God is neither male nor female, he chose to be addressed as 'father' and 'husband', he did not choose to be addressed as 'mother' or 'wife'. To use Matthew 23:37 as Elaine Storkey does: 'How often I have longed to gather your children together as a hen gathers her chicks under her wings' betrays the poverty of the case she is trying to make![23] She might have been wiser to refer us instead to the lone verse in Isaiah 66:13 'As a mother comforts a child, so will I comfort you' – but you cannot make a theology out of a simile!

We may rightly blame men for the cultural tradition that has often marginalised women in society, but as evangelical Christians we cannot avoid the facts that it is the Sovereign Creator, who made both man and woman in his own image and likeness, who nevertheless revealed himself as Father not mother, who chose men not women to act as writers for his revelation, who called Patriarchs not matriarchs to be on centre stage in the formation of his chosen people, who chose priests not priestesses to be the mediators of the Old Testament sacrificial ceremonies, who sent his Son not a daughter to be our Saviour, who called men not women into the inner circle of apostolic leadership, who sent men not women to act as heralds of the good news of the kingdom, and who established men and not women as leaders and teachers in the early Christian community.

If God has merely accommodated himself in all this to contemporary culture and has nothing abiding to teach us in this pattern, then he has gravely misled us, and a modern generation of anti-Christian humanists have proved themselves more wise and more humane that God himself. But what the world regards as just and fair is not *our* standard for reckoning. The alternative is to believe that what is often wrong in the story of the church is not the basic God-revealed pattern of male spiritual leadership but the way the Christian church has abused and misused this pattern.

The issue is not whether women *can or cannot* do the same things as men but whether they *ought to*. Distinct God-given roles of men and women in the church tell us nothing about superiority or inferiority, unless we make an arbitrary decision that some duties and services are more quality-human than others. God no more dehumanises women by barring them from leadership or teaching over men than he dehumanises men by preventing them, for example, from bearing and nursing children. The problem is not what men and women can and cannot do, it is how we perceive the roles God has given them. But the detail of this must wait until a later chapter.

The beautiful picture presented by the Bible in general and the New Testament in particular of the nature, dignity and role of women in relation to men in the home and in the church – a picture of headship, submission, love, harmony and security – convinces me that we should be proud and not ashamed of the biblical teaching on this vital subject. After all, as John Piper wisely says of our Creator: 'He designed our differences and they are profound'.[24]

Notes

1. Mary Daly *Beyond God the Father – Towards a philosophy of Women's Liberation* The Women's Press 1973 reprinted 1985. At the time of writing, Mary Daly was Associate Professor of Theology at Boston College, Massachusetts 'unconfined by the teachings of church or man'.
2. Elizabeth Fiorenza *In Memory of Her – A Feminist Theological Reconstruction of Christian Origins* S.C.M Press 1983 p.xv.
3. *Men, Women and God* Marshall Pickering 1987 ed. Kathy Keay.
4. *What's Right with Feminism?* S.P.C.K 1985 p.123.
5. ibid. p. 124.
6. *Men, Women and God* p. 9.
7. *Men, Women and God* p.39.
8. *Men, Women and God* p.56.
9. *In Memory of Her* p.169.
10. ibid. p.56.
11. ibid. p.57.

12. *Men, Women and God* p.52-53.
13. Donald Guthrie *New Testament Introduction* Tyndale Press 1962.
14. *In Memory of Her* p171.
15. ibid. p.63.
16. *In Memory of Her* pp.105 on.
17. ibid. p.139.
18. ibid. p.161.
19. ibid. p.167-168.
20. There is an excellent chapter by James Borland in *Recovering Biblical Manhood and Womanhood* Crossway Books, Illinois, 1991 pp.113-123.
21. *The Role of Women* I.V.P. 1984.
22. *When is it Right to Die?* Marshall Pickering 1993 p.63.
23. *What's Right with Feminism* p.124.
24. *Recovering Biblical Manhood and Womanhood* p.32.

Interpreting the Bible on Gender

Stephen Rees

Stephen was educated at Manchester
Grammar School and St. John's College
Cambridge where he read classics and
theology. He has been the minister of Grace
Baptist Church, Stockport, since its formation
in 1984. Stephen describes himself as a G.P.: a
pastor whose aim it is to preach in a way that
is exegetical, doctrinal, biblico-theological,
ethical and experimental!

Interpreting the Bible on Gender

When evangelical Christians debate gender issues, the discussion usually focuses on a small number of key texts. The passages generally referred to are Genesis chapters 1-3; 1 Corinthians 11:2-16; 1 Corinthians 14:33-36; Galatians 3:28; Ephesians 5:21-23; Colossians 3:18-19; 1 Timothy 2:8-15; Titus 2:4-5; 1 Peter 3:1-7.

We will not be offering a detailed exegesis of these passages here; some of them are discussed thoroughly in chapters five and six. Our objective in this chapter is to think about the question of how we approach the task of interpreting such passages.

In the past, such a discussion might not have been necessary. Bible-commentators of previous generations apparently found little problem in interpreting these passages. They disagreed, of course, over details of exegesis but to them the broad lines of teaching seemed straight-forward. As they read the opening chapters of the Bible, they discovered that from the Creation there was a certain order in the roles of man and woman. It was clear to them that men and women are different. Man was created first. Woman was created out of man and for man, to be his helper. And when these Bible-readers turned to the New Testament, they found their understanding confirmed. They learned from 1 Corinthians 11 that the secondary (but not inferior) role that woman held in relation to man was mirrored upon the relation of God the Son to God the Father. As they studied the other passages listed, they learned that while man and woman have equal standing before God, they are called to play different roles in the family and the church. Within the family, a wife should submit to her husband: within the church, women should follow male leadership.

That broad consensus no longer exists. In the course of this chapter we will be quoting a number of Bible scholars who call themselves *evangelical* or *biblical* feminists. These scholars hold a high view of Scripture. They speak of its full authority. Many of them would use words like infallibility or even inerrancy. But they deny that Scripture teaches any special priority or leadership role for men.

C. Powell writes in *Themelios* (the journal of the Religious and Theological Studies Fellowship which forms part of the UCCF), 'Scripture teaches equality and mutual submission rather than a hierarchy of sexes'.[1] That sums up well the position of many 'evangelical feminists'.

In the same issue of *Themelios,* Robert Letham (not a feminist) defines evangelical feminists as 'those who hold to evangelical theology (such as the authority of Scripture and the sufficiency of Christ as saviour) and argue for a non-hierarchical relation of full equality and reciprocity between man and woman'.[2] The word 'reciprocity' simply means a mirror relationship: whatever role man plays towards woman, woman can and should play towards man. If, for example, a wife's role is to submit to her husband, then reciprocally, a husband should submit to his wife.

So, the question is this. If Bible-readers down through the centuries have found the Bible's teaching on gender issues so plain, how is it that evangelical feminists can read the same passages and come to such very different conclusions?

The answer obviously lies in the methods of interpretation – the hermeneutics – which are used to read the Bible. Hence the need for this chapter. Some evangelical feminists lay out their hermeneutical system explicitly; some do not. But they all have a system: principles which they bring to the study of Scripture.

As far back as 1977, Grant Osborne, (a leading feminist scholar) wrote, 'the determining factor in the discussion is hermeneutical'.[3]

Powell agrees: '...the debate is not simply a matter of whether Scripture is authoritative, but how that authority may be discovered. We are still left with the dilemma that evangelicals (ie those, including myself, who regard Scripture as primary and authoritative) do not necessarily agree upon the interpretation of the text... Deciding what the text means involves more than merely assenting to its authority.'[4]

In this chapter, we will list five hermeneutical rules which are often found in the writings of evangelical feminists. Not all evangelical feminists would accept all five. But these five rules do emerge frequently in the work of different feminist Bible scholars.

Rule 1: Clear passages have priority over obscure passages

Evangelical feminists have often emphasised that difficult or ambiguous passages should be read in the light of straightforward passages. That, of course, is not a new insight. Few evangelicals would disagree with the principle as stated. But how is the rule to be applied? Consider this statement from Gretchen Gaebelein Hull's book: *Equal to Serve: Women and Men in the Church and Home.* Hull is an evangelical feminist who speaks warmly of the inspiration and inerrancy of Scripture. She writes, 'Everything I know about God indicates that he is indeed love, so loving that He himself came to die for me. Therefore, I put to one side passages like the imprecatory Psalms or the Canaanite wars that I do not understand. But I do not throw out the known truth "God is love" simply because some passages about the nature of God puzzle me'.[5]

We should take note of two things. First, whenever we appeal to 'Rule 1' it is obvious that someone has to decide which are the hard passages and which are the easy ones. Hull has decided that 'God is love' is an easy passage, and she has decided that the imprecatory psalms are difficult. But not all readers will accept her judgement. The statement 'God is love' seems to me far from straighforward. Is it a statement about his essential being? Or about his relationships with his creatures? Does it teach that God is always love? That he is only love? And what does the word 'love' mean in this verse? Is it a feeling? Or is it a relationship? Or is it an attitude? The word love can be employed in all these ways. By contrast I find the imprecatory psalms very easy to understand. 'O Daughter of Babylon, doomed to destruction, happy is he who repays you for what you have done to us - he who seizes your infants and dashes them against the rocks' (Psalm 137:8-9). We may not find such verses pleasant to read, but surely we know exactly what they mean. So it seems that two people may not always agree as to which are hard and which are easy verses.

We are entitled to ask why Hull puts the statement 'God is love' into the easy pigeon-hole and the imprecatory psalms into the difficult. The answer is there in the opening words of her statement. 'Everything I know about God indicates that he is indeed love'. Behind her decision there is a prior decision. She has already decided how she views the nature of God before she looks at either passage. A hard passage is not one where the vocabulary is obscure and the syntax complex, or where it is difficult to establish the writer's intention. The hard one is simply the one that seems to contradict her own experience. The easy one is the one that confirms what she already believes. The application of the rule has become simply a matter of subjective preference.

It is important to note, secondly, what Hull suggests we should do with the hard passages. She says: 'I put to one side passages like the imprecatory psalms or the Canaanite wars'. They are simply discarded. They can be left out of account when we draw up our doctrinal statements.

This is very different from the way Rule 1 has historically been used by evangelicals. Evangelicals have always accepted that when we are formulating Bible doctrine, priority must be given to unambiguous passages. But they have never felt free to 'put to one side' the difficult passages. Rather, we return to them to study them afresh in the light of what we have learned from the 'easy' passages. And often our rereading of the difficult passages forces us to return yet again to our easy passages to refine our understanding of them. The study of Scripture has been described as a 'hermeneutical spiral' where we are constantly refining our understanding. Hull's procedure is more akin to that of a radical surgeon, excising passages that fit awkwardly with her prior understanding.

Having explained the working of Rule 1, Hull applies it to the question of male and female roles. She says, 'So we should also treat the three "hard passages" about women (1 Corinthians 11: 2-16; 14: 33b-36; 1 Timothy 2: 8-15) which we find in the New Testament and which appear to place specific restrictions on women only. To these we could add Colossians 3:18; Ephesians 5: 22-24; and 1 Peter 3:1-6... we may legitimately put these Scripture portions aside for the very reason that they remain hard passages – hard exegetically, hard hermeneutically, and hard theologically'.[6]

Hull has already quoted passages which she considers clear and unambiguous on the subject of women's roles. They include, for example, 2 Corinthians 5:14-21, a passage which says nothing explicit about gender roles at all. By contrast, each of the passages which speak directly about gender roles (and which seemed so clear to readers in the past) are, she claims, so obscure, that they cannot be safely used at all. Hull says that we may simply 'put these Scripture portions aside'.

Our stand as historic evangelicals is that *all* Scripture is inspired by God and is useful for teaching (2 Timothy 3:16). Any hermeneutical approach that allows us to discard vast areas of the Word of God is surely irreverent and must destroy all biblical authority. To hold on to her understanding of 'God is love', Hull 'puts to one side' many of the psalms, as well as the greater part of the biblical histories with their accounts of wars commanded by God. To maintain her understanding of 'we regard no-one from a worldly point of view' (1 Corinthians 5:16) and 'There is neither male nor female, for you are all one in Christ Jesus' (Galatians 3:28) she discards not only the 'hard passages' cited above, but the whole sweep of redemptive history. The lesson is plain. As evangelical Christians, we must never be satisfied with our view of any subject unless we have dealt honestly with *all* the Bible data.

Rule 2: Broad principles have priority over individual texts

A second rule, often appealed to by evangelical feminists, may be summed up in the words of Howard Marshall. 'When we speak of the supreme authority of Scripture, we speak of *the authority of Scripture taken as a whole* rather than of isolated texts within it... isolated texts taken on their own may convey a message which is at variance with that of Scripture as a whole.'[7] Willard Swartley spells out what this implies: 'The interpreter should give priority to theological principles and basic moral imperatives rather than to specific council on particular topics when these two contradict'.[8]

Again we recognise a truth in these statements. Evangelical theologians have always emphasised that no passage should be interpreted in a way that contradicts the teaching of Scripture as a whole. But how is this principle (the *analogia fidei*) applied by evangelical feminists?

A good example would be the manifesto published by the evangelical feminist organisation *Christians for Biblical Equality* in 1990.[9] The introduction to the document includes these words: 'The Bible teaches that God has revealed himself in the totality of Scripture, the authoritative Word of God. We believe that Scripture is to be interpreted wholistically and thematically'. We are warned that we must never take our teaching from individual texts or passages. Rather, we must first decide what 'the totality of Scripture' teaches, and then we must read individual passages in the light of the broad themes of Scripture.

The authors of the manifesto proceed to lay down what they view as the broad themes on gender issues: the principles which emerge from the totality of Scripture. They list 'Biblical Truths' relating to Creation, Redemption, Community and Family: for example, the fact that both man and woman were created in the image of God; that both had a direct relationship with God; that they were created for a 'full and equal partnership'; that both are redeemed in Christ; that both experience the indwelling of the Holy Spirit since Pentecost; that both receive gifts sovereignly from the Spirit.

Few evangelical Christians would disagree with these broad principles. But the question remains: how should we interpret texts that seem to differentiate between the roles of men and women? The authors write, 'The Bible teaches that in the New Testament economy, women as well as men exercise the prophetic, priestly and royal functions... Therefore, the few isolated texts that appear to restrict the full redemptive freedom of women must not be interpreted simplistically and in contradiction to the rest of Scripture, but their interpretation must take into account their relation to the broader teaching of Scripture and their total context.'

The argument is clear. The writers agree that there are texts that *appear* to restrict women's roles but tell us that those texts must not be 'interpreted simplistically' since that would clash with their broad principles. When they come to a text, they rule out *a priori* any interpretation which contradicts their broad principles. They are forced to look for an alternative way of understanding it. But might it not be the case that the way they have formulated their broad principles is over-simplistic? Perhaps the broad principles need to be refined to harmonise with the obvious meaning of these texts.

How would we react if the same methods were applied to other areas of exegesis? Take for example all the Bible has to say about the final state of the wicked. God is love. God loves the world. Christ is the Saviour of mankind. These are great Bible themes. So if there are verses which seem to speak of individuals being finally condemned, then, by this hermeneutical principle, they simply cannot mean what they seem to say. That has always been the approach of liberals to the text of Scripture, but here we have people who call themselves evangelical adopting exactly the same hermeneutical approach.

Rule 3: Narratives have priority over doctrinal statements

Scripture includes both narratives and propositional statements. Which should have priority as we formulate our theology and ethics? Many evangelical feminists are contending that narrative should be given a more prominent role than 'traditionalists' have allowed. Again, Gretchen Gaebelein Hull makes the point clear. She lists a number of narratives from Scripture where women apparently took non-traditional roles, sometimes involving leadership over men. Then she says this: 'Those of us who wish to base our world view on God's Word must take these case studies seriously. When we do, we see that his creative choosing activity included many women and that he used women in a variety of nontraditional ways...'[10]

Hull refuses to accept the response of her 'traditionalist friends' that these cases were rare exceptions. She writes, '...concentrating on the number of these "exceptions" will cause us to miss the basic point: If there is only one "exception" – only one Deborah or Huldah or Phoebe – that single case undermines the traditionalist position. If there is only one woman commended by the text for a nontraditional action, we must draw the conclusion that the Bible does not teach role playing. You see, while we may accept the proverb, "The exception proves the rule", the exception does not prove truth. Truth cannot have exceptions. Truth must be unchangeable.'[11]

The implication is plain. However clear the commands and principles taught in Scripture may appear to be, they may be overruled if a single example can be found where a believer is commended for an action contrary to the command.

Once again, the same approach applied to other issues would have startling implications. The Lord commanded Hosea 'Go, marry a prostitute' (Hosea 1:2). That single example may outweigh all that Scripture says about the dangers of marriage to an unbeliever and the call to keep the marriage bed pure (Hebrews 13:4). Samson is commended for the fact that in his death he slays more than in his life (Judges 16:30). Therefore, all believers are free to commit suicide in order to massacre their enemies. The Hebrew midwives gave a misleading answer to Pharaoh's enquiries and were rewarded by God for their faith (Exodus 1:19-20). We may conclude that Scripture does not condemn lying.

Evangelical theologians have always taken full account of the fact that there may be exceptional situations where one commandment must be put aside in order to keep a higher commandment. At times this may be expressed in terms of 'the lesser of two evils'. (A young believer might for example, be forced to disobey a parent who demanded a sinful course of action). But evangelicals have always insisted that such exceptional cases do not invalidate the general force of the commandments. The Lord Jesus, when challenged concerning the Sabbath law, appealed to the example of the priests who 'in the temple desecrate the day and yet are innocent' (Matthew 12:5). Similarly, a man who labours on the Sabbath to rescue his sheep from a pit is acting lawfully (Matthew 5:12). In such cases, the commandment to rest from all labour is overruled by a higher commandment. But these exceptional cases do not invalidate the general rule.

A crucial principle is at stake here. Responsible evangelical theologians have always insisted that we draw our theology and ethics from the propositional statements and the commands of Scripture and then we read the narratives in the light of those propositions. We formulate, for example, our doctrine of the Holy Spirit's work in the believer from such passages as Romans 8 and 1 Corinthians 12 – and then we apply our findings to the narratives of Acts 2 & Acts 19. (This is in fact only a specific application of the method which Hull herself earlier pleaded for: our Rule 1). Hull here reverses that order. She begins by reading selected biblical narratives, and then interprets the doctrinal passages in the light of those narratives.

Hull's approach would find support from many feminist biblical scholars. 'Narrative theology' is given an increasingly important role. Helen Sterk argues thus for the importance of 'narrative theology': '...women find stories exceptionally congenial forms of expression, well suited to preserving and passing on knowledge... women tend to think narratively...'.[12] 'From the stories of Eve and Adam, Abraham and Sarah, Elijah, Elisha, Ruth, Esther, Job... believers learn lessons for living... While biblical stories are not the only means for guiding Christians, they are a crucial means... people learn from and live by not only principles and rules but also stories. Furthermore, important insights into gender relations can be made through studying narrative...'.[13]

Ultimately, the claim of these feminist writers is that their interpretation of ambiguous stories has priority over clear apostolic statements of doctrinal principle. Reformed scholar A.J.K Köstenberger has pointed out how casually many evangelical feminists treat the NT interpretation of OT narratives. In contrast, a genuinely evangelical hermeneutic will 'submit to the apostolic interpretation of the OT where such is available'.[14]

Rule 4: Bible writers are controlled by their culture
Willard Swartley writes, 'The biblical interpreter should recognise the temporal and cultural distance that exists between the world of the

Bible and the world of the believer today, especially when addressing social issues.' He goes on to say, 'Whether the topic be slavery, war, or the role of women, the meaning of the same word, command, or instruction may differ significantly, depending on the historical and cultural place and time in which it was and is spoken'.[15]

Once more we recognise a truth in this statement. Clearly, the application of particular commands does vary in different cultures. The Lord Jesus washed the feet of his disciples before supper, and then commanded them to do likewise. Most of us do not feel bound to obey that command literally when we have visitors round to supper; the needs of our guests are rather different. So we ask 'what is the appropriate way to obey that command in our culture?'. To obey the command involves thinking out what the unpleasant jobs are today that nobody wants to do, and getting on with them. We all read the commands of Scripture in the light of cultural factors.

So, the argument runs, we must be prepared to reinterpret the key texts on gender roles that we listed earlier. The social and cultural situations for which they were written may be so different from our own that the commands may no longer be relevant – or they may need to be applied in a completely different way.

As an example of this approach, we might consider Ramsey Michaels' comments on 1 Peter 3:1: 'Wives in the same way be submissive to your husbands' (or as Michaels translates it: 'You wives too must defer to your husbands') 'so that, if any of them do not obey the word they may be won over without words by the behaviour of their wives'. Michaels quotes David Balch's verdict that Peter's advice to women married to such husbands 'should be understood against the social background in which a wife was expected to accept the customs and religious rites of her husband.' Michaels adds: 'In society's eyes, these women were already highly insubordinate just by virtue of their Christian commitment, and Peter is concerned that they do not compound the difficulty by abrasive or troublesome behaviour... Peter's unqualified advice to Christian wives 'to "defer to your husbands" must be seen in this light.'[16]

Michaels does not see Peter's call to women to submit to their husbands as arising out of any divinely ordained principle. It is simply a response to a cultural norm which has been discarded by our society.

The same approach has been taken by feminist scholars to each of the New Testament passages that seem to restrict women's roles. Michaels' treatment of 1 Peter 3 may be taken as a test-case for the legitimacy of the approach. Three issues should be considered.

Firstly, we may question how accurately Michaels portrays 1st century Graeco-Roman culture. Michaels pictures a world in which women generally were submissive to their husbands, so that if a Christian wife stepped out of line, others would be shocked. Submission amounted to 'doing what society expects'. Yet Peter's words in verses 1 and 2 imply that these pagan husbands are going to be pleasantly surprised when they see their wives' submissive, and reverent behaviour. The implication is that for a wife to be truly submissive was something very unusual: so much so that a non-Christian husband would take note of it and might even be moved to abandon his opposition to the faith. As to the claim that wives were automatically expected to accept the husband's religious rites, Michaels himself is forced to concede that 'this was what Roman society expected, but it did not always happen among female adherents of Judaism, or Christianity, or such Eastern cults as those of Isis or Osiris'.[17] The case of Poppaea, first Nero's mistress, later his wife, is a good example. She is described by Josephus as a religious woman: either a proselyte to Judaism or at least a Jewish sympathiser – a God-fearer. She uses her influence with Nero to gain favours for the Jewish community. Poppaea's religious independence is seen as neither strange nor disgraceful.[18]

We should not take it for granted that a commentator's statements about first century culture are necessarily accurate! Few New Testament scholars have a training in classical history. Michaels' assumption of a homogeneous culture across the Roman empire is itself suspect. 1 Peter is addressed to Christian communities spread across a vast geographical area marked by extreme cultural diversity.[19] Michaels' appeal to historical data is certainly selective and may be completely misleading.

Michaels' treatment is not unusual. Feminist scholars are prone to repeating unfounded generalisations about 1st century culture. The impression is often given, for example, that women played little or no part in religious leadership. Yet virtually every temple had its priestesses; many pagan cults had exclusively female leadership; the Vestal Virgins exercised considerable religious and political influence in Rome. It is simply a myth that women played no public part in religious worship but it is repeated again and again.[20]

The second problem with Michaels' argument is the assumption that Peter and the other apostles were deeply concerned that Christians should do nothing that would shock the sensibilities of others. How plausible is that assumption? They were, after all, followers of the rabbi who ate with prostitutes and taxcollectors; who drove the money-lenders out of the temple; who allowed his disciples to pick corn for themselves on the sabbath. Jesus defied the sensibilities of others at every point. Peter himself went into the house of Cornelius and ate there with Gentiles, smashing a cultural norm that had lasted for centuries (Acts 10:27-28). It would seem that Peter was far less concerned to uphold the status quo than Michaels would have us believe! If Peter had thought that the subordination of wives to their husbands was something ultimately against God's will, we can be sure that nothing would have prevented him from saying so.

The third problem is that, contrary to what Michaels says, Peter does not in fact argue here from contemporary culture. Peter argues rather that a Christian wife should show submission because that is what *purity* and *reverence* demand (v.2). A woman who goes in for elaborate hair-dos and gold jewellery and fine clothes gains a short-lived external beauty. But a woman who has a *gentle and quiet spirit* (v.4) has an *unfading beauty which is of great worth in God's sight*. Peter's argument is not that it is expected by society but that it is precious to God. When Peter addresses husbands in verse 7, he tells them, for their part, that they must 'treat them with respect as the weaker partner...'. The appeal is to the very nature of man and woman. The wife is the 'weaker vessel' – the finer and more delicate creation – and is to be honoured accordingly. Peter bases his teaching not on changing cultural factors, but on things that do not change.

When we come to examine other passages, in later chapters of this book, we will see the same appeal to unchanging factors. Feminist scholars try to show in each case that what is said about the roles of men and women arises from some aspect of that society which no longer applies. But in 1 Corinthians 11, Paul's whole argument is based on the fact that 'the head of every man is Christ, and the head of the woman is man, and the head of Christ is God' (v.3). He goes on to say: 'he (the man) is the image and glory of God; but the woman is the glory of man. For man did not come from woman, but woman from man.'

In 1 Corinthians 14, Paul bases his argument on the unchanging authority of the Old Testament (v.34) as well as 'the Lord's command' (v.37). In 1 Timothy 2, he appeals once more to the order of creation (v.13) and also to Adam and Eve's fall. In all these passages the appeal is to unchanging realities.

Some feminist writers agree. And so they are driven to a more extreme position. Since the New Testament writers did believe that what they were saying was grounded in unchanging factors, relevant to all cultures, the only conclusion is that these writers were themselves bound by their culture. The whole way they argue springs from their cultural background.

Take Andrew Lincoln's comments on Ephesians 5.[21] Lincoln is quite clear in his mind about what is taught in this chapter: wives are to submit to their husbands. Moreover, it is clear to him that the writer of Ephesians (he does not believe it was Paul) roots this in something absolute. The relation of husband and wife is to mirror the relation of Christ and the church. How does Lincoln respond? 'Nothing is to be gained by pretending that the analogy with Christ and the Church makes this piece of paraenesis a timeless and universal prescription for marriage through the ages'. '...the writer's use of the analogy of the Christ and the Church reveals that the point of view of the passage is pervasively androcentric'. Lincoln contends that the Bible-writer has been conditioned by a male-centred society that dictates his whole thinking. '...it is best then to see this vision of marriage for what it is – conditioned by the cultural assumptions of its time... Contemporary

Christians can best appropriate it by realizing that they are to attempt to do something similar in their own setting – to bring to bear what they hold to be the heart of the Christian message on the marriage conventions of their time.' 'Those who consider love and justice to be the central thrust of the Bible's ethical teaching will therefore want to work out a view of marriage where both partners are held in equal regard, where justice will require that traditional male dominance cannot be tolerated'.

Lincoln and other evangelical feminists argue that in following such an approach, they are not rejecting biblical authority at all. They are simply looking beyond the cultural prejudices of the Bible writers to God's real intention.

We respect their good intentions. Yet the dangers of such an approach should be clear. Perhaps they can best be expressed as a question. If God *had* wanted to say that women should submit to their husbands, how could he do so? Even if a Bible writer were to start with the words 'What I am now going to say has nothing to do with culture – this is God's binding command for all societies in all time,' we would still be able to say 'Ah, the writer believed that, but that was just his conditioning'. Ultimately, this sort of hermeneutic makes it impossible for God to give us any absolute commands at all through Scripture. New Testament writers condemn idolatry. But we may dismiss their stand as due to their monotheistic Jewish background. Even the biblical emphasis on 'love and justice', which Lincoln accepts as absolute, could arise out of the cultural conditioning of the writers.

Lincoln is merely stating in more academic language the reaction of many 'ordinary Christians' to Paul's teaching. We have all heard comments about Paul the chauvinist or the woman-hater. (Mary Slessor, no feminist, wrote in the margin of her Bible alongside 1 Timothy 2:12, 'Nay Paul laddie, this won't do!'). Such views cannot be reconciled with the full authority of Scripture.

Rule 5: Bible readers are controlled by their culture
It is an axiom of modern hermeneutics that all readers of Scripture have biases ('presuppositions') imposed by their own personal and cultural

standpoints. We must be prepared to recognise our biases and revise our reading of Scripture accordingly.

In itself, that is a biblical emphasis. Evangelical hermeneutics must take full account of Jeremiah's words: 'The heart is deceitful above all things...' (Jeremiah 17:9). Our deceitful hearts will often blind us to those biblical truths we would find unfamiliar or unpalatable.

David Wenham puts this movingly in an article entitled 'Men & Women in the Church'. He asks, 'How is the Christian interpreter to escape the distorting influences of his social situation and background in approaching vexed issues of biblical interpretation? The fact is that we will never achieve perfect objectivity. But we can and should seek to reduce the distortion, first by recognising our own sinfulness and self-ishness, and so coming to issues in humility and prayerfulness. We need to recognise that we are often wrong and that we are constantly tempted to read Scripture in ways that suit us; we need therefore, to ask God to correct and mould our undertaking, however hard that may be for us. We must be prepared to change...'.[22]

Feminist theologians have been quick to point out the relevance of this principle. They suggest that generations of Christians who found male primacy in the Bible were unconsciously biased in their exegesis because of their upbringing in a male-dominated society. Now the time has come to recognise those biases and abandon them.

Elaine Storkey puts it strongly: '...theology as normally understood is a male-defined subject... To start with, most theologians have been men, and they have approached the subject with what have been described by many feminists as 'male categories', such as a focus on the cerebral or the abstract, the building of theoretical systems and the construction of specific hermeneutical principles. Under male juris-diction theology has become a highly theoretical and complex series of debates'.[23] '...theology incorporates a male-defined reality into... scriptural interpretation'.[24] The charge is clear: traditional evangelical theologians have been warped in their capacity to read Scripture. We read Scripture from 'androcentric' (male-dominated) presuppositions which are all the more powerful because most of the time we are not aware of them.

We cannot respond to that charge fully within the scope of this chapter. The role played by presuppositions is perhaps *the* key question in hermeneutics today. But one response to our evangelical feminist friends would be along these lines. Surely we are entitled to say to them: 'OK we grant your point. It is true that we all have unconscious biases. And it is true that our biases may affect the way we read Scripture. But doesn't the same apply to yourselves? After all, we're living in a culture dominated by democratic, egalitarian ideals. Couldn't that be warping the way *you* are reading Scripture?'

How would evangelical feminists reply to that challenge? Some would acknowledge its force. They would acknowledge that 'feminist' as well as 'traditionalist' must be willing to recognise presuppositions and to guard against their warping influence.

But there are other evangelical feminists who would take a rather different tack. They would say: 'It is a mistake even to try to be objective.' These writers are perfectly willing to admit that their feminist stance shapes their exegesis. E.Hauge writes, '...feminist theology claims to be developed out of women's perspective or feminist perspective. Its scholarly ideal is not the "impartiality" or "objectivity" of established scholarship, but the conscious "advocacy stance" of liberation theologies in favour of the oppressed'.[25] Feminists of this school make no apology for their bias. They are committed to feminism and they read the Bible accordingly.

Evangelical feminists often claim that 'women's experience' should be allowed to shape the way that Scripture is interpreted. Elaine Storkey points out that 'An emphasis on the importance of women's experience undergirds most definitions of feminist theology...'.[26] Storkey distances herself from radical feminists who make women's experience the ultimate authority, but still emphasises its important role in understanding the Bible. '...in stating that Scripture provides a framework for understanding and interpreting women's experience, Evangelical women are also reserving the right to look again at Scripture with a hermeneutic that does itself take women's experience seriously...'.[27]

In practice this means two things. Firstly, it means that the *questions* feminists bring to the Bible will be dictated by women's experience and concerns. That of course, is true for every believing Christian. We all have questions we bring to Scripture: 'What job should I take?' 'Which church should I worship with?' 'Is embryo research justified?' If we are wrestling with these issues, we will inevitably bring such questions to Scripture looking for answers.

But (and it is a big but) evangelical theologians have always insisted that there is an objective meaning – a primary purpose – in any passage, which is distinct from any questions we may put to it. We may look to Psalm 139 for guidance on the subject of embryo research but that is not what the psalm is *about*. The psalm is a meditation on God's omniscience. That was the intended meaning of the divine and human authors. Bible readers must always beware of bringing their own questions to a passage and failing to hear the central message of the passage. Otherwise, we rob the Bible of its practical authority: the Bible is not allowed to address us and tell us things we are not asking about.[28]

Let us take an example of how a feminist reader might bring her questions to Scripture. We read in Genesis 10 that Abraham hid the fact that Sarah was his wife and allowed Pharaoh to take her into his harem. And we ask 'What is the meaning, the message of this story?' In its context, it seems that the writer intended to show us how God's promise to give Abraham an heir from whom the Messiah would come was threatened by Abraham's lack of faith. But now, our feminist exegete comes to the text. What is her first question? 'What does this passage teach us about the place of women in that society?'[29]

Of course it is not wrong to use a passage like this to point out the oppressive treatment suffered by women at the hands of men. But we must still insist that that is not the *primary purpose* of the passage. And it is the primary purpose (the author's intention) that should be the starting-point for interpretation.

The first way then, in which 'women's experience' can shape interpretation is by dictating the questions which are brought to Scripture. But a second (and more dangerous) claim is that women's experience may also be allowed to shape the *answers*, as well. Some feminists are not afraid to say that the Bible must be interpreted in a way that agrees with their own experience. Hauge writes: 'The typical traditional women's experience of childcare and housework as well as the "feminist" experience of struggling against various kinds of oppression both provide significant insights that until recently have had no place in theology...'[30] For feminists of this school, women's experience is the fixed standard by which we interpret the Bible. Walter Liefeld sums this up well: 'Passages of Scripture that do not say what the contemporary reader determines to be true from a feminist perspective are simply not accepted as "biblical revelation and truth". If one were to charge that this is subjective, the answer is that it is consciously and deliberately so, to balance the patriarchal interpretations of centuries.'[31]

A concrete example may illustrate the point. It is taken from a symposium produced by the Calvin Centre for Christian Scholarship, a study-centre under the auspices of Calvin College, Grand Rapids. Helen Sterk discusses the nature of sin. Evangelical Christians have always seen humanity's greatest sin as being pride: the rebellious desire to be independent of God and self-sufficient. Sterk, however, writes: 'Feminist theologians suggest that the traditional understanding of pride as the besetting human sin rings false with women's experience. They argue that women tend to undervalue rather than overvalue themselves, making excessive self-effacement a woman's besetting sin.'[32]

Thus the Bible is filtered through the grid of women's experience. Theoretically, Scripture may have the final authority but Scripture is not allowed to say anything that 'rings false with women's experience'. Historic evangelical theology has always insisted that all experience is to be tested and interpreted by Scripture. By contrast, feminists of this school insist that all Scripture is to be tested and interpreted by experience. It comes as little surprise that some feminist groups, while identifying themselves as evangelical, can uphold homosexual practice and claim that it is biblical. Their *experience* assures them that homosexuality is good, wholesome, natural, fulfilling. Any Bible passages on the subject must be interpreted in a way that fits with their experience.[33]

IN CONCLUSION

It must be stressed again that not all evangelical feminists would endorse all the hermeneutical approaches discussed in this chapter. The term 'evangelical feminist' is used to cover a very wide spectrum today. The tone of this chapter has been negative. Can we draw out some positive guidelines for interpreting the Bible on gender issues? I suggest eight principles that have emerged in the course of this chapter. As evangelicals committed to the full authority of Scripture as the Word of God:

1. We aim to use *all* the data of Scripture in establishing doctrinal and ethical norms. We give priority to clear and unambiguous passages but we do not overlook difficult and obscure passages. We must be willing to rethink our understanding of apparently straightforward passages in the light of obscure passages and vice-versa.

2. We do not interpret any passage of Scripture in a way that contradicts other passages. We must interpret individual passages in a way that harmonises with the broad themes of Scripture. But we must always be open to the possibility that our understanding of the broad themes needs to be refined in line with the natural meaning of individual passages.

3. We establish our theology and ethics primarily from the propositional statements and commands of Scripture. We do not ignore the lessons to be learned from narratives, but we interpret those narratives in the light of such propositional teaching. Where New Testament writers have given us their interpretation of Old Testament narratives, we are bound by their authority.

4. We distinguish between commands in Scripture that arise out of a particular cultural context, and commands that are grounded in unchanging realities – for example, the attributes of God; the Creation; the Fall. We do not accept that the writers of Scripture were restricted by their cultural background so that they could not give infallible teaching relevant to all cultures.

5. We aim to use all relevant historical information to understand the culture within which the Bible's teaching was given. We must avoid bias, selectivity and anachronism in the use of historical information. We must not allow appeal to background infor-

mation to override the natural meaning of a passage.

6. We aim to be *objective* in our reading of Scripture, giving each passage its natural sense. We recognise the danger of allowing our own sinful biases to distort our reading of Scripture. So we seek God's grace, given through Christ, by the Holy Spirit, to recognise our biases and to submit to the plain teaching of Scripture.

7. We believe that every passage of Scripture has a primary meaning which corresponds with the intention of the author. To use the passage rightly, we should begin from that primary meaning.

8. We accept that Scripture and not our experience has final authority. We must test and intepret all our experience by the Bible. Evangelicals of all shades profess to believe in the supreme authority of the Bible. But it is possible to interpret the Bible in a way that *practically* denies its authority. 'Feminists' and 'Traditionalists' alike must make it their goal to interpret the Bible in a way that demonstrates a whole-hearted submission to its authority as the Word of God written.

NOTES

1. C. Powell, 'A stalemate of genders? Some hermeneutical reflections,' *Themelios* 17/3 (Apr/May 1992), p16.
2. R.Letham, 'The hermeneutics of feminism,' *Themelios* 17/3 (Apr/May 1992), p4.
3. Grant R. Osborne, 'Hermeneutics and Women in the Church', *JETS* 20 (1977) p337.
4. Powell, *op.cit.,* p15.
5. Gretchen Gaebelein Hull, *Equal to Serve: Women and Men in the Church and Home,* Scripture Union, 1989, p26.
6. ibid.
7. I. Howard Marshall, 'An Evangelical Approach to "Theological Criticism",' *Themelios* 13/3 (Apr/May 1988) p81.
8. Willard Swartley, *Slavery, Sabbath, War and Women,* Herald, 1983, p230.
9. Christians for Biblical Equality, 'Men, Women and Biblical Equality', published as advertisment in *Christianity Today,* 9 April 1990. CBE is 'a national chapter of Men, Women and God,

International, an organisation associated with John Stott's London Institute for Contemporary Christianity' (David Neff cited in J.Piper & W. Grudem eds, *Recovering Biblical Manhood & Womanhood,* Crossway, 1991, p403.

10. Hull, *op.cit.,* p118-119.

11. ibid.

12. Helen Sterk, in Mary Stewart Van Leeuwen ed, *After Eden: Facing the Challenge of Gender Reconciliation,* Eerdmans/Paternoster 1993, p186. This volume is a symposium produced by the Calvin Centre for Christian Scholarship, a study-centre under the auspices of Calvin College, Grand Rapids, an accredited seminary of the Christian Reformed Church.

13. ibid.

14. Andreas J.Köstenberger, 'Gender Passages in the NT: Hermeneutical Fallacies Critiqued', *WTJ* 56 (1994) p271.

15. Swartley, *op.cit.,* p230-31.

16. J. Ramsey Michaels: *Word Biblical Commentary 42: Ephesians,* Word Books, 1990, p392-93.

17. ibid., p171.

18. Josephus, *Ant.Jud.,* 20.189-196.

19. cf E.G. Selwyn, *The First Epistle of St Peter,* Macmillan, 1946, p47-52. Selwyn writes, 'The people of Asia Minor in the first century of our era were highly heterogeneous. Successive migrations or invasions had introduced into the original Anatolian or Thracian stock the blood and the culture of other peoples, Phrygian, Celtic, Persian, Greek and Jewish'.

20. On the whole subject of the position of women in the Roman world, cf J.P.V. Balsdon, *Roman Women, their history and habits,* 1962. On the role played by women in Graeco-Roman religious movements cf R.C.Kroeger & C.C.Kroeger, *I Suffer Not a Woman: Rethinking 1 Timothy 2:11-15 in Light of Ancient Evidence,* Baker, 1992 p70-74. The Kroegers (evangelical feminists) quote Strabo (Geography 7.3.3): 'All regard women as the prime movers when it comes to religion. It is they who incite the men to the more devoted worship of the gods, to festivals, and to wild outcries..' Note also the work of radical feminist Elisabeth Schüssler Fiorenza who insists on

the role played by women in hosting and leading cultic groups. cf *In Memory of Her: A Feminist Reconstruction of Christian Origins*, Crossroad, 1985, p176-77.

21. Andrew Lincoln, *Word Biblical Commentary 42: Ephesians*, Word Books, 1990, p392-393.

22. David Wenham, 'Editorial: Men and Women in the Church', *Themelios* 12/3 (Apr 1987) p73.

23. Elaine Storkey, 'The Significance of Mary for Feminist Theology' in David F.Wright, Chosen by God: Mary in Evangelical Perspective, Marshall Pickering, 1989, p184.

24. ibid., p185.

25. E.Hauge, Feminist Theology as critique and renewal of theology', *Themelios* 17/3 (Apr/May 1992), p8.

26. Storkey, *op.cit.*, p187.

27. Storkey, *op.cit.*, p195-96.

28. cf Sinclair B.Ferguson, *Add to your Faith: Biblical Teaching on Christian Maturity*, Pickering & Inglis, 1980, p158-159 for fine practical application of this principle. He writes: '...the patient unfolding of the teaching of Scripture *in its own context...* produces a quality of life which will not be found if we use the Bible merely as a sounding board for our own spiritual experience'.

29. cf the many titles published by Sheffield Academic Press offering 'feminist readings' of Scripture (generally not by evangelicals). A typical title would be J.Cheryl Exum: *Fragmented Women: Feminist (Sub)versions of Biblical Narratives*, 1993. The publisher's blurb for the book tells us:'...the author draws on contemporary feminist literary theory to critique the dominant male voice of the biblical narrative and to construct (sub)versions of women's stories from the submerged strains of their voices in men's stories'.

30. Hauge, *op.cit.*, p11.

31. Walter Liefeld & Ruth A.Tucker, *Daughters of the Church: Women and ministry from New Testament Times to the present*, Zondervan, 1987, p446-47.

32. Helen Sterk, in Van Leeuwen ed., *op.cit.*, p351. cf also p170-71; p409.

33. cf Piper & Grudem, *op.cit.*, p476-477 for documentation. They

write, '...in July of 1986 the Evangelical Women's Caucus International under the influence of Virginia Mollenkott and Nancy Hardesty took a stand affirming the legitimacy of lesbianism to such an extent that members like Katherine Croeger [sic] and Gretchen Hull withdrew their membership'. As this chapter was being completed, notice was received of a book by Michael Vasey of St John's College, Durham, written from an 'evangelical' perspective, apparently arguing that Scripture, rightly interpreted, does not condemn homosexual relationships (*Strangers & Friends: a New Exploration of Homosexuality and the Bible*, Hodder & Stoughton, 1995).

Chapter 5

Headship

Edward Donnelly

Ted Donnelly holds an honours degree in classics and a Master's degree of theology from Queen's University, Belfast, and is a graduate of the Reformed Presbyterian Theological Seminary, Pittsburgh. He studied at the University of Athens from 1972-73 and served in the Greek Evangelical Church in Cyprus for one year. Minister of Trinity Reformed Presbyterian Church, Newtownabbey, he is Professor of New Testament Language and Literature in the Reformed Theological College, Belfast, visiting lecturer in New Testament at Ottawa Theological Hall, Canada, and is joint editor of The Reformed Theological Journal. He is a regular speaker at conferences in the United Kingdom, United States, Canada and South Africa. Ted is married to Lorna and they have three children.

Headship

1 Corinthians 11:2-16 is undoubtedly a difficult passage. Paul refers to cultural customs of the first century about which we have little solid information. Several of his expressions are unusual and hard to interpret. An enormous amount of recent exegetical attention has produced no consensus as to the meaning of these verses: commentators differ over almost every line. It might seem that the passage is beyond understanding, of no practical help in the consideration of gender and leadership. Perhaps we should admit our confusion and leave it to one side in favour of texts which are more accessible. That is certainly what some would have us conclude.

Yet the problems are by no means as daunting as they are sometimes made to appear. Paul's general line of argument is clear and straightforward. While uncertainties of interpretation do remain, none of these affects in any way the main principle being asserted. Previous generations seem to have taken the passage in their stride. We too must maintain the essential clarity of the Word of God. We believe that 'all Scripture' (including even these verses!) is 'useful' to every child of God (2 Timothy 3:16). Technical experts and scholars are superb servants, but bad masters. They cannot be allowed to claim any passage as their exclusive domain, too complex for the ordinary believer to grasp. The difficulties which some moderns have may stem from a reluctance to accept teaching which challenges prejudice or preference. Children are not the only ones who seem strangely unable to understand what they don't want to hear.

We must, of course, beware of our own bias, for we can too easily be guilty of talking to Scripture rather than listening to it. We come with our own agenda – questions to be answered, positions to be defended, opponents to be crushed. 'The head of the woman is man' – what an emotive and explosive phrase! We can treat it as an enemy to be conquered or as a club with which to belabour those who differ from us. The Bible is the raw material we intend to use for our own purposes. But this is misuse, almost blasphemy. God's mighty Word is not at our disposal, but above us and over us – searching, questioning, challenging. 'At the beginning of all Theology', writes Geerhardus Vos, 'lies a passive, receptive attitude on the part of the one who engages in its study. The assumption of such an attitude is characteristic of all truly exegetical pursuit. It is eminently a process in which God speaks and man listens'.[1] We begin listening by trying, as far as we can, to put ourselves into the position of Paul's original readers.

He was writing to people who had been transformed by the Spirit of God. Not only converted, but converted in many cases from lives of extreme wickedness (1 Corinthians 6:9-11). The change was amazing. They had passed from death to life, from the old age of sin to the new age of salvation. They were now 'spiritual', a favourite word. The apostle himself marvelled at what he saw in them: 'I always thank God for you because of his grace given you in Christ Jesus. For in him you have been enriched in every way – in all your speaking and in all your knowledge ... you do not lack any spiritual gift' (1:4-7). The church in Corinth was pulsating with a vigorous new life.

The problem was that this energetic experience was mutating into strange forms. Quarrels and divisions showed immaturity rather than spirituality (3:1-4). In particular, there seems to have been an unbalanced, though perhaps understandable, emphasis on the newness of their life in Christ, sometimes described as an over-realized eschatology. Joyfully aware that they were no longer 'of' the world, they tended to forget that they were still 'in' it. They felt that they had 'arrived' spiritually (4:8). Ernst Käsemann describes their condition as one 'where enthusiasm is rattling at the doors of the existing order and proclaiming its allegedly just claims in the name of the Spirit'.[2] As children of God, ordinary human categories no longer applied to them. They had moved beyond the constraints and structures of earthly life.

Sexual distinctions, for example, were irrelevant to those who had become like the angels in heaven (Luke 20:34-36). This was one of the distortions of the faith, inevitably reflected in unbiblical behaviour, which Paul was writing to correct.

We find him, therefore, concerned to stress that the natural order and relationships of life are not intended to be overthrown by Christianity, but to be preserved as far as possible. In chapter 7, for example, dealing with suggestions that Christians should dissolve the marriage bond or abstain from sexual relations within it, Paul's command is repeated and powerful: 'each one should retain the place in life that the Lord has assigned to him and to which God has called him' (7:17, see also vv. 20, 24, 26). This emphasis is particularly relevant for the passage before us.

Chapter 11:2 marks the beginning of a new section in the letter. From 8:1 the apostle has been dealing with the problem of food sacrificed to idols and has concluded his discussion with an appeal to the duties of love for God and for one's brother: 'So whether you eat or drink or whatever you do, do it all for the glory of God. Do not cause anyone to stumble . . . Follow my example, as I follow the example of Christ' (10:31-11:1). This leads naturally to a section (11:2-14:40) dealing with various improprieties in worship which had arisen within the Corinthian church and which were not bringing glory to God. This is Paul's main concern. Although their life together is marked by a considerable degree of adherence to his teaching (v. 2), their obedience is far from complete in several areas. They are not fulfilling 10:31. He deals first with the issue of women participating in worship with uncovered heads. 'Is it proper for a woman to pray to God with her head uncovered?' (v. 13). It is a practice which detracts from God's glory.

Why is covering the head important?

At first sight this may appear quite bizarre. Is such a trivial matter really worthy of apostolic attention, never mind inclusion in Scripture? What relevance can it possibly have for believers at the end of the twentieth century? As we shall see, however, Paul's interest is in an underlying principle of major importance. It is his common practice to deal with apparently minor behavioural matters by expounding sublime theological doctrines (eg Philippians 2:1-11). Some commentators have argued that the problem here is limited to married women and their husbands, in view of the fact that Greek uses the same word for 'man' as for 'husband' and similarly for 'woman' and 'wife'. But the wider application, which would include the more limited, is preferable. Ronald Y. K. Fung understands the issue to be 'the general principle of the headship of man in relation to woman, a principle which finds its primary application and obvious illustration in the specific husband-wife relationship'.[3] The woman with uncovered head is making a cultural statement about her personal independence. She is rejecting, in public worship at least, the authority of men over her. Paul understands this as repudiation of a divinely-established order and it is with this order, rather than the first-century expression of rebellion against it, that we are primarily concerned.

Paul does not define precisely what practice he has in mind and the expressions he uses are capable of several interpretations. The traditional view has been that he is referring to a veil, or, in more recent commentators,[4] a shawl or the corner of a robe. Jewish women in Jerusalem, for example, were always veiled in public.[5] This still seems the more obvious meaning, and will be adopted in our discussion. Other writers[6] have argued that Paul is describing women who, instead of having their hair piled on top of their heads in the normal way, wore it loose and flowing down their backs, like pagan prophetesses, who prophesied with dishevelled heads. A key statement is in verse 15: 'long hair is given to her as (anti) a covering'. Anti usually means 'instead of', but can mean 'as, for' in the sense of equivalence. Does the phrase mean that, since the woman has been endowed with long hair, no other covering is necessary? Or is it saying that a woman's long hair is nature's symbol of the need for her to cover her head in some additional way?

Both explanations are exegetically possible and, unless we believe that this specific cultural practice is to be copied exactly in our own day, it is relatively unimportant which we adopt. In either case, the argument is the same. Some women in the Corinthian church were praying and prophesying with uncovered heads, either bare or with hair flowing. Paul considered this improper because it implied a refusal to accept man's role of leadership. How does he deal with the issue?

Outline

The passage may be divided into four sections.

I. *Heads and headship – verses 3-6.* The apostle explains the impropriety of the rejection by women of a cultural symbol of man's headship.

II. *Argument from creation – verses 7-10.* Differentiation of role is rooted in the circumstances and purpose of the creation of man and woman.

III. *Important qualification – verses 11, 12.* Functional authority does not in any way threaten the essential equality and mutual dependence of the sexes.

IV. *Appeals to 'nature' and church practice – verses 13-16.* Supporting arguments for Paul's teaching.

I. Heads and headship – verses 3-6

'Now I want you to realise that the head of every man is Christ, and the head of the woman is man, and the head of Christ is God'. 'I want you to realise' has a similar function to the more common 'I do not want you to be ignorant' (10:1; 12:1; 1 Thessalonians 4:13; Romans 11:25). The first person verb 'denotes in Paul the weighty and authoritative discharge of office', when 'he wishes to emphasise an important point of doctrine in instructing the community.'[7] Here is the crux of Paul's argument, his 'text', the basis upon which he will develop his discussion of head-coverings. He chooses the metaphor of the head to describe relationships in three different categories. What does he mean by this metaphor? The traditional understanding has been that 'head' is a picture of authority. Every man is under the authority of Christ, the woman under that of the man, Christ under that of God.

In recent years this interpretation has been called into question by those who reject the concept of authority and claim that 'head' refers rather to source or origin. 'Here *head* seems to carry the Greek concept of source, base or derivation.'[8] 'Paul's understanding of the metaphor, therefore, and almost certainly the only one the Corinthians would have grasped, is 'head' as 'source', especially "source of life".[9] Such assertations, if true, would radically affect the understanding not only of this passage but of biblical teaching on male-female relationships. They do not stand up, however, to serious examination and the identification of head with 'origin' is to be discounted for a number of reasons, chiefly the following.

1. There is no solid evidence for contemporary usage of 'head' as 'source, origin'. Catherine Clark Kroeger makes the sweeping claim that 'the concept of *head* as 'source' is well documented in both classical and Christian antiquity.'[10] This is simply not true. Out of a large number of instances where it is used metaphorically, no more than four can possibly, and even then unconvincingly, be understood to mean 'source'. Authorities cited are mostly late 4th century A.D. onwards) and translations are ambiguous. Although one lexicon does list 'source' as a translation when 'head' is used of the end-points of a rivet, there is not a single clear example anywhere of 'head' meaning 'source' when applied to a person. Hardly 'well documented'!

2. Evidence for the meaning 'authority over' is, on the other hand, indisputable and overwhelming. The word is so listed in all the major New Testament lexicons. Many secular texts use the term of rulers or persons of superior rank. This weight of lexical and historical material in favour of the traditional meaning is quite decisive.[11]

3. Apart from four citations of Psalm 118 (Matthew 21:42; Luke 20:17; Acts 4:11; 1 Peter 2:7), Paul is the only New Testament writer to use 'head' in a metaphorical sense, so his own usage of the term is obviously crucial. We find him employing it as a symbol of authority or rule. In Ephesians 1:20-22 he writes of the risen Christ, seated at the Father's right hand in the heavenly realms 'far above all rule and authority, power and dominion, and every title that can be given . . . And God placed all things under his feet and appointed him to be head over everything for the church, which is his body . . .'. This glorious picture – 'all things under his feet – head over everything' – is of supreme authority, universal rule.

The same concept occurs in Colossians. Christ is 'the Head over every power and authority' (Colossians 2:10), not because he is their source, but because he is their master. Returning to Ephesians, Paul introduces the illustration of the husband as head with a motivating word ('for', *hoti*), providing a reason for the wife's submission to his leadership. 'Wives, submit to your husbands as to the Lord. For the husband is the head of the wife as Christ is the head of the church . . . Now as the church submits to Christ, so also wives should submit to their husbands in everything' (5:22-24). Wives are to submit because the husband is the head of the wife. This clearly refers to 'authority'. 'Source', in the context, would simply make no sense.

4. It is true that in two instances the implications of 'head' are different. Christ is '. . . the Head, from whom the whole body . . . grows' (Colossians 2:19). As we speak the truth in love, 'we will in all things grow up into him who is the Head, that is, Christ. From him the whole body . . . grows' (Ephesians 4:15, 16). But in neither of these is Paul saying that the body originates or is derived from the head or that the head is the source of the body. He is simply bringing out another nuance of the head/body metaphor. Just as, through our mouths, we take in food which strengthens the whole body, so Christ provides spiritual food for the growth and maturing of his people. Even if we allow 'source' in the sense of 'that through which nourishment comes', it is significant that neither of these passages refers to gender or marital relationships.

We have dealt with this issue at some length because it is, in a sense, the pivotal point of the passage. But our conclusions are clear. The evidence for 'head' as 'ruler, authority over' is substantial. Of the meaning 'source', applied to a person, there is not even one unambiguous, contemporary example. When Paul writes 'the head of the woman is man', he is referring to a position of authority in which man is placed over woman. That this should have been questioned owes more to current prejudice than to academic objectivity. Grudem is surely correct in deploring 'a disturbing tendency among evangelical feminist scholars today . . . to search for 'any meaning but authority' for the word *kephale* in the New Testament . . . When this can happen even in texts where authority is so clearly specified in context, one wonders if it is a prior doctrinal conviction rather than sound linguistic analysis that has led to their conclusions in these texts'.[12] But we must return to our passage.

The apostle is explaining that the pattern of authority and submissions is not confined to male-female relationships but is imprinted upon the very nature of being and is already acknowledged by all believers. The woman is to follow man's leadership, accepting his role as initiator and ruler because 'the head of the woman is man'. But this is prefaced by the reminder that the man himself is not to be considered autonomous, subject to no authority but his own. He too is under rule, that of his Lord, for 'the head of every man is Christ'.

Does such a comparison imply inferiority? Christ is certainly far superior in his essential being to the man, whose head he is. Is the man, then, similarly superior to the woman? Lest such a false inference be drawn, Paul adds that 'the head of Christ is God'. God is not essentially greater than Christ, for the Son is of the same substance with the Father. So man is not, in his essential being, greater than woman. The point of this triad is not to describe basic identity, but to illustrate differences in role or function. Christ, first as Son and then as Mediator, is joyfully subject to the Father's authority, a point developed more fully in chapter seven of this book. But this has no bearing on personal worth. Let the woman not feel diminished by her subordinate role, for in this she is following not only man but the divine Saviour. 'Just as Christ is not a second-class person or deity because the Father is his head, so the woman is not a second-class person or human being because man is her head'.[13]

Paul now links the metaphorical with the literal 'head'. As in every age and culture, first-century men were distinguished from women by various features of dress and appearance. In general, men were bareheaded, while women appeared in public with their heads covered. This covering was a protection, a sign of modesty, purity, submission to the authority of their husbands or fathers. For a man to cover his head in worship would be to dress like a woman. In so doing he would 'dishonour his head' (v.4). By 'his head' Paul may mean that he would bring shame on himself by unmanly behaviour or that he would dishonour Christ, his only Head, by appearing in a posture of submission to human authority. Perhaps both meanings are intended.

It is unlikely that this was a real problem in the Corinthian church. What was certainly happening, however, was that some women were praying and prophesying with their heads uncovered. Awareness of their new and liberated status in Christ (Galatians 3:28) had led to the false conclusion that they had been emancipated from all male leadership. Their uncovered heads were a deliberate statement of independence, of rebellion. But they were, in reality, dishonouring their heads (v.5) – shaming both themselves, by their aggressive 'manliness', and their leaders or husbands, by such an open rejection of their authority.

Paul presses upon them the logic of their position. 'It is a disgrace for a woman to have her hair cut or shaved off' (v.6). The shaven head was a mark of public shame, the sign of the adulteress or the sexually promiscuous. The forcible removal of a woman's long hair, her 'glory' (v.15), was a token that she had thrown aside her true womanliness. It left her dishonoured and vulnerable, with little claim to respect or consideration. Were these Corinthian women prepared to go so far? They didn't want to be covered. Very well then, let them be completely consistent! Let them remove nature's covering as well as that of society. 'If a woman does not cover her head, she should have her hair cut off' (v.6). 'If she wishes to be regarded as a reputable woman, let her conform to established usage. But if she have no regard to her reputation, let her act as other women of her class'.[14]

The women of the congregation were to recognise the authority of men, their 'heads', and were to affirm such recognition by their dress and behaviour. But why is the man in this position of leadership? Why is he regarded as the head of the woman?

II. Argument from creation – verses 7-10
It is extremely significant that the main argument which Paul uses to establish his position is taken from the events of creation. His appeal is in no way culturally-conditioned. Man's headship is not based on a patriarchal society. It is not due to male selfishness or oppression. It

derives from the original constitution of man and woman as they came forth from the hand of God. It is written into our very natures as sexual beings, true for all humans in every place and time. Here is a reason which is both permanent and universally valid.

Nor can it be claimed that new life in Christ abolishes such distinctions. The apostle goes back before the Fall, to the perfection of Eden. He will remind us how the man was head before sin entered the world at a time when God looked on all that he had made and declared it good. Christ did not come to abolish the creation structures but to renew them. Believing men and women are restored to what they were meant to be; they are not, yet, taken forward to what they never have been. That new sphere of existence still lies in the future.

Two indisputable facts are now adduced from the creation account in Genesis chapter 2, beginning with the order and method of creation of the sexes. 'For man did not come from woman, but woman from man' (v.8). If he had so wished, God could have created man and woman simultaneously. He did not do so. The man was made first. No other human being existed. He was 'alone' in the world (Genesis 2:18). The woman was brought to him as a new and later creation.

Not only so, but she came 'from man' in the sense that she was made from the material of the man's body. God could have created her quite independently of the man. As he had done with Adam, he could have formed her from the dust of the ground and breathed into her nostrils the breath of life, so that she became a living being (Genesis 2: 7). He did not choose to do so. Instead 'the Lord God caused the man to fall into a deep sleep; and while he was sleeping, he took one of the man's ribs and closed up the place with flesh. Then the Lord God made a woman from the rib he had taken out of the man...' (Genesis 2:21, 22).

The implications of this are breathtakingly beautiful. What is stressed in Genesis 2 is the kinship and closeness of the sexes, their possession of an identical essence. In the world's first poetry the man expresses astonished delight in his God-given partner. Best of all is the awareness that she is literally, part of him: 'This is now bone of my bones and flesh of my flesh; she shall be called 'woman', for she was taken out of man' (Genesis 2:23). Such physical oneness will be restored and consummated in marriage (Genesis 2:24).

The creation of the woman from the man does not in any way imply inferiority. It is, rather, the ground of their unity, rich with promise. Matthew Henry's quaint comment has lost none of its aptness over almost three hundred years: 'not made out of his head to rule over him, nor out of his feet to be trampled upon by him, but out of his side to be equal with him, under his arm to be protected, and near his heart to be beloved'.[15] The fact of priority does, nevertheless, remain and this is the point Paul is making. There is an order in creation. The woman came after and from the man.

Paul now moves to the purpose of woman's creation. 'Neither was man created for woman, but woman for man' (v.9). The preposition 'for' (*dia*) means 'because of, for the sake of' as 'the reason why something happens, results, exists',[16] and the sentence is similar in form to Mark 2:27: 'The Sabbath was made for man, not man for the Sabbath'.[17] Woman was created with regard to man, for his benefit, to make an important contribution to his life. The reference is to Genesis 2:18: 'The Lord God said, "It is not good for the man to be alone. I will make a helper suitable for him".'

These words are often misunderstood. They have been taken to imply that women have no value apart from men. They are adjuncts, accessories whose sole function is to minister to male needs when required. It may be that the modern use of 'helper' has contributed to this misreading. A plumber will bring along his helper (called his 'mate' – a mark of male chauvinism?) to hold the tools, carry out simple or unpleasant tasks, do what he is told. No wonder that women feel little enthusiasm for such a role!

In Scripture, however, 'helper' has no connotation of either inferiority or subordination. The word is used twenty-one times in the Old Testament and fifteen of these refer to God himself as the helper of his people. 'We wait in hope for the Lord; he is our help and our shield... God is our refuge and strength, an ever-present help in trouble' (Psalms 33:20; 46:1). No woman need hesitate to share a role filled by God! That she is man's helper is not a statement of her inferiority but of his inadequacy.

Nor is her help to be understood simply in terms of meeting the man's need for company, assuaging his loneliness, valuable though that is. He needs a helper for the fulfilment of his God-given mandate to multiply and rule. On his own he is incomplete, inadequate for the task. The woman is his necessary partner. She is not a menial or a plaything, but fully involved with the man in propagating the race and in the stewardship of the earth.

Her role is, therefore, one of great value and dignity. But it is her role, let her not abandon it. Woman was created 'for man' in order to help, not to replace or compete with him. Some women in Corinth wanted to deny their femininity, to blur the sexual barriers by behaving like men. But the differentiation of the sexes has a deliberate and permanent purpose. Men and women are not, even in Christ, interchangeable.

These facts of creation have been introduced to establish that 'A man... is the image and glory of God; but the woman is the glory of man' (v.7). Now it is abundantly clear from the Genesis narrative that both man and woman were made in God's image. 'God created man in his own image, in the image of God he created him; male and female he created them' (Genesis 1: 27). It is equally plain that all Christ's people, regardless of sex, 'are being transformed into his likeness (lit. 'image') with ever-increasing glory' (2 Corinthians 3:18). So, if both men and women were created in and are being restored into the divine image, in what sense can the male alone be described by Paul as being 'the image... of God'?

The context supplies the answer. Paul is dealing with authority relationships. Man has a position of leadership with regard to the woman. He is recorded in Genesis 2:23 as naming her. This is a function of rule, since the authority to name implied authority to govern (Genesis 1:5; 2:19; 17:5) It is in that sense that he is the image of God, while in that sense she is not.

As man exercises his authority in a proper way he is the 'glory of God'. 'Glory' (*doxa*) here means 'that which brings honour to someone'. In verses 14 and 15 long hair is described as a 'disgrace' (or 'shame, dishonour') to man, but a 'glory' to woman. Glory is thus seen as the opposite of dishonour. In 2 Corinthians 8:23 the representatives of the churches are 'an honour to (literally 'glory of') Christ'. 'They by their holiness lead men to see the excellence of Christ whose image they bear. [18] Man, in his delegated authority, brings honour to the God who installed him in that position. Woman, in turn, is 'the glory of man' as she submits to his authority, follows his leadership, recognises his God-given role. What an immense honour she thus confers upon him by her loving submission! 'A wife of noble character is her husband's crown' (Proverbs 12:4).

In the presence of God, in public worship, the 'glory of God' should not be covered. 'A man ought not to cover his head' (v.7). The 'glory of man', on the other hand, should be covered in the Lord's presence. 'For this reason, and because of the angels, the woman ought to have a sign of authority on her head' (v.10).

There are two difficult phrases in this verse. Firstly, what does Paul mean when he writes, literally, 'the woman ought to have authority upon her head'? modern translations correctly expand this as 'a sign of authority' (NIV) or 'a symbol of authority' (NASB), but the meaning is still unclear. Is Paul referring to authority which the woman herself exercises, so that on her head is a symbol of her liberty in Christ, her authority over 'the angels' (cf. 6:3)? Or does he mean that she is to wear a sign of the man's authority over her? in favour of the first interpretation is the fact that 'authority' *(exousia)*, when used in other places (e.g. 7:37; Revelation 14:18; 20:6), has an active sense – 'charge of, power over, control over'. We have here, however, a symbolic use of *exousia*, unique in the New Testament, so that the meaning must be determined largely by the context. This tends against this interpretation, as the topic under consideration is the man as head of the woman and how this is to be reflected in headcovering. In verses 11 and 12 he will guard against any idea that women are inferior and this will be introduced by 'however', showing that he is moving to a new topic, a contrasting and balancing truth. It is possible, of course, that Paul is making a double reference. By covering her head, the woman is recognising the authority of the man and is also proclaiming her status as co-ruler of creation.

The unusual term 'authority' may, in fact, have come from the

Corinthians themselves, as one of their catch-phrases. They were eager to insist on their rights. To their proud self-centredness nothing was more important than 'the exercise of freedom' (Greek *exousia*) (8:9). A favourite slogan, 'everything is permissible for me' (6:12), uses the Greek verb from which 'authority' comes. It may well be that Paul is here picking up their boast. 'You are interested in freedom, authority, rights. Well then, recognise one of these rights. Let the woman wear on her head a symbol of the authority which has been given to the man by God, an evidence of her own exalted position as a sharer in his dominion'.

The rather mysterious supporting reason, 'because of the angels', has suffered from the misplaced ingenuity of commentators. We may dismiss the suggestion that the head-covering is to protect women from angelic lust. Angels are portrayed as interested observers of Christian worship and life (Ephesians 3:10; 1 Timothy 5:21). It is important, therefore, that due decorum be observed in the assemblies. The worshippers should remember that they are on a cosmic stage, watched by these mighty, unseen beings, and should conduct themselves in accordance with God's order.

III. Important qualification – verses 11,12

The apostle has been emphasizing male headship and female acknowl-edgement of this. But he knows how ready men are to abuse their position, distorting loving leadership into an oppressive tyranny. He understands how women might feel crushed, frightened, vulnerable under this teaching. So he now introduces a vital qualification. 'In the Lord, however.. ' 'However' or 'nevertheless' brings in something new, an important balancing truth to be kept in mind. He is writing to those who are 'in the Lord'. Their relationships are not to be governed by oppressive tradition or by brute force. As new creatures in Christ, men and women are set free to live according to the Creator's original design. This was one of mutual dependence. The sexes are not separate species, nor are men and women self-sufficient entities. They need each other, they belong together. 'Woman is not independent of man, nor is man independent of woman' (v.11).

Why so? 'For as woman came from man, so also man is born of woman' (v.12). It is true that the man was made first. But it is also true that all men ever since have been born second. Woman is man's mother as well as his wife. The woman cannot boast of her superiority as representative of some great mother goddess, the womb of all life, because 'woman came from man'. The man who wants to claim superiority has the balloon of his self-conceit punctured by the smile on the face of his mother, who held him in her arms as a helpless infant, for 'man is born of woman'.

This is wholesome and relevant teaching. It pours oil on the troubled waters of sexual conflict. Role-distinctions and equality are not contradictory. Neither male nor female is inferior, of lesser worth. Both have functions to fulfil and, in order to do this, they need one other. In valuing the contribution and acknowledging the dignity of each other, they are simply recognising their common creatureliness and confessing that 'everything comes from God' (v.12).

IV. Appeals to 'nature' and church practice – verses 13-16

It may be that some of the Corinthians are still objecting, still reluctant to accept the apostolic teaching. Paul therefore brings the passage to a close by appealing to their own sense of what is 'proper' (v.13), enlisting it as a witness in favour of his teaching. 'Judge for yourselves' (v. 13). He seems to say: ' You claim to be wise. Well then, consult your own wisdom, examine your own sense of right and wrong.' 'Does not the very nature of things teach you that if a man has long hair, it is a disgrace to him, but that if a woman has long hair, it is her glory?' (vv. 14,15).

By 'nature of things' (lit. 'nature') Paul means an inherent awareness of what is fitting. It is an instinctive sense of right and wrong, 'that which is engraven on our natural constitution'.[19] 'Nature' teaches us that there should be a clear distinction in appearance between men and women. Both the effeminate man and the masculine woman are regarded as objectionable. Generally speaking, the distinction is partly signalled by hair length, with women wearing their hair considerably longer than men. When Paul allowed his hair to grow long, it was as a deliberately exceptional act (Acts 18:18). That which is woman's 'glory' (v.15), bringing honour to her person and status, would be a 'disgrace' (v.14) to a man, rendering him an object of contempt. The Corinthians themselves know this. 'Long hair is given to her as a covering' (v.15). It is nature's way of emphasizing her need for covering, her recognition of the man's authority. So 'is it proper for a woman to pray to God with her head uncovered?' (v.13), Why should she boldly uncover her head? Is there not an inner voice, an ingrained sense of propriety which protests against the unnaturalness of what she is doing?

'Does not the very nature of things teach you?' C.S. Lewis was later to argue along similar lines: 'I am not married myself, but as far as I can see, even a woman who wants to be the head of her own house does not usually admire the same state of things when she finds it going on next door... There must be something unnatural about the rule of wives over husbands, because the wives themselves are half ashamed of it and despise the husbands whom they rule.'[20]

The section closes with a final brief message addressed to anyone who still 'wants to be contentious about this' (v.16). 'Contentious' means 'a lover of strife' a war-monger, the person who enjoys an argument for its own sake. This objector may continue to maintain that women may pray and prophesy with uncovered heads. Paul dismisses them crisply; 'We have no such practice (not 'no other practice' as in NIV) – nor do the churches of God' (v.16). Those who persist in following this disorderly practice should realise that against them stand not only Paul and his colleagues but the entire world-wide Christian community.

The message for today

It is unfortunate that study of this passage has often centred on whether or not women should wear hats during worship. Such a preoccupation has tended to obscure an important and fruitful principle. We are living at a time when the respective roles of men and women are matters of controversy. The egalitarian spirit of the age is, of course, hostile to any idea of authority. But within the church itself strong voices have also argued that exclusively male leadership is sub-Christian and out of date. 1 Corinthians 11 shows us that this is no new problem. Corinthian women, intelligent and enthusiastic believers, were claiming equal status with men in the church. Paul does not, here, question their motivation. But he does explain, gently and yet with the full weight of apostolic authority, that they are wrong.

God has established a structure in which 'the head of the woman is man' (v.3). This is evident from creation, witnessed to by 'nature' and supported by universal Christian practice. Man's headship is carefully qualified so that it poses no threat to woman's worth, dignity or meaningful role in life. Still, he is head and the woman rejects his authority to her and his shame and to the dishonour of God. The male-female distinction is to be preserved and to be demonstrated in both behaviour and appearance.

In first-century Corinth the uncovered heads of the worshipping women sent out a deliberate and unmistakable message of rebellion against God's created order. The impact a century ago may or may not have been similar, but such is not the case today. Rejection of divinely-given authority is now manifested in other ways, more often by attitude and demeanour than by details of dress or hair-style. While there seems to be a permanent basis for women wearing their hair significantly longer than men, the precise cultural expressions of subordination will vary with place and time and they are not the basic issue with which Paul is dealing. Compelled to discuss symptoms, his true concern is to treat the underlying disease. So he reminds them that men are to be seen to behave as men. Women are to embrace their role as helpers. Both are to respect and maintain God's order in whatever ways may be culturally appropriate and significant.

For the true follower of Christ this should be neither unwelcome nor difficult. We know already the satisfaction to be gained from submitting wholeheartedly to the One whom God has appointed our Lord and Master. It is added and immense encouragement to reflect that we are following in the steps of the Saviour himself. When all his enemies are under his feet, he too, with gladness, 'will be made subject to him who put everything under him, so that God may be all in all' (15:28).

NOTES

1. Geerhardus Vos, *Biblical Theology,* Eerdmans, 1948, pp. 12,13
2. Cited in *Dictionary of New Testament Theology,* C. Brown ed., Paternoster, 1976, Vol. 2, p. 160.
3. Ronald Y. K. Fung, ' Ministry in the New Testament', in *The Church in the Bible and the World,* D A Carson ed., Paternoster, 1987, p. 186.
4. For example, Gordon D. Fee, *1 Corinthians,* Eerdmans, 1987, ad loc. Fee (pp. 495-497) provides a useful brief assessment of both arguments, together with a third and unlikely suggestion that the contrast is between long and short hair .
5. J. Jeremias, *Jerusalem in the Time of Jesus,* Fortress, 1969, p. 359.
6. For example, J. B. Hurley in *Westminster Theological Journal* 35 (1973), pp. 190-220.
7. G Schrenk, *Theological Dictionary of the New Testament,* G. Kittel ed., Eerdmans, 1979, Vol. III, p. 49.
8. Berkeley and Alvera Mickelsen, 'What does *Kephale* mean in the New Testament?', in *Women, Authority and the Bible,* A Mickelsen ed., Marshall Pickering, 1987, pp. 106,107.
9. Fee, op. cit., p. 503.
10. Catherine Clark Kroeger, ' Appendix III: The Classical Concept of *Head* as 'Source',' in *Equal to Serve,* Gretchen Gaebelein Hull, Scripture Union, 1989, p. 267.
11. Wayne Grudem provides a thorough discussion of *Kephale,* with a devastating demolition of his critics, in 'Appendix 1: The Meaning of *Kephale* ('Head'): A Response to Recent Studies', in *Recovering Biblical Manhood and Womanhood,* John Piper and Wayne Grudem eds., Crossway, 1991, pp. 425-468.
12. Ibid., p 453.
13. George W. Knight III, *The New Testament Teaching on the Role Relationship of Men and Women,* Baker, 1977, p. 33.
14. Hodge, op. cit., p 209.
15. Matthew Henry, *A Commentary on the Whole Bible,* ad loc.
16. W. Bauer, W. F. Arndt, F. W. Gingrich, *A Greek-English Lexicon of the New Testament,* Chicago and Cambridge, 1964, p. 180.
17. Although 'man' in the Marcan verse refers to both men and women.

18. Charles Hodge, *Commentary on the Second Epistle to the Corinthians*, Eerdmans, n.d., p. 212.

19. John Murray, *The Epistle to the Romans*, Marshall, Morgan and Scott, 1967, Part 1, p. 73.

20. C. S. Lewis, *Mere Christianity*, Collins, 1977, p. 100.

Chapter 6

Should Women Preach?

Edward Donnelly

Ted Donnelly holds an honours degree in classics and a Master's degree of theology from Queen's University, Belfast, and is a graduate of the Reformed Presbyterian Theological Seminary, Pittsburgh. He studied at the University of Athens from 1972-73 and served in the Greek Evangelical Church in Cyprus for one year. Minister of Trinity Reformed Presbyterian Church, Newtownabbey, he is Professor of New Testament Language and Literature in the Reformed Theological College, Belfast, visiting lecturer in New Testament at Ottawa Theological Hall, Canada, and is joint editor of The Reformed Theological Journal. He is a regular speaker at conferences in the United Kingdom, United States, Canada and South Africa. Ted is married to Lorna and they have three children.

Should Women Preach?

In the controversy over female roles in the church two passages in particular have been quoted as prohibiting preaching or ruling by women: 1 Corinthians 14:34,35 and 1 Timothy 2:11-15. Do they in fact do this? The traditional understanding has recently been called into question and it is appropriate to consider the texts again.

1 Corinthians 14:34,35 - 'Women should remain silent in the churches'

This statement seems plain enough and, if not, is reinforced by two others: 'They are not allowed to speak... it is disgraceful for a woman to speak in the church' (vv.34,35). Many have taken this to be an absolute prohibition. Women, on their understanding, are never permitted to say anything in a church service. This would, of course, exclude any possibility of public teaching.

Such an interpretation raises practical questions. May women take part in the singing of praise? What about a congregation united in praying the Lord's Prayer, or, in churches with a set liturgy, making response to the prayers? Would this rule out responsive reading of the Scriptures by the whole assembly? Could a mother speak to her child during a service or does silence apply only to speech audible to others? We cannot have much confidence in an interpretation which brings us rapidly to the level of the absurd.

A more substantial difficulty is that an absolute prohibition seems to conflict with 1 Corinthians 11:5,13, where Paul envisages women praying and prophesying in a public service. How can we reconcile his forbidding them to speak here with this previous permission?

The Christian, committed to the inerrancy and perfection of the Word of God, cannot believe that the two passages conflict with one another. Nor is it possible to imagine that a man of Paul's towering intellect would have contradicted himself so foolishly, and within such a short space. It is, indeed, disturbing to note the readiness, almost gleeful, with which some writers allege inconsistency in the apostle. They seem to treat him as a hostile witness, someone to be refuted and made to look ridiculous. One of the Puritans, William Bridge, acutely diagnoses the spiritual malady at the root of such an approach to Scripture and his words are strikingly appropriate to much feminist exegesis. 'You know how it was with Moses, when he saw the two men fighting, one an Egyptian, and another an Israelite, he killed the Egyptian; but when he saw two Hebrews fighting, now, saith he, I will go and reconcile them, for they are brethren: why so, but because he was a good man, and gracious? So also it is with a gracious heart; when he sees the Scripture fighting with an Egyptian, an heathen author, or apocryphal, he comes and kills the heathen... but when he sees two Scriptures at variance (in view, though in truth not), Oh, saith he, these are brethren, and they may be reconciled, I will labour all I can to reconcile them; but when a man shall take every advantage of seeming difference in Scripture, to say, 'Do ye see what contradictions there are in this book, and not labour to reconcile them; what doth this argue, but that the corruption of a man's nature is boiled up to an unknown malice against the word of the Lord; take heed therefore of that'.[1]

So how can we reconcile the two Scriptures? Some argue that, as Paul's main concern in chapter 11 is with head-coverings, his reference there to praying and prophesying is a neutral one. He simply recognizes that it is taking place before forbidding it in 14:34. Calvin says that 'when he takes them to task because they were prophesying bareheaded, he is not giving them permission, however, to prophesy in any other way whatever, but rather is delaying the censure of that fault to another passage'.[2] Yet the clear implication in chapter 11 is that Paul approves of these activities by women, provided that their heads are covered and this seems a strained attempt to defend a traditionalist position.

It has been asserted by others that 14:34-35 is not authentic, but inserted into the text by someone other than Paul. This idea is based on the fact that a few manuscripts, the Western ones, have 34-35 after verse 40 instead of here, their location in the overwhelming majority of manuscripts. It is argued that, since there is no obvious reason why scribes should have moved the verses either backwards or forwards, they must not have belonged to the original text in the first place. Such a claim is quite extraordinary, since these verses appear in every single known manuscript. That they present interpretive problems argues for their retention, not their exclusion, since a cardinal principle of textual criticism is that the more difficult reading is almost always preferable. Ancient scribes tended to remove, not invent, difficulties. To omit verses 34-35 without any textual support whatever would not only be unscholarly but would establish a most dangerous precedent. What 'inconvenient' passage might be next? D A Carson describes G D Fee's recent elaborate argumentation in favour of omission as sounding 'a bit like the application of a first-class mind to the defense of a remarkably weak position'.[3]

Further suggestions, such as that chapter 11 refers to private meetings and chapter 14 to public ones, that chapter 14 is addressed only to married women, that what Paul is prohibiting is idle talk, self-willed speaking or disorderly interruptions, are less than persuasive. The explanation must lie elsewhere.

The most satisfactory interpretation[4] begins with the realization that the prohibition of verses 34 and 35 cannot mean absolute silence in all circumstances. The silence is one which is mandatory only in certain situations and these are defined by the context. Paul has already insisted on such a relative silence in verse 28, where the tongue-speaker, if there is no interpreter, 'should keep quiet (Greek *sigato*, same word as in v.34) in the church'. Clearly this does not mean that the person involved cannot speak again in the service, perhaps in prayer or instruction. The silence intended is that he should cease speaking in tongues. Similarly, a prophet should be silent (*sigato*, v.30) if a revelation comes to someone who is sitting down. He may speak later, but at this point must cease prophesying. So the silence required of women in verses 34 and 35 is not absolute; it refers to speech of a particular kind. They were still free to pray and prophesy. What type of speaking does Paul forbid?

The context would suggest strongly that what he has in mind is the judging or evaluation of prophecy. From verse 26 onwards he is dealing with the regulating of tongues and prophecy in the interests of orderly worship. 'All must be done for the strengthening of the church' (v.26). As far as tongues are concerned, various restrictions are imposed: only two or three are to speak, one at a time, and interpretation must be given (vv.27,28). When it comes to prophecy, two or three should speak, their messages must be weighed carefully and the speakers are to succeed each other in an orderly way so that everyone may profit (vv.29-32). 'For God is not a God of disorder but of peace' (v.33). It is at this point and in this context that the silence of the women is enjoined 'as in all the congregations of the saints' (v.33). Such a general restraint is understandable in view of the widespread occurrence of prophecy in the early church (e.g. Romans 12:6; Ephesians 4:11; 1 Thessalonians 5:20; 1 Timothy 1:18; 4:14). When prophecies are being judged, 'women should remain silent in the churches'.

Why should this be so? If women were enabled and permitted to prophesy, why might they not evaluate prophecies? Paul amplifies his prohibition: 'They are not allowed to speak, but must be in submission, as the Law says' (v.34). Their speaking would show lack of submission, a usurping of authority. A prophet had no authority of his own, but 'was purely and simply an instrument, an organ of the word of God'.[5] A teacher, on the other hand, exercised considerable authority and this office, as we shall see from 1 Timothy 2, was not open to women. The judging of prophecies, probably an evaluation of whether or not they were true or false,[6] was also a teaching role and therefore limited to men. This is according to the pattern of 'the Law' (v.34), the creation order of Genesis 2 and 3 already referred to in 1 Corinthians 11. If any women were tempted to get round this prohibition, expressing their assessment of a prophecy under the guise of questions, 'they should ask their own husbands at home' (v.35).

The above interpretation does not, admittedly, answer every question and dogmatism would be unwarranted. Our information about worship practices in the New Testament church is limited. But it does fit snugly into the context. It conflicts in no way with chapter 11.

It agrees with Paul's general teaching on male-female relationships. The speech prohibited to women is authoritative judging or direction which would be 'disgraceful' (v.35), incompatible with godly submission.

What is the relevance of these verses for the modern church? We conclude that those who would prevent women from any speaking in church services are imposing on this passage a meaning which it cannot sustain. Those evangelicals who accept a continuing in some form of prophecies in the church today are surely under obligation to observe the rule that women shall not judge them. And those who, like the present writer, believe that 'the prophetic word of God has found its perfection with the completion of the new covenant Scriptures'[7], and that therefore there are no prophecies today, can, of course, regard the matter of women judging prophecies as irrelevant now. But the principle of submission is taught, with the implication that such submission extends to refraining from authoritative speaking. This truth is set forth more explicitly in our second passage.

1 Timothy 2:11-15 - 'I do not permit a woman to teach'

We smile in sympathy as we read the apostle Peter's rueful comment on the inspired writings of his 'dear brother Paul' - 'His letters contain some things that are hard to understand' (2 Peter 3:16). It is comforting to know that we are not the only ones to have had difficulty in grasping fully the thought of a theological genius. Some of Paul's statements, in their concise profundity, are indeed 'hard to understand'. But 1 Timothy 2:12 is not one of them. 'I do not permit a woman to teach or to have authority over a man; she must be silent'. Nothing could be clearer. The words are simple, the grammar straightforward, the meaning obvious. For over nineteen hundred years most Christians have understood that Paul is prohibiting women from teaching publicly or holding ruling office in the church. That women have not done so has been due, for the most part, to an acceptance of this emphatic statement as the word and will of God.

How have the proponents of the ordination of women reacted to this seemingly insuperable obstacle? Many, of course, simply do not care what the Bible says. Brainwashed by the spirit of the age, desperate for the good opinion of those outside the church, terrified of appearing to limit the freedom of any individual to pursue a course to which he or she may 'feel called', they follow the path of pragmatism. What seems to work must be right. Where obedience to Scripture would be embarrassing or inconvenient, so much the worse for Scripture.

Others, however, have sought to justify their views by means of biblical arguments. We may leave aside claims that 1 Timothy 2:12 is not authoritative either because Paul did not write it or because he was wrong. The Pauline authorship of the Pastoral Epistles has been ably defended[8] and both these objections are quite incompatible with a reformed and evangelical doctrine of inspiration. A more reasoned position is held by those who agree that Paul did prohibit women from teaching and exercising authority and that he was right in doing so, but who maintain that this prohibition is no longer applicable to the church today. This is held either because cultural changes have rendered acceptable in the twentieth century what would have been unwise and intolerable in the first or because Paul's teaching applied only to a specific and unusual situation in Ephesus which has no modern counterpart. We shall consider these arguments in due course, but must begin, as always, by examining the context of the passage.

The background
The church at Ephesus was in crisis. Believers were confused about how they were meant to live and worship within the fellowship and this was the immediate reason for Paul's letter: 'I am writing you these instructions so that, if I am delayed, you will know how people ought to conduct themselves in God's household, which is the church of the living God, the pillar and foundation of the truth' (3:14,15). The confusion was being caused by a virulent outbreak of false teaching. The apostle cannot have been surprised at this, as he had foreseen it a few years earlier when taking leave of the Ephesian elders (Acts 20:29,30). But he was determined to fight it with all his strength. He had urged his friend Timothy to remain in charge of the church 'so that you may command certain men not to

teach false doctrine any longer' (1 Timothy 1:3).

The precise nature of the heresy is difficult to determine and we should be careful not to attach second-century labels to what was probably a formless mixture of pagan philosophy, Jewish speculation and legend along with elements of Christianity. One factor, in common with the situation in Corinth, seems to have been a mistaken view of the relationship of the new life to the old, leading to commands to abstain from marriage and from certain foods (4:3) and an assertion that the resurrection of believers had already taken place (2 Timothy 2:18). The relations and practices of normal life were being devalued in the interests of a false 'spirituality' and this will illuminate for us what the apostle has to say about the place of women in the church. He describes the false teaching in strong language: 'meaningless talk (1:6), godless chatter (6:20), things taught by demons... through hypocritical liars, whose consciences have been seared as with a hot iron (4:1,2)'.

Why is Paul so vehement? Not just because of the false content but because the issue of teaching (Greek *didaskalia*) is itself so central to the life and health of the church. Truth must be communicated, but, more than that, it must come in an authoritative manner and through those duly appointed. **'Command** and teach these things' he writes to Timothy (4:11). A major concern is 'sound teaching' (1:10; 2 Timothy 4:3; Titus 1:9; 2:1). He himself is a teacher appointed by God (2:7; 2 Timothy 1:11). Timothy is to entrust the apostolic doctrine 'to reliable men who will also be qualified to teach others' (2 Timothy 2:2). Ronald Y K Fung has shown that '(in) the Pastoral Epistles the *didasko* word-group is used predominantly if not exclusively with the nuance of public and official teaching in church or at least of doctrinal instruction'.[9] This official, authoritative understanding of 'teaching' needs to be kept in mind when we come to the prohibition of verse 12.

In the verses immediately preceding this passage Paul has been giving instructions concerning public prayer (2:1-7). The men who pray are to be holy and to avoid angry disputing (v.8). Female worshippers are to adorn themselves with modest clothing and appropriate behaviour, avoiding all showy or shameless personal ornamentation (vv.9,10). Paul then moves on to explain how such appropriate conduct will manifest itself during worship. First comes a positive injunction followed by a prohibition (vv.11,12). Reasons for the prohibition are then given (vv.13,14) and the section ends with a reference to woman's true role (v.15).

Command and prohibition - verses 11 and 12.

It seems that there was a problem in Ephesus over women[10] disrupting the meetings. Christian women, perhaps newly-emancipated from the limitations of the synagogue, where they had no part in the service and were usually restricted to a separate section or a gallery where they could not be seen, appear to have been abusing their freedom in Christ by claiming a prominent vocal part in the services. So Paul's first word to them, repeated at the end of verse 12 for emphasis, is 'quietness' (Greek *hesychia*). The word can mean absolute silence (e.g. Acts 22:2) or a spirit of restful contentment (e.g. 2 Thessalonians 3:12) and there is no need here to distinguish too sharply between these. 'She must be quiet'. Paul wants the women to have a quiet spirit which will evidence itself in quiet behaviour.

This is not a negative or passive quality, for silence is the best posture for learning, which is precisely what they are to do - 'a woman should learn'. Paul is in advance of his time. The rabbis discounted such a possibility, holding that men came to the synagogue to learn, the women, at most, to hear. In Roman and Greek society also, apart from a few wealthy and prominent women, female education was neglected. In the church, however, women are equal with men in the privilege and responsibility of receiving instruction from the Word of God. The learning is to be 'in full submission' - the highest degree of humble receptivity to what God the Lord will speak. But they participate fully in this glorious spiritual duty. They are to imitate Mary of Bethany, who 'sat at the Lord's feet listening to what he said' and who was commended by the Saviour for having 'chosen what is better' (Luke 10:39,42).

They are not, however, to teach. The prohibition is emphasised by an unusual word order, with 'to teach' being brought forward to the beginning of the verse, immediately followed by 'woman'. 'But when it comes to teaching - by a woman' would be a fair paraphrase. Here is something very different from submissive learning and the apostle's verdict is 'I do not permit it'. The statement is authoritative, with no room for compromise. Paul is not making a suggestion or merely offering advice. He is 'an apostle of Christ Jesus by the command of God our Saviour' (1:1) and he is using his divinely-given authority to prohibit women from engaging in this activity.

Although attempts have been made to discredit this restriction by making it seem absurd or inconsistent, it is obvious that Paul is referring here to official, public teaching of the Scriptures. We have seen already that this is the predominant meaning of the 'teaching' word-group in these letters. There are certainly some circumstances in which women should teach. It was in this very city that, after hearing Apollos, Priscilla and Aquila 'invited him to their home and explained to him the way of God more adequately' (Acts 18:26). Timothy himself had been taught by a godly mother and grandmother (2 Timothy 1:5; 3;15). Titus was to instruct older women to be teachers of good things to younger women (Titus 2;3,4). These are valuable ministries in which women's gifts may be fully exercised. But the public ministry is not open to them.

This is confirmed by the additional restriction - 'or to have authority over a man'. Are these two separate prohibitions? Is Paul saying that a woman may neither teach nor rule in the church? Or does he mean simply that she may not teach in an authoritative manner? It seems a distinction without a difference. The teaching of the Scriptures must by its very nature be authoritative. In Lenski's words, 'the public teacher of God's people does not only tell others what they need to know, but... he stands before his audience to rule and govern it with the Word'.[11] If the woman may not rule in this way, she cannot rule in other ways. The issue is of the exercise of authority, whether in the ministry of the Word or in the office of elder, with which Paul, very significantly, is about to deal (3:1-7).

We have then two clear antitheses in verses 11 and 12. A woman is to learn, not to teach. She is to be quiet and submissive, not to exercise authority over a man. The distinctions are marked and the conclusion clear. It seems impossible to evade or obscure Paul's meaning. But that has not prevented some feminist writers from trying.

Does Paul's prohibition still apply?

Although reinterpretations of the passage are many and various, two main suggestions have emerged.

1. It is argued that first-century society would have been scandalized by women teachers and that women, in any case, were not sufficiently educated for teaching. 'Whether because the women were uneducated and thus particularly susceptible to error, or because their seizing authority would have injured the church's witness in a tense social situation, or (most likely) both, the specific situation Paul addresses invites his specific response'.[12] The prohibition does not, therefore, apply today when women are as well educated as men and their role as teachers is socially acceptable. This is, in fact, what the apostle had in mind as his ultimate goal. Paul is offering a short-term solution and, in affirming their duty and ability to learn, 'he proposes educating them as a long-range solution to the current problem'.[13]

2. A view which in some form or other is currently more favoured by feminists is that Paul is addressing a unique and complex situation in Ephesus. It is alleged that the city was dominated by a feminist religious culture in which the priestesses of Artemis, the Great Mother who took second place to no male god, exercised supreme spiritual authority. Into this matriarchal context came a gnostic heresy which reinterpreted the story of the Fall in Genesis so as to make Eve a heroine, the teacher who brought to Adam salvation by knowledge. Women were claiming to be the leaders and instructors of men. Bruce Barron's assessment is that 'The gospel is struggling in Ephesus with gnostic-influenced women trumpeting a feminist reinterpretation of Adam and Eve as precedent for their own spiritual primacy and authority'.[14] Catherine Clark Kroeger, the best-known proponent of this view, suggests that the rare Greek verb authenteo, rendered in the NIV as 'to have authority', should instead be translated 'to proclaim oneself the author or originator of something'.[15] Paul would then be saying 'I do not allow a woman to teach nor to represent herself as the originator or

source of man'. His words would have no relevance where such a distortion of truth does not exist. This is not, therefore, a permanent prohibition of women teachers but, as he develops his argument in verses 13 and 14, 'a coherent counter-argument to a specific problem - namely, a false interpretation of Genesis by heretical women'.[16]

Are such interpretations valid? What can be said in response to them? Three points should be made.

1. The reconstructions outlined above are almost entirely speculative, devoid of solid supporting evidence. There is no reference anywhere in the text to women's lack of education or to societal disapproval of their assumption of a teaching role. The suggestions about gnostic teaching have been subjected to the most searching criticism.[17] The proposition that religious society in Ephesus was dominated by women has been comprehensively dismantled and shown to be without foundation.[18] *Authenteo* is certainly a rare verb, used only here in the New Testament and with a range of meaning elsewhere, but Kroeger's interpretation is highly questionable, to say the least. It is equally implausible to argue, as some do, that the reference is only to an excessive use of authority, women abusing their right to rule by displaying an objectionable spirit. There is no hint in the context of any such meaning. These verses address women alone, whereas such abuse would be equally inappropriate for men. The biblical alternative to *authentein* is submission and silence, not exercising authority in a gracious way. George W Knight III, who has made an extensive study of the word, states that it 'shows no inherent negative sense of grasping or usurping authority or of exercising it in a harsh or authoritative way, but simply means "to have or exercise authority"'.[19] Unsubstantiated assertions, however popular, can scarcely claim to be credible biblical interpretation.

2. We may readily agree that these verses were framed in the light of a specific pastoral problem at Ephesus. The false teaching does appear to have had a particularly damaging impact upon the women in the church (2 Timothy 3:6,7). These women, deceived and led astray, may be the very ones who themselves want to teach. Paul will not permit them to do so. Not, however, primarily because they are in error but

because they have no right to exercise such a ministry.

Dealing with an activity which will be carried on in every church until the end of the age, Paul is expressing his permanent policy. His prohibition has been evoked by the immediate situation, but would remain the same whether or not the needs of the moment required him to mention it. Most of the practical teaching of the New Testament epistles is similarly addressed to specific circumstances. Its genius, however, is that it is based on theological principles which transcend the particulars and are eternally and universally relevant. The logic is clear. 'These women may not teach or exercise authority because I do not permit any women to do so'.

3. Any interpretation must take into account Paul's own reason for the statement which he has made. If he argues from local circumstances or contemporary cultural norms, we may be justified in dismissing the prohibition as limited and temporary. If, on the other hand, his reasoning is based on theology or redemptive history then the principle established must be permanent and universal. That reason is given in verses 13 and 14.

The Reason - verses 13 and 14
As in 1 Corinthians 11, Paul bases his teaching on what happened when man and woman were created, and then moves on to their fall into sin. He is drawing upon the whole narrative of Genesis 2 and 3, arguing from the early events of redemptive history. This is something which is unaffected by cultural changes, true for all humans and for all earthly time.

His reasoning has been misunderstood, distorted, made to look ridiculous. It has been suggested, for example, that, if Adam has authority over Eve simply because he was created before her, then the animals, created earlier still, should rule over Adam. But Paul's argument is not a purely chronological one. Male prejudice has been evident in the claim, made by some eminent commentators of the past, that women are not to teach because they are inherently more gullible than men. 'It was the woman who was deceived' because the serpent realized that her powers of reasoning were inferior to those of her husband. This is not only insulting but preposterous, for we have seen that Paul expects women to carry out vital teaching responsibilities in their families and homes. If they are so constitutionally lacking in discernment, how could they ever teach anyone? In any case, he uses the same event to warn men as well as women in 2 Corinthians 11:3: 'I am afraid that, just as Eve was deceived by the serpent's cunning, your minds may somehow be led astray...' Men are no more resistant than women to the wiles of the devil.

Paul argues, rather, from the hierarchy, or order, established by God. 'Adam was formed first'. This priority has been considered already in the previous chapter, but it is important to note here that the word 'first' is not, as might appear, an adverb but an adjective. One of Adam's attributes is 'firstness'. He is in a position of primacy or headship. The command of Genesis 2:17 not to eat from the tree of the knowledge of good and evil was given directly to him alone, before the woman was created. He was the representative of the race, acting on behalf of all who would follow and responsible for instructing them regarding this divine prohibition.

Here is the theology of the covenant, the background to Paul's mighty argument in Romans 5, discussed in chapter 7 of this book, in which he compares and contrasts Adam and Christ, the two covenant heads, each acting on behalf of his people. It is because of his 'firstness', his position of leadership, his representative status, that the man's failure meant the ruin of the race. In the words of the Westminster Shorter Catechism, 'The covenant being made with Adam not only for himself but for his posterity, all mankind, descending from him by ordinary generation, sinned in him and fell with him in his first transgression' (Answer 16). God entrusted to him the fulfilment of the covenant obligation. His obedience was the crucial issue.

But what happened? The devil deliberately bypassed the divinely-established order. 'Adam was not the one deceived; it was the woman who was deceived and became a sinner'. 'The serpent... more crafty than any of the wild animals the Lord God had made... said to the woman, "Did God really say...?"' (Genesis 3:1). He approached Eve directly and urged her to act independently of her husband. Her first mistake was in not referring him to Adam. God had not given to her the responsibility of unilaterally assessing his commandment or deciding whether or not to obey. This was the prerogative of the man, the 'first'. Even before she yielded to the Satanic temptation she had put herself in the wrong by acting as if she were the covenant head, usurping a role which was not hers.

What comes across in the Genesis narrative is the degree of leadership taken by the woman and the astonishing passivity of the man. 'When the woman saw... she took... and ate. She also gave to her husband'. Adam's activity is described in one phrase, 'he ate it' (Genesis 3:6). When called to account, the covenant head shelters whimperingly behind the figure of his wife: 'The woman you put here with me - she gave me some fruit from the tree, and I ate it' (Genesis 3:12). God's condemnation of his sin begins with a scathing reference to his abdication of responsibility: 'because you listened to your wife...' (Genesis 3:17).

Paul is not saying that Eve was easier to deceive than Adam would have been. Nor is he blaming her for the Fall. He is simply stating facts. Adam was created "first". Yet Eve acted as 'first' in being deceived and in sinning. God's pattern had been turned back to front. The divine order of communication and responsibility was from God to man, from man to woman, from man and woman to creatures. Genesis 3 shows us an influence which comes from the devil to a creature, from the creature to the woman, from the woman to the man. As Lenski puts it, 'both Eve and Adam had to violate not only the command of God not to eat but also their respective positions towards each other in order to effect the fall: Eve her position of subordination, Adam his headship'.[20] Such a direct reversal of the divine order could bring only disaster.

The apostle's reasoning is clear. The prohibition is not due to any innate female incapacity nor does it depend on cultural or societal norms at any particular time. It is based upon the order of creation, illustrated negatively by the tragedy of the Fall. God's entrusting to Adam the responsibility of leadership is a permanent pattern for male-female relationships. Eve's disruption of this structure is a permanent warning, applicable in a still imperfect world to the would-be female teachers in Ephesus and to all their descendants, of the harm which is caused whenever women usurp a leadership role. This is why a woman is not permitted to teach or to have authority over a man.

Woman's True Role - verse 15

Paul concludes the section with a contrasting truth introduced by 'but'. 'But she will be saved through childbearing - if they continue in faith, love and holiness with propriety'. The nature of the contrast will depend on the interpretation we adopt of what 'must rank among the most difficult expressions in the whole of the Pastorals'.[21] Is this an assurance of safety in the face of risk or of salvation from the penalty of sin? Is it a description of woman's true role as opposed to the would-be teachers and the bad example of Eve? Three possible interpretations deserve consideration.

1. Verse 15 is a promise that the woman will be kept safe through the process of childbirth. God stated that as part of the punishment for Eve's sin he would 'greatly increase your pains in childbearing; with pain you will give birth to children' (Genesis 3:16). She is now reassured that, although she will experience this suffering, her life will be preserved. There is still a curse, but God will not permit it to be life-threatening.

This seems an implausible reading. Although the Greek 'to save' (sozo) can refer to physical safety, Paul always uses it in a theological sense. He is almost certainly referring here to salvation as we commonly understand it. And what could we make of the second half of the verse? Are all faithful, loving and holy women guaranteed safe delivery? Are those who lack these graces particularly at risk? Such a statement sounds banal as well as inaccurate.

2. This is a reference to the birth of the Messiah. At that dreadful moment in Eden when condemnation was being pronounced, God spoke in mercy about the coming 'seed of the woman' who, at cost to himself, would crush the serpent's head (Genesis 3:15). It was a prophecy of the Saviour who was to be born of a woman and this is the 'childbearing' to which Paul now alludes. Women will experience pain as they give birth to children, a reminder of mankind's fatal lapse into

sin. Yet the glory of God's plan is that it was precisely through such labour that the Redeemer of the world would come. Sin has entered the world and the unique role of the mother still bears its imprint. But let her not be discouraged. There is a remedy. 'She shall be saved through the birth of a child'.

Commentators have tended to dismiss this interpretation much too readily; in some respects it is an attractive one. Knight defends it eloquently[22] and it would harmonize perfectly with the second part of the verse, since the birth of Christ brings salvation only to those whose lives demonstrate a true and fruitful faith. Against it, however, is the considerable objection (to many, insuperable) that the rare word teknogonia ('childbearing') seems an extremely obscure and ambiguous way of referring to Christ. If such were his meaning, Paul would surely have expressed himself more clearly.

3. The simplest and most probable interpretation is to understand 'childbearing' as metonymy, a figure of speech where part of something is used as a symbol for the whole. We might speak, for example, of 'the crown' when we mean the monarch, even bareheaded! While not all women are mothers, childbearing is the most unique feature of femininity and is therefore an appropriate symbol for a woman's role. This would fit in well with Paul's use of Genesis 3, where the typical activities of the man and the woman to be affected by sin are agriculture and the bearing of children. Women are saved by grace through faith alone, but the practical outworking of that salvation will be experienced not through insisting on being teachers or rulers, grasping for responsibilities which are not theirs to exercise, but in becoming and accomplishing more fully what they were created to be and to do. Motherhood is, despite modern devaluation, a supremely important role, but it is by no means the only one. Women, whether married or single, childless or mothers, 'will be saved through childbearing' - that is, through developing true womanlinesss in whatever spheres are available to them.

The situation in Ephesus provides support for this interpretation. As we have already seen, some women were being affected by the false teaching, one strand of which was a disparagement of marriage (4:3).

Paul describes the heresy as 'things taught by demons' (4:1), so he is obviously referring to it again when he mentions younger women who have 'already turned away to follow Satan' (5:15). What advice does he give them? What practical steps are they to take in order to combat the tenets of this devilish teaching? 'I counsel younger widows to marry, **to have children** (*teknogonein,* same word-group as in 2:15), to manage their homes and to give the enemy no opportunity for slander' (5:14). A pressure point in the church is an abandoning of the woman's role in home and family. Young Christian women are to resist this partly by bearing children, which is what was previously alluded to in 2:15: 'she will be saved through childbearing'.

The life of salvation has to do not only with serving in God-given roles but with the inner spirit in which duties are discharged. Outward conformity is never enough, so Paul closes with a reminder that a true experience of the life of God in the human soul depends on continuing 'in faith, love and holiness with propriety'. The Christian woman will rest upon God's promises, yield loving service to her Lord and pursue increasing holiness of character. The closing word, 'propriety' *(sophrosyne)* is especially significant. It has already been used in verse 9 and seems to bracket the passage, sounding the echo on which we leave it. Difficult to translate briefly, *sophrosyne* means moderation, self-respect, doing what is fitting or appropriate, 'a suitable restraint in every respect',[23] 'habitual inner self-government, with its constant rein on all the passions and desires'.[24]

This is not a popular virtue today, when the emphasis is on self-expression, freedom, rejection of authority or restraint. But it is recorded here, in the book which is the Christian guide and rule, as being pleasing to God, an essential component of the new life. Is it perhaps an absence of this beautiful grace, rather than new exegetical insights, which has recently made the phrase 'I do not permit a woman to teach' so objectionable to so many?

NOTES

1. Quoted by J I Packer in *Among God's Giants,* Kingsway, 1991, p.134.

2. Calvin's Commentaries, *The First Epistle of Paul The Apostle to The Corinthians,* St Andrew Press, 1960, p.231.

3. D. A. Carson, 'Silent in the Churches', in *Recovering Biblical Manhood and Womanhood,* Piper and Grudem eds., Crossway, 1991, p.145.

4. For this interpretation I am indebted largely to James B Hurley, *Man and Woman in Biblical Perspective,* InterVarsity Press, 1981, pp.185-194.

5. O Palmer Robertson, *The Final Word,* Banner of Truth, 1993, p.104.

6. The argument remains unaffected if, with Robertson, ibid. pp.16,17, we understand the 'weighing' as deciding which prophet is to speak. This too is an authority function.

7. Ibid., p.20.

8. As, for example, in Donald Guthrie, *New Testament Introduction,* revised edition, Apollos, 1990, pp. 607-649.

9. In 'Ministry in the New Testament', in *The Church in the Bible and the World,* D A Carson ed., Paternoster, 1987, p. 207.

10. Although the Greek *gyne* can mean either 'woman' or 'wife', it seems clear that it is used here of women in general. Verses 9 and 10 can hardly be limited to those who were married.

11. R C H Lenski, *The Interpretation of St. Paul's Epistles to the Colossians, Thessalonians, Timothy, Titus and Philemon,* Augsburg, 1964, p.564.

12. C S Keener, 'Man and Woman', in *Dictionary of Paul and His Letters,* Hawthorne, Martin and Reed eds., InterVarsity Press, 1993, p.591.

13. Ibid.

14. Bruce Barron, in 'Putting Women in Their Place: 1 Timothy 2 and Evangelical Views of Women in Church Leadership', *Journal of the Evangelical Theological Society,* Vol.33, No.4, 1990, p.458.

15. In '1 Timothy 2:12 - A Classicist's View', in *Women, Authority and the Bible,* A Mickelsen ed., Marshall Pickering, 1987, p.232.

16. Barron, op. cit., p.455.

17. For example in *Calvin Theological Journal,* Vol.28, 1993, pp.208-213.

18. By S M Baugh in 'The Apostle among the Amazons', *Westminster Theological Journal,* Vol.56, No.1, 1994, pp.153-171.

19. George W Knight III, *The Pastoral Epistles: A Commentary on the Greek Text,* Paternoster, 1992, p.141.

20. Op. cit., p.568.

21. Donald Guthrie, *The Pastoral Epistles,* Tyndale, 1961, p.77.

22. Op. cit., pp.146-148.

23. U Luck, *Theological Dictionary of the New Testament*, G Friedrich ed., Vol.VII, Eerdmans, 1971, p.1103.

24. R C Trench, *Synonyms of the New Testament,* James Clarke, 1961, p.68.

Chapter 7

How feminism affects your theology

Stephen Rees

Stephen was educated at Manchester Grammar School and St. John's College Cambridge where he read classics and theology. He has been the minister of Grace Baptist Church, Stockport, since its formation in 1984. Stephen describes himself as a G.P.: a pastor whose aim it is to preach in a way that is exegetical, doctrinal, biblico-theological, ethical and experimental!

How feminism affects your theology

Biblical theology is a seamless robe. Try to reshape it at a single point and the whole garment may begin to unravel.

Evangelical feminists believe that it is time to rewrite the historic Christian understanding of male and female roles. They want to discard any suggestion that man was created to lead, woman to follow. Christians of past generations emphasised the complete equality of man and woman before God. But they also believed that God had assigned to man and woman very different roles. They used such words as authority, headship and even *rule* to explain man's relation to woman (especially within family and church). They used such words as *submission* and even *obedience* to express woman's relation to man. By contrast, evangelical feminists speak of partnership and mutuality. If the word 'submission' is used, they emphasise that it must be *mutual* submission. The practical implications of such a rethink are obvious and are discussed elsewhere in this book. But what about the theological implications?

William Oddie has written, 'The incarnation of Christ and the doctrine of the Trinity; sin and the fall of man; the doctrine of grace; the very notion of revelation and the authority of the Bible as the inspired word of God; the feminist theologians... are bent on the undermining of all these great supporting arches of the Church's tradition'.[1] Is that an overstatement? In this chapter we discuss three areas of Christian doctrine and assess how they are affected by the feminist rethink. We shall consider the first area at some length, and then deal more briefly with the second and third.

1. THE DOCTRINE OF THE TRINITY

The doctrine of the Trinity is the foundation-stone of all Christian faith and experience. J.I.Packer sums up the historic doctrine thus:

'Within the complex unity of his (God's) being, three personal centres of rational awareness eternally coinhere, interpenetrate, relate in mutual love, and co-operate in all divine actions. God is not only *he* but also *they* – Father, Son and Spirit, co-equal and co-eternal in power and glory though functioning in a set pattern whereby the Son obeys the Father and the Spirit subserves both'.[2]

We must try to unpack that typically high-density statement ('Packer by name; packer by nature'). We can break it down into four key assertions. The first three are relatively uncontroversial (at least among evangelical Christians) and can be stated briefly; the fourth will require more thought.

(1) God is *one*. Packer speaks of the '...unity of God's being'. In contradiction to all the polytheistic systems of pagan religion, Moses declared: 'Hear, O Israel: The LORD (Jehovah) our God, the LORD is one' (Deuteronomy 6:4). Paul, in New Testament days shared the same certainty. 'Is God the God of Jews only? Is he not the God of Gentiles too? Yes, of Gentiles too, since there is only one God...' (Romans 3:29-30). The universe is created, sustained and controlled by one infinite, eternal, and unchangeable Spirit.

(2) Within the single being of God, there are three persons. The term 'person' (borrowed from the Latin, *persona*) should not be misunderstood. It does not mean individual beings, independent of one another. Packer speaks of 'three personal centres of rational awareness'. Jesus commanded his disciples to baptise 'in the name of the Father and of the Son and of the Holy Spirit...' (Matthew 28:19). Jesus speaks of three distinct persons – yet the three persons have only one name. The Father is Jehovah. The Son is Jehovah. The Holy Spirit is Jehovah.

(3) The three persons of the Trinity are equally divine. This follows from the fact that the three are one God. They are, says Packer, 'co-equal and co-eternal in power and glory'. They share the same 'essence'. They are equal in every divine perfection. The attributes of God are not shared out between the three persons. Each person of the Trinity is eternal, all-powerful, all-knowing. Each person of the Trinity is to be loved, trusted and worshipped as fully God.

(4) The three persons of the Trinity relate to one another according to a fixed and unchangeable order. They function, says Packer, 'in a set pattern whereby the Son obeys the Father and the Spirit subserves both.'

Wherever we turn in the New Testament, we will find glimpses of this order, but it is in John's gospel that it is most fully explored. Consider these statements about the relationship of God the Father and God the Son. '...the Son can do nothing by himself; he can do only what he sees his Father doing, because whatever the Father does the Son also does. For the Father loves the Son and shows him all he does... the Father judges no-one but has entrusted all judgement to the Son...' (John 5:19-23). 'The work that the Father has given me to finish, and which I am doing, testifies that the Father has sent me' (John 5:37). 'All that the Father gives me will come to me... I have come down from heaven not to do my will but to do the will of him who sent me. And this is the will of him who sent me, that I shall lose none of all that he has given me...' (John 6:37-39). 'I do nothing on my own but speak just what the Father has taught me. The one who sent me is with me; he has not left me alone, for I always do what pleases him' (John 8:28-29). 'I have authority to lay it (my life) down and authority to take it up again. This command I received from my Father' (John 10:18). 'I did not speak of my own accord, but the Father who sent me commanded me what to say and how to say it... whatever I say is just what the Father has told me to say' (John 12:49-50). 'I am going to the Father... the Father is greater than I' (John 14:28). 'Jesus... looked toward heaven and prayed: "Father, the time is come. Glorify your Son, that your Son may glorify you. For you granted him authority over all people... I have brought you glory on earth by completing the work you gave me to do. And now, Father, glorify me in your presence with the glory I had with you before the world began..." ' (John 17:1-5).

This is only a small selection of the passages, even within John's gospel, where the relation between Father and Son is glimpsed. The Father sends, commands, instructs the Son. He initiates all that the Son does; he gives the Son words to teach others, he hears the Son's prayers; he grants the Son authority; he rewards the Son's labours. In all these senses, the Father can be said to be *greater* than the Son: within their relationship the Father has the priority, the place of authority; or (to use a word from elsewhere in the New Testament) the headship.

We have only to consider reversing these statements to see how central this order is in Christian thought. Would we ever speak of the Father praying to the Son? Or of the Son sending the Father? The priority of the Father is written across the whole New Testament revelation.

When we come to think about the role of the Holy Spirit, we have fewer passages – but the pattern is just as clear. Jesus said: '...I will ask the Father and he will give you another Counsellor to be with you for ever – the Spirit of truth' (John 14:16). '...the Counsellor, the Holy Spirit whom the Father will send in my name, will teach you all things and will remind you of everything I have said to you' (John 14:26). 'Unless I go away, the Counsellor will not come to you; but if I go, I will send him to you' (John 16:7). '...when he, the Spirit of truth, comes, he will guide you into all truth. He will not speak on his own; he will speak only what he hears and he will tell you what is yet to come. He will bring glory to me by taking from what is mine and making it known to you' (John 16:13-14).

The Holy Spirit is sent by the Father at the request of the Son. Indeed it can be said that he is sent by the Son himself. His work is to glorify the Son – and when the Son is glorified, the Father is glorified too (ch 17:1). If the work of the Son is to teach words given to him by the Father, the work of the Spirit is to teach words given to him by the Son.

Here then is the pattern. The Son acts under the authority of the Father. The Spirit acts under the authority of Father and Son. It is right to speak, in this sense, of the subordination of the Son to the Father and of the Spirit to the Father and the Son. We may even speak of the relationship of the three persons as a *hierarchical* relationship.

It was during the earthly ministry of the Son of God that this pattern of relationships was most clearly seen. But the pattern did not begin with the incarnation. The Father *sent* the Son. The Son's coming into the world was the result of the Father's initiative. His submission was the cause not the consequence of his coming.

Orthodox theologians have always taught that the pattern of relationships seen during the earthly ministry of Jesus is the visible outworking of an eternal order within God's Triune being. To deny this implies that the life and work of Jesus Christ are not a true revelation of God's nature. What the three Persons *do* in relation to one another corresponds with what they *are* in their eternal relation to one another. The submission of the Son to the Father rests upon the fact that the Son is eternally begotten by the Father.

Louis Berkhof writes of the eternal order that exists between the persons of the Trinity: '...this order does not pertain to any priority of time or of essential dignity, but only to the logical order of derivation. The Father is neither begotten by, nor proceeds from any other person; the Son is eternally begotten of the Father, and the Spirit proceeds from the Father and Son from all eternity. Generation and procession take place within the Divine Being, and imply a certain subordination as to the manner of personal subsistence, but no subordination as far as the possession of the divine essence is concerned'.[3]

This is surely biblical. The very word 'Son' implies that the second person of the Trinity derives his personhood from the Father. Scripture writers are not afraid to say that the Son, who is himself God, was 'begotten from God': *gennētheis ek tou Theou* (1 John 5:18). The eternal Son of God who had no beginning is nonetheless 'begotten' from the Father. Each of the pictures used in Scripture to express the eternal relationship between Father and Son carries the same idea of the Father as the Eternal Cause of the Son. The Son of God can be spoken of as the *Word of God* (John 1:1). The Father expresses himself: he speaks out the Word. The Word is derived from the heart and mind of the Speaker. The Son can be described as the *'radiance of God's glory'*

(Hebrews 1:3). The Father is seen as the source; the Son as the outshining of the divine glory. In the same verse, the Son is *the exact representation of God's being*, eternally deriving all his perfections as Son from the Father.[4]

What of the eternal relationship of the Spirit to the Father and the Son? We have less information to go on. But it is clear that his very name marks the fact that the Spirit derives his Personhood eternally from Father and Son. The Spirit is the *breath of God*. (Both in Hebrew and in Greek, the same word may be used for spirit or breath). As the Father eternally speaks forth the Word, so he eternally breathes forth the Spirit.

Not all orthodox theologians would want to use the word 'subordination' as Berkhof does to describe the relationship of the Son to the Father, or of the Spirit to the Father and the Son. (Dabney: 'You will perceive that I have not used the word subordination, but derivation, to express this 'personal relation').[5] But all would emphasise that there is a real and eternal order of derivation between the persons of the Trinity. This has been enshrined in the historic creeds. The Nicene creed of 381 AD reads:

'I believe in one GOD THE FATHER Almighty; Maker of heaven and earth, and of all things visible and invisible. And in one Lord JESUS CHRIST, the only-begotten Son of God, begotten of the Father before all worlds, God of God (*ek theou*: from God), Light of Light, very God of very God, begotten, not made, being of one substance with the Father; by whom all things were made... And I believe in the Holy Ghost, the Lord and Giver of Life; who proceedeth from the Father and the Son;[6] who with the Father and the Son together is worshipped and glorified...'.[7]

Some writers have tried to maintain that the Son's submission to the Father was only a temporary arrangement, limited to the period of his earthly ministry. But orthodox Christians, following the Bible, have always taught that the pattern of relationships within the Trinity goes back to that eternal order of derivation. And of course, the pattern did not end with Christ's exaltation. The Son still prays to the Father (Romans 8:34). He still works to bring glory to the Father

(Romans 15:18). Likewise, the Spirit is still sent into the world, and to individual believers, by the Father through the Son (Acts 2:33; Galatians 4:6). When Jesus Christ, the Son of God returns, he will again come, *sent by the Father* (Acts 3:19-21). He will judge the world on the day which the Father has appointed (Acts 17:31). And finally, he will 'hand over the kingdom to God the Father after he has destroyed all dominion, authority and power'. (1 Corinthians 15:24). In this age, Christ is establishing the kingdom that he won by his life, death and resurrection. But his ultimate goal is to offer up that kingdom in willing submission to the Father. 'When he has done this, then the Son himself will be made subject to him who put everything under him, so that God may be all in all' (v.28).

This latter passage is particularly significant. The phrase used by the NIV translators – 'will be made subject'- translates the Greek word *hupotasso* – a precise equivalent etymologically to the Latin, *subordinare*. Paul has used the same verb in the preceding verses to speak of the subordination or subduing of 'all things' (i.e. the universe) to Christ. (The NIV translates the word as 'put under' in v.25, v.27, v.28). Paul is not afraid to picture the eternal state as involving hierarchy: the universe sub-ordinated to Christ; Christ the Son sub-ordinated to the Father.

Some have suggested that this sub-ordination refers to Christ only in his humanity. But this is ruled out by Paul's deliberate shift from the name 'Christ' (used throughout vv. 12-27 – 12 times in all) to the title 'The Son' in v.28. Paul insists that it is as *the Son* that Christ takes the subordinate place to the Father. The pattern of authority and submission within the Trinity is to go on into all eternity.

The glory of the Christian doctrine of the Trinity is that it shows us that within God's eternal being, there is an eternal pattern of loving headship and loving submission. The words themselves, 'Father and Son' express a relationship of love between the Begetter and the Begotten. The nature of the Father's headship over the Son is revealed in the fact that he 'loves the Son and has placed everything in his hands'. The nature of the Son's submission is expressed in his declaration that he loves the Father and does exactly what the Father has commanded

(John 14:31). The nature of the Spirit's service is that he 'he will not speak on his own; he will speak only what he hears', bringing glory to the Son (John 16:13-14). 'Ultimate reality is good, personal, relational. And these relationships are other-person-centred... This is the character of God'.[8] John's statement that 'God is love' (1 John 4:8,16) makes it clear that the pattern of headship and submission within the Trinity is a pattern of perfect love.

It is often suggested today that for one person to hold a position of authority over another must by definition involve self-seeking and tyranny. But the pattern of authority that exists within God's triune being is neither self-centred nor despotic. It is an authority exercised in perfect love. And the submission that is shown within the Trinity is neither a degrading nor a reluctant submission. ' "My *food,*" said Jesus, "is to do the will of him who sent me and to finish his work" ' (John 4:34).

'When Christ came into the world, he said: "...Here I am – it is written about me in the scroll – I have come to do your will, O God" ' (Hebrews 10:5-6). The writer is quoting Psalm 40:8: 'I desire to do your will, O my God; your law is within my heart'. For the Son to submit to the Father's will was infinitely costly. Yet it was, and is, his joyful choice.

We are now in a position to consider the relevance of the doctrine of the Trinity to the debate about men's and women's roles. We may sum up the Bible's teaching in a sentence. The relationship of man and woman is intended to mirror the relationship of Father and Son within the Trinity.

We read in Genesis 1:26: 'Then God said, "Let *us* make man in our image, in our likeness, and let *them* rule over... all the creatures..." '. As Calvin pointed out: 'Hitherto God has been introduced simply as *commanding;* now when he approaches the most excellent of his works, he enters into *consultation...* Christians, therefore, properly contend, from this testimony, that there exists a plurality of Persons in the Godhead.'[9] There was consultation between the persons of the Trinity concerning the creation of man in God's likeness. God planned to create *man* – a single being. Yet it is explicit that within the one man created in God's likeness, there was to be a plurality of persons: 'let *them* rule...'

'So God created man in his own image, in the image of God he created him; male and female he created them' (v.27). The statements in the first and second halves of the verse are parallel. To create man in the image of God was to create him male and female.[10]

The implications of this are shown in the verses that follow. God created a single being – the first man. From that man he derived a second being – the woman, taken out of man. The woman was created out of the man and for him, to be his helper. Among the beasts, there was none fit to be man's partner. But the woman was his equal, for she shared his nature. He could say of her: 'This is now bone of my bones and flesh of my flesh; she shall be called woman, for she was taken out of man'. They were two, each an individual with consciousness and will. Yet they remained one. And (the writer adds) whenever there is true marriage between a man and a woman, the two again become one: 'they will become one flesh' (Ch2 V24).

The man and the woman were created as two persons, one deriving her personhood from the other. They were created sharing a single nature yet made to relate to one another. Thus their relationship mirrored the relationship of Father and Son within the Trinity. In their created and finite unity, they were to reflect the pattern of God's uncreated and infinite unity.

The implications of this are brought out explicitly in 1 Corinthians 11. Paul writes (v.3): 'Now I want you to realise that the head of every man is Christ, and the head of the woman is man, and the head of Christ is God.' This passage is discussed elsewhere in this book. At this point, it is sufficient to observe that Paul parallels the relationship of the Son and the Father (designated here Christ and God[11]) with that of the man and the woman. As the Father is the 'head' of Christ, so the man is the 'head' of the woman. Their relationship is a created analogue of the uncreated fellowship of Father and Son within the Trinity. This viewpoint raises the relationship of man and woman (especially within marriage) to the highest conceivable dignity. Paul's statement accomplishes three things.

First, it establishes that in the relationship between man and woman, man has a certain priority. As the Son eternally derives his personhood from the Father, so in creation the woman derived her personhood from the man. 'A man ought not to cover his head, since he is the image and glory of God; but the woman is the glory of man. For man did not come from woman, but woman from man; neither was man created for woman, but woman for man' (vv.7-9).

It is clear moreover, that this priority must express itself in authority and leadership. Feminist scholars have tried to show that in contemporary usage the term 'head' does not imply authority. In my judgement they have failed.[12] But even if their linguistic observations were sound, Paul would still be telling us that the behaviour of man and woman in relation to each other should mirror the roles of Father and Son within the Trinity. And we have seen how pervasive is the Bible's witness to the Father's position of initiative and authority.

Some scholars have restricted the application of this passage to husband and wife. However, Paul's teaching at this point is in the context of congregational worship. It is difficult to imagine that it applies only to married persons present. Paul's words appear to establish a more general principle: that men should exercise authority within the church. (Whether the principle of the man's headship can be further extended to contexts other than marriage and church, and what this would mean in practice, is a question outside the scope of this chapter.)[13]

Secondly, Paul's teaching rules out forever any suggestion that woman is inferior to man by nature or status. The Son shares the nature of the Father and is equal to the Father in power and glory. Likewise, the woman shares the nature of the man and is equal to the man in every dignity. We are called to honour the Son even as we honour the Father (John 5:23; see Revelation 5:6,13). Likewise we honour the woman even as we honour the man. Paul is anxious to make this plain as his argument unfolds (1 Corinthians 11:11-12): 'In the Lord, however, woman is not independent of man, nor is man independent of woman. For as woman came from man, so also man is born of woman. But everything comes from God'. Clearly Paul is concerned to correct any misunderstanding of his teaching that would lead men to think of women as their inferiors.

Thirdly, Paul's words establish the quality of the relationship that should exist between man and woman, especially within marriage but also within the life of the church. The headship that man is to exercise is a loving headship mirroring that of the Father towards the Son. It is authority without a hint of domination, exploitation or self-centredness. The submission that woman is to show is a loving submission without a trace of compulsion or self-depreciation. It is the glad, loving, union of equals, each delighting in his or her assigned role. Those who claim that primacy must, by definition, involve (or lead to) tyranny while submission must be degrading have failed to grasp the beauty of the other-person-centred order that exists within the Trinity.

The implications of Paul's teaching in 1 Corinthians 11 for those who call themselves 'evangelical feminists' should, by now, be obvious. Letham defines feminism (in a Christian context) as including 'all who reject the idea of a relation of authority between the man and the woman and instead prefer to talk simply in terms of complementarity'.[14] Since Paul teaches that the man/woman relationship mirrors the Father/Son relationship, Christian feminists must ultimately deny all the biblical testimony to the pattern of authority and subordination that exists within the Trinity.

Some feminists, calling themselves evangelical, have not shrunk from making that denial. Explicitly, they deny that within the Trinity there is any pattern of subordination. More alarming still, they seem unaware that by so doing, they have abandoned historic Christian doctrine. Gretchen Gaebelein Hull attacks the idea that man's headship over woman involves authority. In her book *Equal to Serve*, she writes: 'If we define *head* as "authority over" then 1 Corinthians 11:3 can mean that there is a dominant to subordinate hierarchy within the Trinity, a position that does violence to the equality of the Persons within the Godhead. Early in its history, orthodox Christianity took a firm stand against any teaching that would make Christ a subordinate figure. To say that God is somehow authoritative over Christ erodes the Savior's full divinity and puts a Christian on dangerous theological ground'.[15] In an appendix to the same book, Katherine Kroeger says: 'The heretics would argue that although the Son is of the same substance as the Father, He is under subjection'.[16] As Wayne Grudem comments: 'These statements by Hull and Kroeger are simply false'.[17] The position that these writers call heretical is in fact the position of orthodox Christianity throughout the centuries. It is their own position that is a deviation from the historic stance of the Church.

Letham has pointed out the seriousness of such attempts to jettison the biblical and orthodox view of the relations between the persons of the Trinity. If feminists wish 'to preserve the eternal coequality of Father, Son and Holy Spirit without such internal relations...' they must ultimately be 'driven toward tritheism, with three coequal but subsistentially undifferentiated *personae*'.[18] We can no longer worship God as One God, the Father who eternally expresses himself in his Son by His Spirit. Rather, we worship three independent and self-existent powers who happen to have chosen to co-operate with one another. Letham adds: 'Evangelical feminism, as we have defined it, is on a dangerous path... one fails to see how evangelical feminism as such can consistently or for long preserve the historic Christian doctrine of the Trinity'.

We may be sure that few evangelical feminists have understood the danger to which their chosen path leads. The great majority of those who use that label remain, we hope, within the bounds of orthodox Trinitarianism. But deviations from the path of orthodoxy in one generation have a habit of leading to full-blown heresy in the next. And what more serious heresy could there be than the abandonment of the biblical doctrine of the Trinity?

2. ADAM AND CHRIST

By any standards, Romans 5 is a foundational chapter for evangelical theology. In this chapter, Paul paints with sweeping brush-strokes the whole history of the fall and redemption of humanity. The history of mankind, declares Paul, hangs on the acts of two men. 'Just as through the disobedience of the one man the many were made sinners, so also through the obedience of the one man the many will be made righteous' (v.19).

Debates have raged around this chapter. They can be reviewed in any major evangelical commentary. For our purposes, we need only to highlight the most obvious point. Paul declares that it was through Adam alone that the human race was subjected to sin: v.12: '...sin entered the world through one man, and death through sin, and in this way death came to all men, because all sinned...'; v.15: '...the many died by the trespass of the one man...'; v.17: '...by the trespass of the one man, death reigned through that one man...'. Paul does not speak of sin and death entering the world through Eve, nor through Adam and Eve together, but through Adam alone.

This is the more striking because in Genesis 3, it is Eve who first eats in disobedience to God's command and it is Eve who gives to her husband to eat. Paul elsewhere highlights the woman's personal guilt. He writes, 'Adam was not the one deceived; it was the woman who was deceived and became a sinner' (1 Timothy 2:14). Yet Paul insists in Romans 5 that it was through *Adam's* action alone that mankind became subject to condemnation, sin and death.

Paul is, in fact, stating explicitly what is implicit in Genesis 3:8-20. After the account of Eve's and Adam's shared disobedience, we read (3:8-9): 'Then the man and his wife heard the sound of the LORD God... and they hid from the LORD God among the trees of the garden. But the LORD God called *to the man*, "Where are you?" ' (The pronoun is singular). It is the *man* who is called to speak and to give account for the rebellious couple.

In vv.14-19, God pronounces his judgements in turn upon the serpent, the woman and the man. To the woman he says (v.16): 'I will greatly increase your pain in childbearing; with pain you will give birth to children. Your desire will be for your husband, and he will rule over you'. The woman's sin brings pain and oppression upon her. But it is restricted to herself personally. By contrast, God says to the man: 'Cursed is the ground *because of you* (again the pronoun is singular); through painful toil you will eat of it all the days of your life. It will produce thorns and thistles for you...'. The sin of the man brings God's curse not merely upon himself, but upon the whole created environment. Furthermore it is to the man, not to the woman, that God speaks the words of verse 19: 'By the sweat of your brow you will eat your food until you return to the ground, since from it you were taken; for dust you are and to dust you shall return'. It is the sin of the man that has provoked this sentence of death – a sentence that will ultimately fall on each of his descendants. It is clear that the man, carries in a distinctive way, not shared with Eve, responsibility for the sin and for its consequences.

Paul has good reason, therefore, to insist that 'sin entered the world through one man, and death through sin...' (Romans 5:12). Some scholars have nevertheless tried to avoid the plain meaning of Paul's words. Leon Morris (usually the most careful of interpreters) writes, 'Elsewhere Eve is linked with Adam in the first sin (2 Cor.11:3, 1 Tim.2:13-14) and her part is emphasized in some Jewish writing (e.g., "From a woman sin had its beginning, and because of her we all die" ' Sir.25:24). Paul does not mention her here, probably because he is thinking of Adam and Eve as one in their sin (cf. God "created them male and female... and called them Adam" Gen 5:2').[19]

It is true that the word Paul uses throughout this passage, anthrōpos, signifies man generically – human being – as distinct from anēr: the male. It is equivalent to the name 'Adam' which, as Morris points out can be used for man and woman together. But Paul's insistence here is that sin and death came through *one* man (vv.15,16,17,19) a single human being. He contrasts the *one* through whom sin came and the *many* who died in consequence (vv.15,19). The act of a single rebellious will brought ruin to the many. Morris's quotation from the apocryphal book of Ecclesiasticus only makes Paul's words more striking. Where Ben Sira attributes man's ruin to Eve, Paul insists that it is due to Adam's sin alone.

The real importance of Paul's contrast between the 'one' and the 'many' becomes evident as Paul draws the parallel with the work of Christ. As the disobedience of one, Adam, brought ruin and death to the many, so Paul argues, the obedience of one, Christ, brought grace and life to the many (vv.15,17,18,19). It is crucial for Paul's argument that in either case, it was one individual, exercising his single will in obedience or disobedience, who affected the many.

The relevance of all this should be clear. Feminist theologians have denied emphatically that man, as created, had any position of headship in relation to woman. Elaine Storkey sums it up succinctly: '...nothing in the first chapter of Genesis would support any hierarchical view of man and woman. *Whatever applies to one applies equally to the other'* (my italics).[20] Such writers deny that Adam in his relationship with Eve, held any primacy other than the purely chronological.

As we have shown, that view is difficult to square with Genesis 3, and it is impossible to reconcile with Romans 5. Douglas Moo comments, '...the sin that enters the world... is the bridgehead that paves the way for "sinning" as a condition of humanity... The fact that Paul attributes to Adam this sin is significant, since he certainly knows from Genesis that the woman, Eve, sinned first (cf.2 Corinthians 11:3; 1 Timothy 2:14). Already we see that Adam is being given a status in salvation history that is not tied only to temporal priority'.[21] Paul makes it plain that Adam had a status in salvation (or rather, condemnation) history that Eve could not share.

How is that status to be described? John Murray speaks of Adam as 'the head of the whole human race'.[22] Charles Hodge terms him 'the representative of his race'.[23] J.D.G.Dunn speaks of him as 'the one epochal figure... in trespass to condemnation...'.[24] However we express it, it is clear that Adam stood uniquely responsible for all other human beings, so that his actions affected them in a way that Eve's did not.

If evangelical feminists assert an absolute equality of role between Adam and Eve as created, they must reject Paul's claim that Adam stood, uniquely as head and representative of the human race. That is to say, they must deny the Bible's understanding of the fall and its explanation of human sinfulness.

But that is not all. As we have seen, Paul draws a parallel between Adam's unique status and that of Christ. Adam was 'a pattern of the one to come' (v.14). As Adam's sin brought judgement and death to many, so Christ's obedience brought justification and life to many. If feminists deny that it was the sin of *one* – Adam – that brought ruin to humanity, they must deny also that it was the obedience of *one* – Christ – that brought grace to the new humanity. If we cannot speak of Adam as uniquely the Head of the old humanity, we cannot speak of Christ as uniquely the Head of the new humanity.[25]

Most treatments of Scripture by evangelical feminists comment on the event of the Fall, recorded in Genesis 3. But the majority of such writers apparently see no need to consider Paul's interpretation of that event. P.K. Jewett offers one paragraph on the issue in a footnote. 'When the apostle traces the sin of mankind back to the "disobedience of the one" in Rom. 5:18-19, this, of course, is not to blame the man instead of the woman. He speaks in the singular because of the contrast and comparison with Christ, the one man who accomplished our salvation'.[26] Jewett does not seem to have grasped that if we do not 'blame the man instead of the woman', the 'contrast and comparison' Paul draws between Adam and Christ becomes false.

Storkey's words, quoted above, may seem harmless enough. But ultimately, her denial that Adam held a unique and unshared position of headship at creation, undermines the very foundation of the gospel. Thomas Goodwin, the seventeenth-century Puritan, summed up Paul's understanding of the Christian message in a graphic sentence: 'In God's sight, there are two men – Adam and Jesus Christ – and these two men have all other men hanging at their girdle strings'.[27] If the feminist claim is true, that most fundamental Bible viewpoint must be abandoned.

3. THE MESSIANIC PROMISE

The Bible is the story of a promise fulfilled. The Lord God said to the serpent, 'I will put enmity between you and the woman, and between your offspring and hers; he will crush your head, and you will strike his heel...' (Genesis 3:15). God promises that the woman will bring forth offspring (literally, a seed) who will destroy the serpent and his offspring. The word 'seed' in itself, could apply to many descendants. But the statement '*he* will crush your head' makes it plain that one figure, above all, is in view. The promise does not make clear whether the promised Saviour will be the immediate child of the woman or whether many generations will elapse before he appears. But the promise is sure.

From that first promise develops the Messianic hope that runs through the Old Testament. The writer of Genesis lists the generations through which the promise was inherited: the line of men between Adam and Noah (Genesis 5). We read how each in turn fathered an heir who in turn fathered his heir. When we come to Noah's father, we read, 'When Lamech had lived 182 years, he had a son. He named him Noah and said, "He will comfort us in the labour and painful toil of our hands caused by the ground the LORD has cursed."' (Genesis 5:28-29). Lamech was conscious of the curse pronounced upon the earth after the Fall (Genesis 3: 17-19) but he was also looking for the promised seed who would relieve mankind of the consequences of disobedience.

The story of Genesis unfolds with the division of the nations after the Flood and the election of Abraham. To Abraham, God says, 'I will make you into a great nation and I will bless you; I will make your name great, and you will be a blessing. I will bless those who bless you, and whoever curses you I will curse; and all peoples on earth will be blessed through you' (Genesis 12:2-3). The earth was cursed through Adam, but through Abraham blessing is to come to all the peoples of the earth. In the chapters that follow, the promise to Abraham is amplified. It is to be fulfilled through his offspring: his seed (13:14-16, 15:4-5, 17:3-8, 18:18-19). It culminates in the declaration of 22:18: '...through your seed all nations on earth will be blessed, because you have obeyed me.' All the earth is to be delivered from the curse through the promised seed.

The familiar stories of Abraham are the stories of how the promise of the seed was threatened: by his folly in handing his wife over, first to Pharaoh (12:10-20) and then to Abimelech (ch 20); by his attempts to obtain an heir through the slave-girl Hagar; and finally by the Lord's command to sacrifice Isaac his son.

Isaac lived and inherited the promise. 'The LORD appeared to Isaac and said..."I will make your descendants as numerous as the stars in the sky and will give them all these lands, and through your offspring (seed) all nations on earth will be blessed..."'. Jacob, despite all his follies and misadventures in turn inherited the promise from Isaac (Genesis 27:27-29; 28:13-14) and then passed it on to his son Judah. 'The sceptre shall not depart from Judah, nor the ruler's staff from between his feet, until he comes to whom it belongs' (Genesis 49:10). The promise of the seed had become the promise of the King.

The book of Ruth tells the story of one strange providence by which the line of promise continued from Judah. The book closes with the list of men through whom the promise was passed – from Judah down to Boaz, Obed, to Jesse and finally to David.

So David of the tribe of Judah became king, and heir to the promise, despite the premature calling of Saul the Benjamite. And the Lord promised him through the prophet Nathan: 'When your days are over and you rest with your fathers, I will raise up your offspring (seed) to succeed you, who will come from your own body, and I will establish his kingdom. He is the one who will build a house for my Name, and I will establish the throne of his kingdom for ever. I will be his father and he will be my son... Your house and your kingdom shall endure for ever before me, your throne will be established forever' (2 Samuel 7:11-16).

Again, it was not made clear whether the promised seed was to be David's immediate heir or his distant descendant. The books of Kings tell the story of the line of kings that descended from David. Solomon the first of them was a figure of unsurpassed majesty. But his successors in many cases were far less impressive figures and eventually the line of kings petered out with the fall of Jerusalem and the Babylonian exile.

Yet the promise was not forgotten. Isaiah had prophesied centuries earlier that the tree of Jesse's line would be reduced to a stump. But from that stump, he said, 'a Branch will bear fruit. The Spirit of the Lord will rest on him...'. In his day, 'the wolf will live with the lamb, the leopard will lie down with the goat... the earth will be full of the knowledge of the LORD as the waters cover the sea'. So, when the people finally returned from the Babylonian exile, all their hopes rested upon the man descended from David's line, Zerubbabel the Branch (Zechariah 3:8, 4:6-10).

But Zerubbabel was not the promised King. And the prophets continued to look forward. 'Rejoice greatly, O Daughter of Zion!

Shout, Daughter of Jerusalem! See, your king comes to you, righteous and having salvation... He will proclaim peace to the nations. His rule will extend from sea to sea...' (Zechariah 9:9-10).

And at last the King came. A child was born in Bethlehem the city of David – a male child. Matthew and Luke record his genealogy: his descent through Abraham's male heirs right down to Joseph, husband of Mary. And through Joseph, Jesus inherits promise and Kingship. Joseph is no more than an adoptive father, but when it comes to establishing this child's right to lead God's people, it is the father's line which is all-important. It is through the father that Jesus inherits the right to David's throne, and to Abraham's blessing.[28]

The story of the Old Testament is the story of a promise and an inheritance handed down from Eden to Bethlehem. And written large across the story is the fact that the promise, all the way from Adam to Christ, was inherited through a line of men. Every genealogy proclaims that fact.

We have surveyed the Bible story at length in order to make one point: the absolute centrality of this line of inheritance to the plan of salvation. Now in contrast, consider a statement by a consistent evangelical feminist, Gretchen Gaebelein Hull. Hull quotes with approval the definition of *patriarchy* found in 'Webster's New Collegiate Dictionary'. Patriarchy is 'social organisation marked by the supremacy of the father in the clan or family, the legal dependence of the wife and children, *and the reckoning of descent and inheritance in the male line*' (my italics).[29] Hull acknowledges that 'there is no question but that Scripture records a patriarchal society'. The question, she says, is this: *'Is patriarchy a true record of a false idea? Is male domination a true idea, or is it simply an account of fallen man's discrimination against a fellow human being, woman?'* (her italics). Hull's answer is clear. 'Patriarchy fosters continued discrimination against women, denies their human rights, and encourages less than truthful conduct in both men and women'.[30]

After a diatribe stretching to some twenty pages, she concludes: 'Our overview of patriarchy has exposed it as an unjust and sinful system'.[31] She is specific in condemning the practice of inheritance in the male line.

'Possibly worst of all, with the highest premium being placed on male heirs, patriarchy has its own built-in mechanism to perpetuate the system – but what a system! At its crudest, as Judges 19-22 proved, patriarchalism spawned the most inhuman actions because of its overriding compulsion: "Anything to keep the clan going" '.[32] 'In rigid patriarchalism a desire for sons as heirs not only puts a premium on a particular woman's child-bearing ability, it also quickly leads to the acceptability of 'many wives and concubines.'[33]

The implication of Hull's claim takes one's breath away. The whole plan of salvation, centring as it does upon a line of male heirs is simply a record of injustice and sin. In the end, Hull implies that it was never the will of God that Isaac should be the heir of the promise; that Jacob should receive it in turn; that David should pass it to Solomon; that Jesus should inherit it through Joseph. All this was simply 'fallen man's discrimination against a fellow human-being, woman'.

It is difficult to imagine a professed evangelical propounding a view that cuts across so much biblical evidence. The Bible writers tell us plainly that *God* chose Abraham; that *God* promised him a son not a daughter to inherit the promise; that *God* appointed David and his sons after him as King (in a world where other nations had women rulers – witness, for example, the Queen of Sheba); that God sent his Son into the world as a man. Hull must discard all this to maintain her claim that patriarchy is invariably and inevitably wrong.

Not all evangelical feminists would state their position as boldly as does Hull. But her statements serve to highlight the dilemma of any evangelical who wishes to claim that 'patriarchy' is by its very nature evil. The whole story of redemption establishes beyond refutation that God did assign to *men* a special role. He decreed that the line of promise should be a line of male heirs. The Christian who holds that fundamental biblical perspective cannot accept that God wills an absolute equality in the roles played by men and women.

How serious is the feminist reshaping of Christian doctrine? In this chapter, we have argued that, when worked out consistently, it subverts the biblical doctrine of the Trinity; it undermines the twin pillars of evangelical doctrine – our fall in Adam and our redemption in Christ;

and that in the end, it destroys the whole fabric of the Bible story.

Throughout this chapter, and in chapter four, the present writer has used the term 'evangelical feminist'. I do so in the conviction that there are many who believe in the authority of Scripture and love the gospel, but who have unthinkingly absorbed the tenets of feminism. But my deeper conviction is that in the final analysis, evangelicalism and feminism must be viewed as mutually contradictory systems of thought. Ultimately, Christians will have to choose whether they wish to be evangelicals or feminists. We cannot be both.

NOTES

1. William Oddie, *What Will Happen to God? Feminism and the Reconstruction of Christian Belief,* SPCK, 1984, p118.
2. J.I.Packer, article 'God' in Ferguson, Wright and Packer (eds), *The New Dictionary of Theology,* IVP, 1988, 274-277.
3. Louis Berkhof, *Systematic Theology,* Banner of Truth, 1958, p88-89.
4. cf P.E.Hughes, *A Commentary on the Epistle to the Hebrews,* Eerdmans 1977, p43-44: 'The Greek word translated 'the very stamp' here means an engraved character or the impress made by a die or a seal, as for example, on a coin... The principal idea intended is that of exact correspondence. This correspondence involves... a true and trustworthy revelation or representation of the Father by the Son'.
5. R. L. Dabney, *Systematic Theology,* Banner of Truth ed, 1985, p204. The word 'subordination(ism)' is a slippery word and is used differently by different writers. Herman Bavinck uses the word to denote the teaching that 'the Son is indeed eternal, generated out of the essence of the Father... nevertheless, he is inferior and subordinate to the Father.' Among the examples he cites is Eusebius of Nicomedia who 'assigned to the Son a place "outside the Father" and called him "*similar, not same*" in essence to the Father.' (Bavinck, *Doctrine of God,* Banner of Truth ed, 1977, p288-89). When defined in this way, subordinationism is indeed heretical. But as used by Berkhof, to define 'the manner of personal subsistence', the term is unobjectionable.
6. 'Proceedeth from the Father *and the Son*'. The phrase 'and the Son' was not part of the original wording of the creed and is not accepted by

the Eastern Orthodox Churches. For reasons that should be evident from this chapter, I would prefer to speak of the Spirit 'proceeding from the Father, *through the Son*'.

7. For an excellent short survey of the debates leading to the formulation of the Nicene creed, see Christopher B.Kaiser, *The Doctrine of God*, Marshall Morgan & Scott, 1982, p47-71.

8. D.Broughton Knox, *The Everlasting God*, Evangelical Press, 1982, p52.

9. John Calvin, *Genesis*, Calvin Translation Society ed (1847), reprinted Banner of Truth, 1965, p91-92.

10. This understanding of Gen.1:27 has not been widely held by reformed theologians. Paul King Jewett calls it ' "novel" as theological opinions go...' Yet it appears to be the natural reading of the passage and to concur with 1 Cor.11:3. cf. P.K.Jewett, *Man as Male and Female: A Study in Sexual Relationships from a Theological Point of View*, Eerdmans, 1975, p23-48.

11. Charles Hodge contends that "the word Christ is the designation, not of the Logos or second person of the Trinity... but of the God-man. It is the incarnate Son of God, who in the great work of redemption, is said to be subordinate to the Father..." (C.Hodge, *A Commentary on 1&2 Corinthians*, Banner of Truth ed, 1974, p 207). But, as we have argued, whatever role Christ takes in his historical appearing, must reflect his eternal relation to the Father.

12. cf Wayne Grudem, 'The Meaning of Kephalē ("Head"): A Response to Recent Studies', in W.Grudem & J.Piper (eds), *Recovering Biblical Manhood & Womanhood: A Response to Evangelical Feminism*, Crossway, 1991. A. J. Köstenberger warns of the tendency to exaggerate the value of lexical studies while under-playing the importance of context. He insists that while word-studies may set parameters for possible meaning, ultimately we must decide the meaning of a word such as *Kephale* (head) by its usage in a particular context. Judged on this basis, it is hard to deny that both in 1 Cor 11 and in Ephesians (1:21-23; 5:21-33), the term must naturally be understood as implying authority and leadership. cf. Köstenberger, 'Gender Passages in the NT: Hermeneutical Fallacies Critiqued', *WTJ* 56 (1994), p265.

13. cf D.B.Knox, *op.cit.*, p70-71. Robert Letham writes: '...the headship of the man, while it receives expression in marriage and the church, is not to be confined to these areas but is instead applicable to the entirety of human contexts'. cf. Letham, 'The Man-Woman Debate: Theological Comment', *WTJ* 52 (1990), p74.

14. Letham, *op.cit.*, p66.

15. Gretchen Gaebelein Hull, *Equal to Serve: Women and Men in the Church and Home,* Scripture Union, 1989, p 193-194.

16. ibid., p283.

17. Grudem & Piper, *op.cit.*, p540. cf. also comments by Thomas R Schreiner, *ibid.*, p128-29, p486. Grudem and Schreiner cite a number of other evangelical feminists who fall into the same error. Grudem speaks of the 'attempt to shift the understanding of the doctrine of the Trinity as it has been held through the history of the church'.

18. Letham, *op.cit.*, p78.

19. Leon Morris, *The Epistle to the Romans,* Eerdmans/IVP, 1988, p229.

20. Elaine Storkey, *What's Right With Feminism,* SPCK, 1985, p153.

21. Douglas Moo: *The Wycliffe Exegetical Commentary: Romans 1-8,* Moody Press, 1991, p331.

22. John Murray, *The Epistle to the Romans (NICNT),* Eerdmans, one vol ed 1968, p178.

23. Charles Hodge, *A Commentary on Romans,* Banner of Truth ed, 1972, p163.

24. James D.G.Dunn, *Word Biblical Commentary 38A: Romans 1-8,* Word, 1988, p285.

25. Evangelical Christians have rejected vigorously the Romanist claim that the 'one man' who obeyed shares his place as Saviour with a *co-redemptrix* – a female co-redeemer. Evangelical feminists, in order consistently to maintain their position are forced to view Eve as *co-peccatrix* – a female co-transgressor – sharing Adam's place as the cause of our ruin.

26. Jewett, *op.cit.*, p117.

27. cited by F.F. Bruce, *Romans: An Introduction and Commentary (TNTC),* IVP, 1963, p127.

28. There is some variation between the genealogies in Matthew and Luke. But both writers give us the genealogy of Joseph, rather than of Mary, and each traces the genealogy through a line of men. For discussion of possible solutions of the seeming discrepancies between the two gospels, see the commentaries in loc., and J.Gresham Machen, *The Virgin Birth of Christ*, James Clarke, 1958 (first pub 1930), p202-209.

29. Hull, *op. cit.*, p83.

30. ibid., p87.

31. ibid., p104.

32. ibid., p99.

33. ibid., p87.

Husband and wife–and the church

John Benton

John's doctorate is in the discipline of theoretical chemistry which he gained from the University of Sussex, England. After five years teaching mathematics, John studied theology and became pastor of Chertsey Street Baptist Church, Guildford, Surrey in 1980. John has written a number of evangelistic books and Bible commentaries designed for the ordinary church member. Together with his pastoral responsibilities John is Managing Editor of Evangelicals Now. He is married to Ann and they have four children.

Husband and wife–and the church

At about eight o'clock each weekday morning in our home, we all sit down around the table together for breakfast. We sometimes join hands. We pray together, saying grace, giving thanks for God's provision of our daily food. This scene of tranquil prayerfulness then dissipates pretty rapidly as the cereals and toast are quickly demolished, the doorbell rings, coats are flung on and brief cases grabbed as it is time to rush off to school or to work. We are the classic nuclear family, sitting targets for the sneering comments of secular sociologists and liberal clerics. But there we are, for what we are worth, for that brief moment together: the Benton household, father, mother and children with heads bowed before God.

Paul calls the church 'God's household'. In 1 Timothy 3:15, he is referring particularly to the local congregation at Ephesus, where Timothy is working for the Lord. It is a description which can be applied to all local churches, and finds echoes throughout the New Testament as the apostles refer to 'brothers' and 'sisters', 'mothers', 'fathers' and 'sons' in the faith (1 Peter 1:22, Romans 16:1, 22, Titus 1:4, 1 Corinthians 4:15). In New Testament terms the church is the congregation, and that congregation is thought of as God's family. While the idea of a family is not the only description used in the New Testament for the local church, the church and the family do go together and relate closely to each other.

In this chapter I will maintain that the biblical teaching concerning the family and marriage is of crucial significance when it comes to considering male and female roles within the church. First, we shall see that the clear pattern of the headship of the husband and the submission of the wife as envisaged by Scripture provides a clear example of authority which is servant-like, and submission which does not involve oppression but rather blessing. This provides a model for the role of men and women within the church. Secondly, we shall see that so close is the relationship in God's eyes between family and church, that the apostles specifically underline and guard the likeness between the two in their instructions. Not to do so is to violate the intention of Scripture.

Leadership in the family

The 'headship' of the husband in a marriage is taught both explicitly (Ephesians 5:23; 1Corinthians 11:3) and implicitly (Colossians 3:19; 1 Peter 3:7; Matthew 1:25; 2:13,14; 2:19, 20 etc.) throughout the New Testament. Alongside this the wife is instructed to submit to her husband in their relationship (Ephesians 5:22, 24; Colossians 3:18; Titus 2:5; 1 Peter 3:1). Though this submission is clearly limited by the fact that it must be 'as is fitting in the Lord' (Colossians 3:18), nevertheless it does involve a voluntary subjection. What is this headship and submission business? Does it really mean that somehow the husband is actually superior to his wife? Do men have a scriptural warrant to behave autocratically and oppressively within the home?

Jim Callaghan, the former Labour prime minister, once said, 'A lie can be half-way around the world before the truth has got its boots on', and he was right. It certainly seems true in this matter of the biblical teaching on the relationship between husband and wife. So before we come to the positive exposition of the husband/wife relationship, we need first to clear the ground and deal briefly with five misunderstandings which are sometimes promoted concerning male headship in the family. We will look at some of the things which are said:

First. 'The Bible does not teach male headship at creation.'

That is not true: it does. In Genesis 1 and 2, it teaches it in a number of ways. Here are two examples. In Genesis 1:27 we read 'God created man in his own image, in the image of God he created him, male and female he created them.' The generic name for the human race used here is 'man'. That is not just a tradition, it is the way God chose to express it in his Word. That itself indicates male headship. In Genesis 2:23, Adam having named the animals, also names the woman. He names her with a most exalted name, indicating that she is utterly equal with him, but nevertheless he names her. Alister McGrath has correctly written, 'For biblical writers, to name someone is to have authority over them (as when Adam was allowed to name the living creatures)'. [1] Male headship goes back to creation.

Secondly. 'Male headship is the result of the Fall.'
That is not true: it had already begun! But here are more reasons. It was because Adam was already the head of their relationship before God, that he is held responsible for the Fall in a way in which Eve is not. Though Eve ate the fruit first, yet we read 'as in Adam all die', and 'sin entered the world through one man and death through sin' (1 Corinthians 15:22; Romans 5:12). Adam is responsible in a way that Eve is not. He is the head.

Thirdly. 'You cannot have headship and equality at the same time.'
According to Scripture that is not true. 1 Corinthians 11:3 says, 'Now I want you to realise that the head of every man is Christ and the head of every woman is the man and the head of Christ is God.' If you say that you cannot have headship and equality at the same time then you have to conclude from that verse that Christ is less than God, and if you do that you depart from orthodox Christian teaching on the Trinity. Though Christ is eternally begotten of the Father, and though he submitted himself in obedience to the Father in the plan of redemption, yet Christ is no less than the Father in deity, any more than one of my children, though begotten by me, and obedient to me, is of any less value than I am. Headship does not necessarily imply inequality.

Or think again about another text, Galatians 3:28. In Galatians Paul is defending the gospel of justification by faith alone in Christ alone, which makes sinners acceptable to the holy God. He says in this context, 'There is neither Jew nor Greek, slave nor free, male nor female, for we are all one in Christ Jesus.' Paul plainly believed that in Christ male and female are equal. We are all one and equally heirs of God's promises. Yet Paul is the same person who wrote, 'the husband is the head of the wife', Ephesians 5:22. Is Paul being inconsistent? Does he not know what he talking about? Of course he does. In Paul's mind headship and equality of privilege are not at all inconsistent with each other.

Fourthly. 'The word "head" means source and has no connotation of authority.'
That is a gross half-truth and is dealt with extensively in chapter six. In ancient literature on some occasions it seems the word 'head' can mean source, just as we may speak for example of the 'head of a river'. But the overwhelming New Testament use of the word has distinct implications of authority and responsibility (Matthew 10:25; 1 Corinthians 11:3; 11:10; Ephesians 1:10, 4:15; Colossians 2:10). Think for example of the use of the same word 'head' referring to Christ in the same letter of Ephesians where Paul describes the husband as the head of the wife. Ephesians 1:22: 'And God placed all things under his [Christ's] feet and appointed him to be head over everything to the church.' Of course Christ has authority over his church as its head, though we must remember that his headship is not oppressive - he is the servant King.

Fifthly. 'Male headship in Scripture simply reflects the culture of New Testament times and can now therefore be set on one side since we live in a different culture.'
It is possible that the way male headship is expressed may vary a little, legitimately so, in different cultures. But the notion that headship itself is purely cultural is not true. Male headship is rooted back to Adam and Eve as we have seen. It is pre-cultural, not cultural.

Indeed the idea of the husband's headship must be above culture, for it is a reflection of an eternal reality. Dr. Edmund Clowney has written, 'When Jesus came to gather to Himself the people of God, He revealed Himself as the Bridegroom come to claim His church as His Bride. The figure is not accidental. It is not that God looks down from heaven to discern some human relationship that might prove a fitting symbol of His love. The reality is the other way round'.[2] In other words Christ's relationship to the church is not patterned on human marriage, but human marriage is patterned on the relationship between Christ and the church, which transcends all human cultures. And Christ is in the most fundamental way the head of the church.

Having dealt with these five misunderstandings, we are now in a position to look positively at what the Scriptures teach about male headship and female submission in marriage. We will concentrate our attention on Ephesians 5:21-33 and see that it involves no diminution of the status of women, but rather gives them the highest value. The corollary to be drawn is that a Christlike male leadership in the church can only be interpreted as an attack upon the status of women if we move outside biblical categories of thinking about gender issues.

It would be best if the reader had the text of Ephesians 5 to refer to as we look at these verses. It is a passage which highlights the meaning of 'submission' (vv.21, 22, 24) and what it is to be a Christlike 'head' (v.23). We will focus on six points concerning the husband's headship in marriage, not because headship is the be-all and end-all of the subject of husband/wife relationships but imply because it takes us to the heart of the passage.

Headship for the husband
First. The context of headship - verse 21

Flowing out of the Spirit-filled life (v.18) there should not only be thankful praise to God (v.19, 20), but also mutual submission to one another as Christians (v.21). Putting others before ourselves is something to which all Christians are called and it is in this context that Paul introduces both the husband's and the wife's role within marriage. With that as the context we can immediately see that the headship which Paul envisages has nothing to do with male oppression and unfeeling dominance of women. Indeed that is the complete opposite of what Paul has in mind. Rather it is almost as if Paul expects a newly-wed husband to say 'out of submission and love to my wife, I will take on this exacting job of headship.'

'Submission to one another' assumes the fundamental equality of male and female (Genesis 1:27) though their roles may be different. Also this attitude of mutual submission is inculcated 'out of reverence for Christ'. We are motivated by respect and worship, for the Lord also saved us. The way of submission and servanthood is his way (Philippians 2:3-11).

Secondly. The metaphor of headship - verses 22-24
The only picture of true headship is that of Christ, and husbands are to model themselves on that (v.23,24). The husband is to be the head 'as Christ is the head of the church'. Apart from the initiative and leadership implicit here, Paul fills it out by telling us that the church is Christ's body (v.23) and therefore Christ acts with nothing but care and concern towards her (v.28, 29). He also tells us that Christ's headship over the church means that he is the Saviour of the church (v.23). His headship therefore involved him giving himself up for the church (v.25). Christ himself is the picture of headship which provides Paul's metaphor, no other.

Since Christ is our pattern the leadership of the husband should be respected (v.33). Christ does have authority over the church and, under God, a husband does have a certain authority over his wife. But we need to underline that the pattern of the exercise of that authority is the way of Jesus and no other (Mark 10:42-45). Male leadership in the church is modelled precisely on that. So biblically, headship is a caring, sacrificial leadership.

Thirdly. The practice of headship - verses 25-27
We have already begun to touch on this, and of course much more could be said. But to get to the heart of the matter we ask one simple question of these verses. Headship does involve a certain authority and leadership, but for whose benefit did Christ make every decision and every action he took? The answer from Ephesians 5 is 'for the good of the church'. At a later time his decisions will in a wonderful way bring pleasure to himself as he contemplates and presents to himself his

spotless bride (v.27). But all Christ did for the Father's glory was primarily for the good of the church. He 'loved the church and gave himself up for her... cleansing her.' (v.26) As Christ loves the church, so husbands must love their wives. So if Christ's actions and decision-making were all focused on the good of the church, we must ask for whose good is the husband's headship to be exercised? The clear answer of the passage must be not for his own good, but for the good of his wife.

Here then is a headship which is servant-like, not self-serving. Here is a male headship which is sensitive, listening and tender towards the woman. The biblical teaching on marriage gives a wife far more 'rights' than any women's liberation cause. It gives her the 'right' to be loved sacrificially.

Fourthly. The vision of headship - verse 27
The intention of Christ's headship over the church is that he presents her to himself as a 'radiant church, without stain or wrinkle or any other blemish, but holy and blameless' (v.27). So the love of Christ is a visionary love. It sees the church in all its sin and decay, but it sees beyond that and it acts to bring the church to the fullness of her potential under God. In the same way the husband's headship should be guided by the vision of bringing his wife to her full bloom under God. His headship, like that of Christ, should be such as to provide the protecting care, affection, resources, and encouragement which will enable his wife to develop her feminine gifts, graces and personality to the full. Some modern women reject such an attitude as patronising. It is not however intended in that way. Just as the husband's loving headship should cause a wife to flourish, she too has the power through her loving respect for him, to cause him to flourish as a man. This is implicit in Paul's words 'husbands ought to love their wives as their own bodies. He who loves his wife loves himself' (vv.28, 33).

Here then is a mutual edification between husband and wife which is not in the least patronising. They need each other. The original Sylvester Stallone film 'Rocky' provides an illustration of this. At the beginning of the film Rocky is a down-at-heel slob of a failed boxer, who takes an interest in a drab, shy, bespectacled girl called Adrienne who works at the local pet shop. Through Rocky's big break to fight the world heavy-weight champion, this relationship persists and develops and by the end of the film the drab, shy girl has become quite an attractive woman, and Rocky is a little smarter and has grown as a person. As a man loves his wife with a self-sacrificial leadership, she grows. As a woman loves her husband and gives her respect to him, he grows too!

Fifthly. The response to headship - verses 22 and 33

How is the wife to respond? The wife is to respect her husband as we have said (v.33) and in doing so, to submit to the man's love (v.22), 'Wives, submit to your husband as to the Lord'. Wives are not to submit foolishly, or to surrender all responsibility, for a wife is answerable first of all to the Lord, not to her husband. But she is to submit to his love and his attempts to do good to her and the family, and for the Lord's sake to back him up and support him, and to help him when he does make mistakes.

Sixthly. The presupposition of headship

The assumption behind the biblical teaching concerning male and female roles in a marriage, implicit in the passage, is that there is an essential difference between maleness and femaleness. Though male and female are equally made in the image of God, there is equality in diversity. This assumption is not fully explored, but it finds its origin in Genesis 2, and is highlighted for example in 1 Peter 3:7: 'Husbands, in the same way be considerate as you live with your wives and treat them with respect as the weaker partner and as heirs with you of the gracious gift of life.' To deny this essential difference between male and female is to fly in the face of Scripture and of common sense. The husband is called to be gracious, Christlike, protector and provider for 'the weaker partner'. Men and women are different.

So far we have reviewed something of the biblical teaching concerning male headship within a Christian marriage. Such leadership is seen not in terms of superiority, but in terms of servanthood which elicits the respectful love of the wife. The purpose in this headship is very much to enable the wife to flourish as a woman in the fullest sense. The idea that men and women must have precisely the same roles and opportunities in order to be equal is puerile and flies in the face of God's wonderful design of unity in diversity which pervades both creation and Scripture. It is founded on a narrow individualistic approach to life which is alien to the biblical world view.

Matching the church and the family

The relationship between husband and wife as envisaged by the New Testament gives a pattern of male leadership which completely safe-guards the dignity and equality of women. The next step is to see that this pattern within the family must not be contradicted by the roles which men and women take in the church. The structure of the church and the structure of the family must match each other. This is a persistent theme throughout the New Testament.

First, when Paul sets out the qualifications for eldership in the local church in 1 Timothy 3 and Titus 1, the terms he uses indicate that he is speaking about male candidates (1 Timothy 3:2), and he also makes it clear that successful exercise of headship in a family is the normal training ground and prerequisite for being a leader in the church. 'If anyone does not know how to manage his own family, how can he take care of God's church?' (1 Timothy 3:5). Though this does not neces-sarily preclude single people from leadership in a congregation, it certainly precludes married women, if as we have seen the Scriptures teach male headship in the family. The candidate for church leadership must 'manage his own family well and see that his children obey him with proper respect' (1 Timothy 3:4). Paul's underlying thought here (as we noted at the beginning of this chapter) is expressed in verse 15; it is that the church is God's household. While the apostles do use other similes to describe leadership in the church (shepherds of the flock etc.) these are never used to give requirements for normal necessary practical experience prior to taking on church leadership. The only practical management experience which the New Testament points to is domestic leadership.

Secondly, although the modern application of Paul's instructions about head-coverings in 1Corinthians 11:3-16 may be a matter of legitimate dispute, the overall thrust of the passage is unmistakeable. Paul's concern is clearly that the headship role of the male be not only maintained, but be clearly seen to be maintained in the practicalities of local church life. His remarks in verses 11 and 12 of that chapter refer back to the creation of male and female, and therefore indicate that what he has to say applies to all men and women, whether married or not. Similarly in 1 Corinthians 14:33-35, although there may be dispute over the particulars of Paul's commands that women should be silent in the church, and if they wish to enquire about something they should ask their own husbands at home, nevertheless Paul's main interest is clear. His concern is that church activity should never be seen to undermine, threaten or contradict the roles of husband and wife in the family.

Such considerations must inevitably lead us to conclude that if we believe Scripture teaches male headship in the family, then male leadership in the church inevitably follows. And male leadership in the church is, as we have seen for example from 1 Timothy 3, what we find in the New Testament.

Thirdly, as Paul indicates how people from different families and of different genders and ages are to behave towards one another in the local church, it is the pattern of family relationship to which he turns for his explanations. When he tells Timothy how to lead the local congregation at Ephesus Paul says, 'Do not rebuke an older man harshly but exhort him as if he were your father. Treat younger men as brothers, older women as mothers, younger women as sisters, with absolute purity' (1 Timothy 5:1,2). Family terminology is used. In the church we are to relate to one another as if we are a family together. Indeed, that is what we are - members of God's family. What we have learned about roles within a family cannot simply be ignored in church. We cannot conclude that the structure of the family can be squashed in church. We cannot say that the family is irrelevant to ecclesiology. What the Bible says about the roles of male and female within a family has to be appropriately and sensitively transposed into the life of the church, and this will include the eldership of a church (those who 'rule' the congregation 1 Timothy 5:17) being male.

A practical application

How do the principles we have established work out in practice? First, given the fact that Scripture insists that the domestic structure must be reflected in the ecclesiastical structure, and although that precludes women from eldership, it does give us a proper vision for women's ministry within the church. In the family the wife is very much to be her husband's helper. Men's abilities are often either greatly enhanced by the help and wisdom of their wives, or greatly hindered by the lack of it. In the same way, though leadership in the church is to be male, that leadership needs help. In the New Testament, the diaconate is the general helping hand for the eldership, and with appropriateness and sensitivity women's ministry in the church can sit in just that creative, responsible and helpful position. Different church traditions may wish to work this out in different ways, but a male eldership which is faithfully supported and encouraged and served by mature women, is always an eldership which is greatly enhanced.

Secondly, we must take seriously what the outcome will be if the church generally ignores the biblical pattern of male leadership in God's household. As we have seen, the New Testament is concerned that the local congregation should match the family both in structure and ethos. There are many agencies in our culture which either consciously or unwittingly are undermining the family at the present time. While the nuclear family is not to be idolised, it is the basic building block of society which God has designed. For the church to pursue female leadership will bring a contradiction between the church and the family which the New Testament warns us against, surely for good reason. To abandon male leadership in the church will indirectly be another blow to the family and hence to society generally. Richard Baxter, the great Puritan, was right in his memorable words from 1656, 'Family is the seminary of the Church and State and if children be not well principled there, all miscarries'.

Notes

1. McGrath, Alister NIV Bible Commentary, Hodder & Stoughton, p.234
2. Clowney, Edmund The Unfolding Mystery, IVP, p.26

Presuppositions, Freedom and Self-Worth

John Benton
John's doctorate is in the discipline of theoretical chemistry which he gained from the University of Sussex, England. After five years teaching mathematics, John studied theology and became pastor of Chertsey Street Baptist Church, Guildford, Surrey in 1980. John has written a number of evangelistic books and Bible commentaries designed for the ordinary church member. Together with his pastoral responsibilities John is Managing Editor of Evangelicals Now. He is married to Ann and they have four children.

Presuppositions, Freedom and Self-Worth

Problem-solving is fraught with problems of its own! When tackling any problem we bring with us various assumptions or presuppositions. Our presuppositions are of immense importance: very often they make all the difference between solving a problem and not being able to do so. Take this little conundrum as an example:

			How can you cover all 9 dots with just
.	.	.	How can you cover all 9 dots with just
.	.	.	4 straight lines without taking your pen
.	.	.	off the paper or retracing any lines?

If you inadvertently assume that you cannot take your pen-lines outside the square of the dots, the problem is insoluble. But if you presuppose that you can move outside the square then the answer is not too difficult.[1] The assumptions make all the difference.

As people talk together around the matter of male and female roles in the church, they often have different sets of presuppositions. This is not only true when Christian debates with non-Christian, it is often also true as Christian debates with Christian on the subject. Ideally Christians should agree on most presuppositions, but often they are things we are not aware of or have not really thought through, and so even Christians come at problems from different angles.

This is not always bad because our discussion forces us all to go back and check up where we are coming from. On the other hand it can be disastrous. Different presuppositions can be so pervasive that we can end up using the same words but meaning totally different things by them and so talking completely at cross purposes. A few such words which spring immediately to mind in the debate over gender and leadership are words like 'justice', 'freedom', 'dignity' and 'value'. Is it 'just' for women to be debarred from leadership in a local church? Does a male necessarily have more 'freedom' because the option of leadership is open to him? If a church insists on male leadership what does that mean concerning their view of the 'dignity' or 'value' of women? Such terms are crucial to the debate. But what do we mean by them?

What then are the Christian's presuppositions which dictate meaning? The writers of this book come from the background of the historic Christian faith, which believes in the inerrancy of Scripture as God's revelation to us, and that the Bible is our final authority to shape all our thinking and assumptions. We believe that this basic position should be the position of every Christian, and we have been trying to come to the subject of gender and leadership with this as our basic assumption. The Christian lives in a world which by and large rejects that great assumption. Our world at the end of the twentieth century functions from a secular outlook with very different presuppositions about life, and therefore very different ideas about what is 'valuable' and what it is to be 'free' for example. The goals of secular society are very different from biblical concepts of what the goal of human life should be. Ideas of personal fulfilment and justice will inevitably be conditioned by these assumptions.

Unearthing Our Presuppositions
The aim of this chapter therefore is to outline briefly the different basic assumptions of the biblical and secular worldviews (we realise there are other world views which we do not have space or time to cover), and to investigate how those assumptions colour our understanding of the two concepts of freedom and self-worth which are crucial to the gender debate.

The Secular Approach to Human Life

Secularism is the approach to life which leaves God out as either non-existent or irrelevant. Reinhold Niebuhr, the influential professor of Applied Christianity at Union Theological Seminary in New York, who died in 1971, spoke of secularism as 'a way of living which denies the Holy, the Ultimate, the Sacred; in more explicit terms it denies God.' Secularism is now the majority culture in the Western World. It dominates our media, our politics and our public debates. It is the general public's framework of thought.

Of course this has not always been so, but in the second half of the nineteenth century secularism came into its own. The leader of the flourishing secularist movement in England then was George J. Holyoake, and the *Oxford English Dictionary* summarises Holyoake's idea of secularism as 'the doctrine that morality should be based solely on regard to the well-being of mankind in the present life, to the exclusion of all considerations drawn from belief in God, or in a future state.' Human beings are not the creation of God, they are the result of blind evolutionary processes and our only saviour to guide us for this life is our reason. It was believed that, on the basis of reason alone, it would be possible to ascertain a public morality for the well-being of all. However since Holyoake's day, more and more, secularism has shifted away from the idea of public morality into a philosophical individualism. This drift is actually inevitable given what secularism stands for.

First, secularism divides the world we experience into two categories, the public and the private. Secularists would for example, rarely want to deny people the option of having a religious faith. But what they would say is that this must be kept as a private matter and kept out of public life.

So, secularism brings about what we might call the Great Divide between the public and the private, the objective and the subjective aspects of life (diagram see next page). In the public, objective category are things of which people would agree we can be certain, like the results of mathematics or with parts of science (this is simplistic). In the private, subjective area of the divided world are things such as personal

THE GREAT DIVIDE

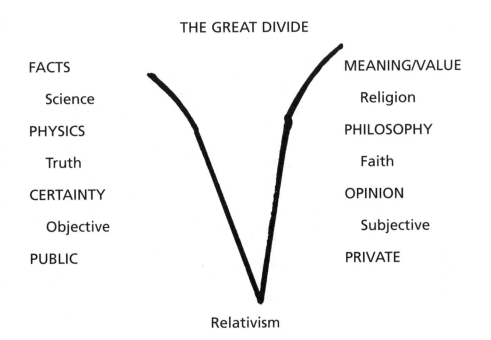

FACTS	MEANING/VALUE
Science	Religion
PHYSICS	PHILOSOPHY
Truth	Faith
CERTAINTY	OPINION
Objective	Subjective
PUBLIC	PRIVATE

Relativism

opinions, values and feelings. So secularism splits the world, since there is no God who transcends both public and private and unites the whole.

But, secondly, this view of life leads to the inevitable failure of the idea of a public morality which Holyoake and his ilk so treasured. Once we accept the secular framework we are left with the task of seeking to construct a public morality from the brute facts of the world round us to the good of everyone. It cannot be done, it is the philosopher's nightmare of trying to produce an 'ought' from an 'is', and it just does not work. To take a simple example we could cite the debate over smoking. On one hand it seems quite clear form the medical evidence that smoking tobacco drastically raises the chances of people dying from lung cancer and other illnesses. However, since many people enjoy their smoke and many others make their living by the sale of tobacco products, any suggestion of a legislated ban on cigarettes is met with howls of protest as an infringement of individual liberty. The idea of human 'well-being' is not something which is readily transferable from the private to the public domain.

If you move away from the use of pure reason and seek to set up a public morality based on what the majority of people see as best for them, then it turns out that 51% of the population can dictate to the other 49%. That hardly seems fair.

It is problems such as this which cause Holyoake's ideals of a secular public morality for the good of all to founder; after all, God has been left out of the reckoning. Once we accept this framework of thinking then we are inevitably led to the conclusion that there are no absolute guidelines for life. What is meaningful or valuable and therefore 'right' for one person or group of people may not be so for others. Our assessments are purely private and personal, and so are called 'value judgements'. Since there is no possibility of God telling us the difference between right and wrong we must decide these things for ourselves. So secularism leads to various degrees of moral relativism. The idea of public morality becomes emaciated to a shadow of the former ideals which Holyoake hoped for. Rationally consistent secularism leads to total moral relativism. Only the individual can decide what is right for him/her. Whereas secularism ideally sets a limit on the individual's freedom by saying that what is acceptable is only that which does not hurt other people, in reality the view of individual freedom sails as close as possible to an outlook of 'no limits', 'do as you like'. Often the 'other people' aspect is looked upon as a burden. Indeed in the famous words of Jean Paul Sartre, the attitude which underlies a veneer of concern for the public good is that 'hell is other people', for they place limits and make demands on the individual. So although secularism holds the public good as an ideal, secularism in reality fails this ideal.

Thirdly we are led to secularism's practical deification of the human self. Later we will be comparing the secular view with the Christian worldview, so it is helpful to put it in these terms. In the secular system the individual is put, as closely as possible, in the position which Christians reserve for God. The entity of highest value in Holyoake's system is not God, but mankind, and mankind is made up of individuals. The self in the secular system ideally sits in God's position as the law-giver; for the individual, arbiter of right and wrong and what is good, is the master of the individual's destiny.

Since there are other people in the world, the individual cannot completely set his/her own agenda. So the proviso has to be that individual choices can be pursued so long as more choices do not hurt other people. Here as we have already seen there is a turn around from Holyoake's initial intention. He looked for a secularism to promote the positive well-being of mankind, but the facts of the case force secularism into a stance simply of not causing another's hurt, as the bottom line. However it is actually not possible for secularism even to hold the line there.

It is at this very point that the idea of political correctness becomes very relevant. As we have said, the secular outlook essentially deifies the human self. The individual is defined in terms of the basic make-up of their gender, sexual orientation and ethnic background. Political correctness is a movement which seeks to take seriously the idea of not offending or causing hurt to others. It therefore seeks to control the use of language so as to make sure that all statements are neutral, and make no 'value judgements' in those three areas of what is seen as an individual's basic make-up. In this sense political correctness is almost the secular equivalent of the Christian law against blasphemy. To make politically incorrect statements is hurtful to the human deity.

The attempt of political correctness to take seriously the desire to cause offence to no one actually turns into an oppressive denial of human freedom as far as many people are concerned. Sarah Dunnant writes concerning the political correctness debate, 'According to both its right and left critics it represents a form of Orwellian thought police on the campus exercising power and surveillance both explicitly and implicitly. Some commentators see political correctness as a conspiracy of 1960s radicals who are not only subverting the teaching of the canon of Western culture, but are denying free speech by institutionalising speech codes and codes of behaviour in order to eliminate racism, sexism, homophobia etc.'[2] Even Shakespeare must be discarded as too heterosexual in his 'Romeo and Juliet'.

Here then we have something of the secular outlook. It denies God.

Its highest goal necessarily becomes the self-styled fulfilment of the individual in this world, with the boundary condition of not hurting other people. Its outlook is exploratory of life, there is no fixed guide book, only the compass of personal reason. It is this outlook which colours the secularist's view of matters which pervade the gender debate, such as freedom, justice and self-worth.

The Biblical View of Humanity

By contrast, the biblical outlook on the world begins at the opposite extreme from secularism. Christians believe in God. The reality of the living God as revealed through the Lord Jesus Christ, the God of the Bible is the primary Christian assumption. This prime assumption provides the key to understanding the Christian view of human identity, as we consider the biblical drama of creation, fall and redemption.

First. Creation

The Christian believes in God as the Creator. That is so fundamental as to be non-negotiable. He is the Creator and we, both men and women, are his creation. Our fundamental identity therefore is that of creatures. We are very special creatures, as we, both men and women, have a dignity given to no other creature. We are made in God's own image (Genesis 1:26,27). We were originally made as personalities to reflect the character of God. Is God holy? Then that is reflected in that we have a conscience. Is God personal and spiritual? Then we are personal and spiritual too. As God's image we were made to signify God's sovereignty over the world, and under God together to rule, and care for the world on his behalf (Genesis 1:26, 28). As God's creatures we are also accountable to God. He is the one who defines us and commands us (Genesis 2:17). We are planned beings. Male and female is the design of God, not an evolutionary accident. This is markedly different from secular assumption.

Secondly. The Fall

But the human drama unfolds in the Bible and tells us that we are no longer as God created us. Equally, as men and women, we have (starting with Adam and Eve) rebelled against God. We are still in one sense God's image (James 3:9), but we are a fallen race. Our hearts have become hostile to God and his commands (Romans 8:7), and we are guilty before him and deserving of his wrath because of our sin. We have become subject to death and our human nature is desperately flawed.

Again this is very different from the secular view of human beings. The secularist usually wishes to speak of human beings as fundamentally good. There is indeed a lot of good in people for we are made in God's image. But according to Scripture it is not true that people are basically good. Rather we are intrinsically self-centred and sinful. Even our minds are corrupted. This unpleasant fact must be born in mind as we consider concepts which are fundamental to the gender debate.

Thirdly. Redemption

All of us as human beings stand in need of and are the objects of the love of God. We are all invited to accept God's redemption for us in the Lord Jesus Christ, who died for us at Calvary. Christ is risen, and ascended, and his Spirit is poured out on 'all flesh' (Acts 2:17). God's salvation knows no boundaries of gender, race, or social class for any repentant sinner, no matter how self-righteous or immoral. Eternal life is for all who believe. The prime feature of redemption is that it is the work of God's grace. It is all a free gift. It had to be that way, because the effects of the Fall are such that we cannot redeem ourselves. Again this leads to a very different approach to life from that of the secularist. The secularist believes in humanity's ability to solve its own problems. For the secularist 'redemption' (the well-being of society for example) is down to our efforts and achievements, and is therefore something to be proud of. For the Christian redemption is all of God's grace, and therefore the corresponding attitude is one of thankfulness.

In the scope of this thrice-fold drama of humanity, creation, fall and redemption, men and women are caught up equally together. Before we are either male or female we are human. According to the Bible, to be human is to be related to God in the ways already described.

What is Freedom?

Freedom is a crucial concept for human beings in many ways, and it is crucial to the gender debate in that the concept of freedom is determinative of our view of justice. The Declaration of Independence of the United States, for example states that among the 'inalienable rights' of every human being are 'life, liberty and the pursuit of happiness'. To deny people their liberty is to deny them their rights, which is to deny justice. The Christian, with a background in the Old Testament prophets, should have no difficulty in endorsing such an approach to human rights, freedom and justice. However, we need to ask the fundamental question, 'What is freedom for human beings?' When we ask that question, because of our differing presuppositions we find two very different answers from the secularist and the Bible-believing Christian.

The secularist has put the individual human being as closely as possible in the place of God. The human being is autonomous. People are to decide for themselves what is best for them. The political philosopher of the nineteenth century, John Stuart Mill, sums up the secular position admirably: 'The only freedom which deserves the name is that of pursuing our own good in our own way, so long as we do not attempt to deprive others of theirs or impede their efforts to obtain it.' But although such an approach to freedom is applauded by our secularist society it is in fact deeply flawed, both in its own terms and certainly in biblical terms:

First. There is a saying from ancient Greece, 'The free man is one who lives as he chooses'. But what is the instrument to guide a person in his/her choosing? Is it to be their reason or feelings? Even the secularist realises that the inner passions of human beings can be more enslaving than any outward coercion. Does the individual really know what is best for them? If so, what do we have education for? So the rock group Pink Floyd sang:

> 'We don't need no education
> We don't need no thought control,
> No dark sarcasm in the classroom
> ...Teacher leave the kids alone...'

Secondly. This brings us to the second flaw in the secularist's view of freedom. If this view is accepted then we should never seek to restrain the suicide attempt or rescue the drug addict from their slavery. In their own thinking (which is all that ultimately matters in this system) they are either doing no harm to others or the least harm to others.

Thirdly. In biblical terms of course, we see the human mind, emotions and will in bondage to sin as part of our fallen nature. To trust purely to individual choice is to trust to a corrupt heart in rebellion against God. It is to trust to a blind heart which cannot see its own best interest (2 Corinthians 4:4). How can we make such a virtue of 'unconstrained' personal choice? If this is the case, to adopt a view of freedom which acts along the lines even of seeking to remove an individual's felt frustrations is no sure guide to the right way to proceed. Some of our frustrations as sinners can be the product of our fallen natures.

So when we come to look at the Bible we find a very different view of freedom, in some ways almost an opposite view. For the Christian the idea that freedom is ultimately to do with self-determination is an impossible view. True freedom is not independence from God. We are essentially God's creatures. That is our place, and to resist the idea of him setting our basic agenda is to behave against what we are ultimately made for and is hence self-destructive.

All through Scripture, freedom is seen in this light. It is never the 'no limits' or 'set your own boundaries' view of secular culture. Think of the Exodus. God's people are in bondage in Egypt and through Moses God brings them out. But having rescued them he does not cast them adrift to do as they choose. "I have borne you on eagles wings and brought you to myself that you might serve me and that I might bless you" says God (Exodus 19:4, 5 paraphrase). Only in God's service is there real freedom.

Think about what the Lord Jesus Christ said: 'You will know the truth and the truth will set you free' (John 8:32). Modern secular individuals often say in effect, 'I don't want the truth, I want to make my own truth, I will decide what is right and what is wrong for me.' That is especially the case in issues surrounding gender and male and female roles. However, Jesus speaks not of making our own truth, but of our learning his truth. It is Christ who is the way, the truth and the life (John 14:6). The apostle Paul and other New Testament writers underline the fact that the Christian view of freedom is intrinsically tied to willing service to God (Romans 6:18; Galatians 5:13 etc.). It is the freedom of obedient children, who, with transformed hearts and minds, love to obey their Father who loves them.

This does not mean that the Christian view of freedom has no place for individual choice or creativity. We are made in the image of God and therefore creativity is part of our true humanity as reflections of our Creator. We can view the commands of God as fences which are demarcation lines around a great area of individual freedom of action. God has set the boundaries. Within those boundaries we have a God-given 'safe area' in which to be free. Within those boundaries we have all the liberty to use the God-given resources of our gifts and capabilities to enjoy all that God has provided for us in serving Him and other people with thankfulness. This is the path to true fulfilment and happiness. For Christians, the individual's happiness and true well-being is always a derivative. We never find true liberty and joy by aiming at pleasing ourselves. We always find it as a derivative of serving God and others. We are to pursue those great goals with all the imaginative, and ingenious, individual skills at our command.

Here perhaps is the crux of the debate between the Christian and the secular view of freedom. It comes back to a matter of faith in God. The Christian is content to let God set the boundaries of individual liberty and to trust him to know what is best for us. We believe that the secularist's boundary conditions of 'not hurting others' are not guidelines peculiar only to them. Rather we believe that as we obey God's commands we automatically do what God knows is best for our neighbour and do no harm to our neighbour. Love is the fulfilment of God's law (Romans 13:10). The Christian not only trusts God to set the limits, but also sees God's service and the service of other people (made in God's image) as the correct avenue for self-expression.

By contrast the secularist does not trust God, but trusts only his/her own perceptions of what is right. The secularist wishes to set his/her own boundaries based on their own fallible ideas of what might be best for others. Also the goal of the exercising of individual liberty and self-expression, is self-pleasure and self-fulfilment as their primary aim. In the words of J.S. Mill already quoted, it is 'that of pursuing our own good in our own way.'

In coming to the question of roles of male and female therefore, if we have a proper concern for the true freedom of the individual from a biblical perspective we have to ask seriously the question, 'Has God set boundaries on the behaviour and attitudes of men and women?' The secular approach which often rubs off on Christians is simply to ask if something is possible, and if in our estimation it will cause any immediate hurt to other people if we proceed to do it. But that is not good enough. No sensible person doubts for example that in many areas of life women are just as capable as men, and individual women may surpass many individual men, perhaps even all men, in some areas. At a first glance, it may look as if a woman has just as much right to lead a congregation as a man. 'What harm does it do?' we ask, 'It may have many benefits'. Such an approach is flawed and it is certainly not the biblical approach. Because something is possible that does not make it right. Because there are some evident immediate benefits that does not prove its validity. Take an example from the world of ecology. Obviously we have the machines and the abilities to cut down the South American rain forests. Obviously there are immediate practical benefits for the furniture and building industries, and land can be cleared for agriculture. But what is it doing to the local culture and to the balance of global ecology? Its long term effects are disastrous. Just so, though women have every ability to lead a congregation and gifts which are able to be used in this way, is this really the right avenue of service and deployment for those gifts? What does women taking leadership in church do, for example, to the spiritual 'ecology' of marital rela-tionships and family life more widely? Is that just?

We must come back to the question of whether or not God has set boundaries on the freedom of men and women. The answer from Scripture, with which we agree in this book, is that he has. God debars men from taking the soft option of avoiding tough tasks and responsi-bilities. God restricts men from indulging in certain activities, which are allowed to women. God positively calls men, to take on the role of servant-leadership within the family for example. These guidelines are to be respected. They are God's good gift to us. When men throw off those restrictions they receive in themselves the due penalty, and hurt themselves (Romans 1:27). When men throw off God's guidelines for true manliness, then society generally suffers as men misuse that physical strength. In her book *What's Right with Feminism?* Elaine Storkey writes, 'Christian feminists are not wanting any power struggle with men. That would be entirely foreign to their agenda. Nor are they wanting to construct an all-female reality which washes its hands of any involvement with the other sex. But they are not happy simply to slip into a slot marked 'woman' and live their lives according to a set of prescribed cultural and essentially non-biblical values. The message they bring is a message of liberation, and it is for men also.'

We can agree with all that Elaine Storkey says there. However suppose, as I have been arguing, that part and parcel of true biblical freedom is a safe-area of boundaries set by God, in which we can be secure to express ourselves without infringing on others or doing despite to God's glory. Suppose there are 'slots' marked 'men' and 'women', which are not defined by our culture or by non-biblical considerations, but by God. If, as the writers of this book believe, that is the case then it is in no way a restriction of a woman's freedom to insist on male leadership in the church, neither is it unjust. Rather it is a stance which tends to true freedom and justice for both women and men as they are both prepared to submit to God in all their masculinity and femininity. We believe the biblical case for the differing roles of men and women is irrefutable and we have sought to demonstrate that plainly in the rest of the volume.

What About Self-Worth?

Having looked at the subject of freedom we now turn to the subject of self-worth and personal fulfilment. If Christianity is different from secularism in its approach to the question of who is to set the boundaries on our liberty, it is also different with respect to the goal of our self-expression. The secularist wishes to be free to pursue his/her own fulfilment as a person. Self-esteem, or self-worth, is to do with the way we see ourselves. It consists of our evaluation of our personal worthiness to be loved and accepted. It carries with it either pleasant or unpleasant feelings about ourselves. To have a strong sense of self-worth will therefore mean that we feel fulfilled as people. In many ways our self-worth is a measure to us of our personal fulfilment.

But this self-evaluation is closely linked not just to what we think of ourselves, but to what we think that other people think of us. The way we perceive others as thinking of us will be important in determining how we evaluate ourselves. We are always more influenced by other people than we realise. Now it is not necessarily about what they actually think of us. It is about what we think they think of us. So for example, if a son thinks his father thinks him useless (no matter how able he may actually be, or how secretly proud his father is of him), the son will probably have low self-esteem. On the other hand when parents are openly supportive and loving, even a youngster who has failed somewhere in his/her life, can see themselves in a more positive way.

In secular society people's self-worth is often tied up with various forms of personal achievement. This may be why the area of leadership is such a big deal for our generation. To become a leader is perceived by society to be someone who has achieved a high position. It is perceived as having proved yourself to be better than others. Especially if by our achievement we gain the approval of people whom we see as significant people, we feel good about ourselves.

So all the time we are interpreting and evaluating events in our lives. 'Have I performed adequately?' or 'What did they think of me?' we tend to ask ourselves. Sometimes that evaluation is honest. But sometimes self-esteem is a crooked game. For example, those who are good at demeaning others and putting them down with a sharp word, often do so in order to boost themselves by comparison.

What does positive self-esteem do for people? Feeling fulfilled and good about ourselves usually goes with a stable and resilient personality. We are able to handle relationships well and generally feel on top of life. But low self-esteem is often linked to anxiety or depression. So there is a real case for positive self-worth.

At this point we can see a woman's frustration in modern society. Our culture is materialistic and puts value on earning power, jobs which produce money, and careers in the market-place economy. The ethos of the market-place is one of competition and the creation of wealth. These are the indication of real achievement in our modern secular society. It is wealth which gives the individual the power to choose and to 'pursue his own good in his own way'. It is achievement in competition with others which allows a person to stand tall and fulfilled in society. With these attitudes dominating society, it is clear that the traditional role of wife, mother and homemaker, which women have been generally content to fulfil, is at a discount. By fostering the idea that the Bible teaches a male leadership in the church, Christians who take such a line, are seen as demeaning women and excluding them from being able to achieve their potential and so find fulfilment in this area. Pressed further, the stance is seen as undermining the self-worth of women and therefore inflicting psychological harm on women.

What then is the answer to such challenges? The answer is to see that through the gospel of the Lord Jesus Christ, the Christian is to have a totally different approach to the whole matter of self-worth. We are to see that true self-worth is not to do with personal achievement. We do not believe in a gospel of works, but in a gospel of grace. We certainly do not believe that the world's idea of wealth and the ability to choose from many options in life, are true indications of a human being's value.

Self-worth, we have said, is to do with status. It is to do with the status we perceive we have in the eyes of others who are important to us. For the secular person, the significant audiences to their lives, are their own circle of friends, or the public at large. But for the Christian, surely God himself is the most significant person in the universe. The heart of the gospel is about God bestowing a new status of eternal significance upon us, even though we may not only be low achievers in the world's estimation, but sinners in the estimation of a holy God. He bestows on us a new status, when we come to Christ. He justifies us (Romans 5:1). That is, he gives us a free gift, and not something we have achieved. God loves us. The answer to our need to feel valued, lies all in God and in Christ.

We can get this in perspective as we look at the cross. Calvary says two things to us. First, it tells us that morally we are all totally offensive and unacceptable to God. We are sinners who can do nothing to justify ourselves in his perfect eyes. It tells us that our sin is so serious that only the death of the Son of God as our penal substitute could expunge it and appease God concerning it. But secondly, the cross tells us that God values us just as we are. God the Father did not have to send Jesus. So why did he do it? 'For God so loved the world...' And that love is not a colourless, detached decision on God's part; it is not as if God flipped a coin saying 'Heads I save them, tails I won't bother; they don't mean anything to me.' It was because even in our sins and our lack of achievement, God values us, as made in his image and as potential heirs of heaven. The biblical picture is that God values lost sinners as a woman values a lost coin, a shepherd values a lost sheep, a father values a lost son (Luke 15).

Now all this totally changes the basis for the Christian's self-worth. It is no longer about my position in life, or my performance in the market-place. It is all about what God has done for me. It calls for a total re-orientation of outlook. It calls us away from the question 'What is it about me and my achievements that makes me worth loving...?' to the radically different question, 'What is it about God that drew him to give his Son and see me as acceptable to him?" It points away from a self-centred, performance-led view of life, to a God-centred, faith-oriented approach to life.[3]

As we consider the question of gender and our roles as men and women in the world, all this needs to be translated into our every day experience. First, we have eternal acceptance with God. If God has loved you and accepted you in Jesus Christ, who are you not to accept yourself? And who are other people that we should be so worried and perhaps controlled by their estimate of us? The gospel helps us to see the values of the society around us in a totally different light. Is it really wealth and competitive achievement which makes for fulfilment in life? Or is it about knowing the love of God, whatever our circumstances or abilities? Surely it is the latter.

Secondly, does this Christian approach to our own work mean that we should not have any ambitions? Does it mean that our achievements at work, or in a family, or in sport, mean nothing? No. But the gospel makes us see achievements in a completely different and more wonderful way. They take on a new meaning. They are no longer 'What I have done', but what God has done through me (Philippians 2:12,13). This both excites us and humbles us at the same time. It delivers us from foolish pride in our own abilities, and invites us to Christlike joy, purpose and humble lowliness.

Lastly, the gospel sets us free from ourselves to serve God and others. It turns us away from ourselves and what is open or not open to us, as the centre of our world, to God filling our horizon. We are not so concerned with what we do in life, as who we do it for. In the eyes of God one who serves at tables is just as great, if not greater, than any king or ruler, and though there are a wide variety of options open to women, the role of wife and mother is just as great as that of any church leader or preacher (Mark 10:42-45).

Eventually our Christian presuppositions not only redefine what we mean by freedom and true self-worth, they actually give us a totally different view of human greatness.

Notes
1. Starting at the top left corner move out to the right beyond the furthest dot, swing back diagonally to the bottom left, then up the left side of the square and down diagonally to the bottom right.
2. The War of Words: The Political Correctness Debate, edited by Sarah Dunnant, Virago p.2.
3. The Dilemma of Self-Esteem, by Joanna and Alister McGrath, Crossway Books.

'You're a man, aren't you?'

Jonathan Stephen

Jonathan is pastor of Carey Baptist Church in Reading, England, member of the FIEC Pastoral and Theological Committees and a former chairman of the Christian Citizenship Committee. He lectures for the Prepared for Service training course and holds degrees from the Universities of Wales and Birmingham in sociology and social and political anthropology. Jonathan is married to Sheila and they have one son.

`You're a man, aren't you?'

It was only a few years ago that 'women's issues' became 'gender studies'. This was due to a growing recognition amongst academics in the field that there was no earthly reason why research into men and masculinity should not prove to be the next growth industry. However, the best laid plans of mice and people do not always come to pass and the shelves of the serious bookshops remain as dominated as ever by contributions both by and about women.

Things were rather different at the level of pop psychology. The men's movement of the seventies led to numerous paperbacks and magazine articles largely sympathetic to a burgeoning feminism. Readers over thirty-five will recall 'New Man'. Driven by guilt, men started radically redefining their roles and sought desperately to get in touch with their emotions.

The eighties saw a reaction setting in. A new wave of publications declared that feminism had gone too far and made a bid to restore a lost masculinity. [1] Men were 'confused and resentful' and were no longer going to accept the blame for the lot of women. The new men's movement that arose was very different from the old one. In the United States, men signed up eagerly to attend seminars and spend their weekends running around bare-chested at tribal-oriented 'Wild Man' events. Here in Britain, we saw it all on *News at Ten,* but the weather was against those who thought it more than just a good idea. By the mid nineties, the whole project had run out of steam, anyway. It had nowhere to go. But as the secular men's movement waned, the

Christian men's movement, claiming a far sounder footing, in the pages of Scripture, was just beginning to take off.

The undoubted leader in the field is Promise Keepers, an organisation dedicated to transforming Christian men. And because it intends to attain the same high profile in the UK as it undoubtedly has in the US, it deserves more than a passing mention. Huge rallies filling vast football stadiums with exuberant Christian men set on re-establishing man's God-given role in home and church are the hallmark of the Promise Keepers. Challenging messages on leadership and accountability are delivered by well known evangelical conference speakers.

The Feminisation of the Church

One of their commonest themes is the necessity of reversing what they see as the ever-increasing feminisation of the church. This is not just a reaction to women in leadership positions. In most of the churches represented by the Promise Keepers, women are hardly likely to be pastors and elders or be found preaching in the pulpit in any case. No, their understanding of feminisation is of a far longer-standing and more deep-rooted phenomenon.

They would ask the question, why are women so often the driving force behind the vast majority of evangelical church activities, not least in getting the family to church in the first place? Even more fundamentally, why do more women than men attend church and why is the discrepancy growing? [2] Why is church seen by the unchurched as a female preserve? Why, when you knock on the door and say where you are from, does the man of the house tell you he will fetch the wife?

The fact is that women do shoulder much of the work in evangelical church life. Beneath the visible veneer of male leadership, it is often womanpower that enables the church to function. They are the ones who pray in the prayer meetings, keep in contact with the missionaries and ensure that the family offering finds its way into the church treasury week by week. Of course, this is probably merely a reflection of the fact that the spiritual welfare of the family is usually left in the hands of the wife and mother as well.

Promise Keepers traces the feminisation of the church and family back to the social disruption that occurred at the time of the Industrial Revolution. From that period on, men were removed from work that revolved around the home to factory and office jobs that separated them from their families. The spiritual consequences for church, family and society as a whole have been far reaching.

Historian Anthony Rotundo remarks that the increasing absence of husbands and fathers from the home 'entrusted women with the care and nurture of communal values - of personal morality, social bonds, and, ultimately, the level of virtue in the community.'[3] Women were forced to take a leading role in areas where previously men had assumed responsibility. The absent husband and father has meant that women became primary providers of moral and spiritual leadership firstly in the home and then, by natural extension, in the church itself.

This simple scenario is persuasive in that it has been stated and restated in so many different ways and places. The separation of the workplace from the home did not, of course, only affect spiritual roles. Conservative evangelicals who are keen to blame the Industrial Revolution for the feminisation of the church are not generally so eager to accept that it was also largely responsible for the now traditional division of labour between the male 'breadwinner' and the female 'breadmaker'.[4] In pre-industrial times, the family income was usually a joint responsibility. Biblical examples reveal women working alongside their husbands on the land, reaping and threshing the crop or pressing the olives. There are instances in Scripture of cottage textile industries, weaving and dyeing cloth, tentmaking etc. No wonder wives were to be 'busy at home', literally 'homeworkers' (Titus 2:5). Through the cultural spectacles of modern, British, traditional evangelicalism, it is easy to read the words, 'Christian wives shouldn't go out to work', a meaningless statement in any pre-industrial society.

Not only did husbands and wives generally work together to meet the family budget in biblical times, as in nearly all times and places in human history, but child rearing was seen very much as a joint project as well. In fact, fathers bore the ultimate responsibility in this area. Notice, for example, Colossians 3:21, where the symmetry of the passage would have led us to expect the command to come to 'parents' jointly and not just to 'fathers'.

The rigid demarcation between husbands' and wives' roles, so often fiercely defended by evangelicals, proves to owe more to a tradition born of societal upheaval than to the Word of God. This is not intended to be a plea for a return to some long lost co-labouring, co-nurturing family culture, no matter how good that would be for family, church and nation. Though it must be said that that may not be just a romantic pipedream. The eventual effects of the present microchip revolution through which we are just beginning to pass may serve to undo the harmful effects of the previous industrial one. For instance, the idea of commuting to a place of work might well be seen in time to come as a destructive, social aberration of the twentieth century.

All this aside, my purpose here is simply to highlight the fact that if the roles of men (or women) are to help us in our search for an essential masculinity (or femininity) then we must be careful to distinguish between those determined by biblical principle and those based purely on cultural factors. Because of the scope for differing judgments at this point, I shall be endeavouring to concentrate on those biblical texts where roles and relationships are not in view.

Masculinity or Masculinities?

To return to the diagnosis offered by the Christian men's movement, industrialisation meant that men lost touch with the broad social context in which they had always expressed their masculinity. The expectation for men to be the prime breadwinners and their virtual exclusion from other settings has driven them to correlate their self-worth with their earnings.

The entertainment industry has added to the confusion of the modern male who wants to find out what he is supposed to be and do. Which stereotype is he to follow? Is he to join the movie tradition that stretches from John Wayne via Clint Eastwood to Sylvester Stallone and Arnie Schwarzenegger? Or does he take his cues from the androgynous camp, more to the fore in the rock music scene? Whether he adopts the strong, silent approach to life or the one that seeks to obliterate all gender distinctions, or even if he tries to steer some middle course, he is conscious that the way he expresses his maleness in our society is to a large extent a matter of personal choice.

Current historical and sociological research accommodates itself to what is undoubtedly an extremely diverse picture by asserting that there is no such objective phenomenon called 'masculinity'. All we can talk about and investigate are 'masculinities', plural. There are working class and middle class masculinities, there are black and white masculinities. And that is just the start: endless variations can be played on these themes. We would also need to look at the very different masculinities of unfamiliar cultures and sub-cultures around the world. And then we could begin to examine the way masculinities have changed over time or the way they interact with and modify each other...

What is the Bible-believing Christian to make of all this? Is there an essential masculinity, a universal masculinity? Or is it all just an ever shifting product of social psychological conditioning? Is it true that, 'There is no masculine entity whose occurrences in all societies we can generalise about?' [5] Or are all the gender doubts and ambiguities that have crept into our society merely seedlings sown by feminists bent on the destruction of male domination? The Christian man needs to know. And if, after all, there *is* an essential masculinity, is there a clearly discernible biblical model that can be followed?

The Promise Keepers would have no problem in answering 'Yes!' to the last question. 'Coach' (ex-American football) Bill McCartney, the founder of this exploding Christian men's movement, has unearthed hundreds of thousands of men in the US who have been only too ready to hear such a message and flock to his banner over the past six years. In that time, the organisation has known phenomenal growth. In the year 1993-4, the number of full-time employees rose from 29 to 150 and the annual budget from $4 million to $22 million. Men return from the mega-rallies to set up men's groups in their home churches and to demonstrate support for their pastors and other local leaders. [6]

But is such a Christian men's movement simply a cultural backlash to the growing emancipation of women in western society? Is it a desperate and ultimately doomed attempt to turn back the clock to the bad old days of male supremacy? Or do Promise Keepers and allied organisations have a watertight Scriptural foundation for the positions they hold and the agenda they intend to carry out? It is to the Bible that we now turn in an attempt to answer these questions.

Playing the Man - the Use of *Andrizo*

Previous generations of schoolchildren, though almost certainly not our own, thrilled to the words of Hugh Latimer to his fellow Bishop, Nicholas Ridley, as they were burned at the stake during the reign of Queen Mary. 'Be of good comfort, Master Ridley, and play the man. We shall this day light such a candle by God's grace in England, as I trust shall never be put out.' [7]

No one ever found it necessary to ask what Latimer meant when he encouraged the Bishop of London to 'Play the man'. What he said meant the same in the mid-sixteenth century as it did four hundred years later in the mid-twentieth. It is only in recent decades that we would profess uncertainty. Few today would use the phrase except in jest or with considerable embarrassment. What is the truth of the matter? Are there fundamentally manly qualities which have been instinctively recognised in all times and cultures? Or have we in the last few years finally recognised that it was all a massive confidence trick and that the myth of an essential masculinity is as threadbare as the Emperor's new suit of clothes?

Before we congratulate ourselves on being the first generation to be able to loose its hold on a particularly heavy piece of cultural baggage, we should do well to reflect on the matter. It is worth considering, for example, just why it should be that Latimer's sentiments would most certainly have been perfectly comprehensible to all the alien tribes and races that people the pages of Scripture.

In fact, the Apostle Paul gives the same command to the believers in Corinth. 'Be on your guard; stand firm in the faith; be men of courage; be strong' (1 Corinthians 16:13). The single word translated 'be men of courage' comes from the verb *andrizo* and could well be simply translated, 'play the man', or just, 'be manly'. The men of the church are to set the tone and example that should characterise the fellowship in what were perilous times. The four commands of the verse belong together and constitute a single composite thought in the apostle's mind. Watchfulness, constancy and particularly, as we shall see, strength, accurately summarise the scriptural definition of manliness.

While *andrizo* appears nowhere else in the New Testament, it is nevertheless to be found in the Septuagint. This Greek translation of the Old Testament, completed by the second century BC, was widely regarded as the standard version in the days of the early church. Andrizo is used twenty or more times in the Septuagint to translate just one very common Hebrew verb, *hazaq*. This verb has a circle of meanings connected with prevailing strength and courage. Originally it meant to seize or take hold of something. It always implies the idea of taking the initiative.

In the instances of the use of *hazaq* rendered *andrizo* in the Greek Old Testament, the English versions always translate, 'be strong'. In his final address to Israel, Moses bids the people, '**Be strong** and courageous' (Deuteronomy 31:6). He then twice repeats the command, but on these occasions personally, to Joshua (verses 7 and 23). Exactly the same combination of verbs, '**Be strong** and courageous' are spoken four more times to Joshua, but now, after the death of Moses, directly by the Lord himself (Joshua 1:6,7,9,18). For the translators of the Septuagint there was no doubt that the essence of true masculinity lay in the strong and godly leadership embodied so clearly by Joshua.

Subsequently, Joab insists that the troops of Israel, '**Be strong** and... fight bravely for our people and the cities of our God' (2 Samuel 10:12). David also, according to the Septuagint, twice urged his son Solomon to 'be a man' and not to be afraid or discouraged as he contemplated the building of the temple (1 Chronicles 22:13; 28:20).

The Greek version of Psalm 27:14 was surely in Paul's mind when he wrote 1 Corinthians 16:13: 'Wait for the Lord; act like men, take heart and wait for the Lord'.

When the prophet Daniel confesses to the intimidating figure who has appeared to him on the bank of the Tigris river that his 'strength is gone' and he 'can hardly breathe', the reply comes as a great encour-

agement: ' "Do not be afraid, O man highly esteemed," he said. "Peace!
Be strong now; **be strong** "' (Daniel 10:19).

Playing the Man - in Plain Hebrew

The use of *andrizo* in the Septuagint as a rendering of *hazaq* leaves us in
little doubt as to what the Jews of the time felt was the essence of
masculinity. [8] Direct Old Testament references to what was expected of
a man do not however depend on the Greek version. Nor was the
accepted understanding the preserve only of the Israelites.

When the Philistines learned that Israel had brought the ark of the
covenant into the camp, they were afraid, recalling the plagues that had
fallen upon Egypt in former years. But then they pulled themselves
together: 'Be strong, Philistines! Be men, or you will be subject to the
Hebrews, as they have been to you. Be men, and fight!' (1 Samuel 4:9).
Philistine men, apparently, were not supposed to be weak, frightened,
submissive or passive.

The quotation I have used as the heading to this chapter is an interesting
case in point. The outlawed David has refused to murder the sleeping Saul,
but is filled with disgust for Abner, who should have been protecting the
king. From the safety of a hillside, and brandishing the spear and water jug
he had silently removed from beside Saul, David mercilessly mocks the
king's general in front of his troops. 'You're a man, aren't you? And who is
like you in Israel? Why didn't you guard your lord the king?' (1 Samuel
26:15). Here it is not simply strength that is regarded as essential to
manliness, unless it be the strength required to stay awake. He is rebuked
rather for his shameful lack of leadership in not setting an adequate guard.
A real man will protect those for whom he is responsible.

Nor was a life of spiritual faith and obedience something that David
felt was the province and preserve of women. Quite the reverse. On his
deathbed, he gave a detailed charge to his son and successor, Solomon,
which began: 'I am about to go the way of all the earth. So be strong,
show yourself a man, and observe what the Lord your God requires....'
(1 Kings 2:2,3). A true man was faithful to the revealed will of God in
everything. The reward, incidentally, for David's descendants
remaining spiritually obedient was that he would 'never fail to have a

man on the throne of Israel' (verse 4). As long as an anointed man exercised spiritual leadership, anointed men would retain it.

The fact that it was God himself who thought in gender terms when speaking in Scripture is reinforced at that dramatic point in the Book of Job when, having had to listen to the interminable opinions of mere mortals, the Lord finally speaks out of the storm. The devastating four chapter barrage of relentless, unanswerable questions that follows begins: 'Who is this that darkens my counsel with words without knowledge? Brace yourself like a man; I will question you, and you shall answer me' (Job 38:2,3). The same words are repeated halfway through the humbling, disciplinary procedure (40:7).

What the NIV reasonably paraphrases, 'Brace yourself' is in fact the familiar biblical injunction, 'Gird up your loins'. This natural preparation for any severe form of physical exertion is of course suggested ironically. The contest is infinitely unequal. Job is speechless from the start. Nevertheless, the desired effect is achieved and, spiritually enlightened, Job repents in dust and ashes (42:5,6).

From the point of view of our study, we may infer that the Lord requires a man to speak and behave circumspectly in matters bordering on and beyond his frail capacity. We sense that it is precisely because he is a man that he needs to be taken to task. This is in line with God's response in the Garden of Eden. Despite the fact that Eve was the first to sin, it is the man who must take responsibility for the disaster (Genesis 3:22-24).

The Strong/Weak Axis

All the incidental pictures sketched in Scripture of what a man ought to be portray clearly the qualities of strength and leadership responsibility as being paramount. Incidental references to women reinforce this conclusion, with the concept of women ruling over the people of God evidently seen as a severe judgment. This is not because women are regarded as inferior beings, but because the Bible unquestionably views such a state of affairs as a reversal of nature, shocking to all right-minded men and women alike (eg Isaiah 3:12).

The same is true when men are condemned for acting like women, as they not infrequently are, particularly in the Prophets: 'In that day the Egyptians will be like women. They will shudder with fear at the uplifted hand that the Lord Almighty raises against them' (Isaiah 19:16). 'Ask and see: Can a man bear children? Then why do I see every strong man with his hands on his stomach like a woman in labour, every face turned deathly pale?' (Jeremiah 30:6). 'Babylon's warriors have stopped fighting; they remain in their strongholds. Their strength is exhausted; they have become like women' (Jeremiah 51:30). 'Look at your troops - they are all women!' (Nahum 3:13).

What are we to make of these and similar texts? Seen through modern eyes, they are breathtakingly chauvinistic. But this is only because our culture deems it shocking for men and women to be regarded and treated differently, whereas the cultures of the Bible deemed it shocking for men and women to be regarded and treated as the same. The essential 'weakness' of women, while considered disgraceful in a man was highly honoured as the essence of femininity. (I felt compelled to place weakness in inverted commas in the previous sentence because it needs a good measure of contextual explanation in these hypersensitive days!)

The NIV is not particularly helpful when it refers to the woman as the 'weaker partner' in marriage (1 Peter 3:7). It is quite contrary to all the scriptural evidence to suggest that the husband brings more to the marriage relationship than the wife. But we are not talking about marriage or marriage roles in this chapter and neither is the Apostle Peter, if we isolate and correctly translate his concept of the 'weaker **vessel**'. When a man marries, he is to 'live with (his wife) according to knowledge **as with a weaker vessel, the female,** assigning honour as co-heirs of the grace of life' (literal translation).

The 'knowledge' he is to bring into the marriage is the awareness and understanding of the differences between men and women enshrined in Scripture, expressed in the world around him and, as I shall later suggest, imprinted on his own psyche. Obviously, this knowledge will be all the greater, the more he is consciously aware of these three sources of information and instruction. The 'honour' he is to assign derives from the essential spiritual equality of men and women in Christ, an equality in no way affected by the marriage relationship or by the fact that the woman is the weaker vessel.

Presumably, if woman is the 'weaker vessel', then the Apostle Peter would not object to our calling man the 'stronger vessel'. But what do these expressions mean? It doesn't appear as though Peter imagined he was saying anything overly controversial. No explanation is given because none was thought to be required. The ordinary Christians 'scattered throughout Pontus, Galatia, Cappadocia, Asia and Bithynia' (1:1) were apparently considered well able to take the thought on board and apply it to their lives.

The older Bible commentators did not appear to have any particular trouble at this point, either. Most merely noted the 'obvious' allusion and passed quietly on to more problematical issues. Not so today, as contemporary evangelical exegetes struggle (manfully?) to elucidate the deep mysteries that must lie behind the apostle's deceptively simple words. Is it every other human culture that has always had a blind spot here or could it possibly be our own?

Can we in fact define more closely what the apostle means by the weaker vessel? His use of the term is as an incentive to the man to be understanding and protective. The emphasis therefore is on the aspect of the woman's vulnerability. Let me enter three important caveats before continuing. First, it ought to be obvious that Peter is speaking in generalities. Many men will be more vulnerable ('weaker') than many women in the areas I am about to mention. Secondly, this strong/weak axis in Scripture is not to be associated with superiority and inferiority. It would have done both men and women a great service if both Jewish and Christian commentators over the centuries had tumbled to this truth. Just because a man can lift heavier weights no more makes him superior to a woman than it makes an elephant superior to him. Thirdly, the strong/weak axis is to be considered as a help to comprehending and evaluating the complementary nature of masculine and female characteristics. I hesitate to bring in an alien religious concept but the Eastern idea of Yin (the feminine or passive principle) and Yang (the masculine or active principle) manages to reflect what is surely a universal human perception without pejorative overtones. The 'weakness' of women enables the exhibition of qualities that, in a context where there was no possibility of confusion, we should unquestionably call 'strengths'.

Few would care to dispute that men are stronger than women in sheer physical power. Of course women can run marathons and, maybe, endure greater physical pain. It is a simple fact that proportionately more women survived concentration camps and everyone knows that they live longer than men. But not even the most ardent feminist would suggest that the International Olympic Committee should combine the men's and women's events. When physical danger threatens, the man is designed to protect the woman and not the other way round. Her physical 'weakness' fosters the qualities of sympathy and tenderness.

The emotional makeup of the woman also renders her more vulnerable. She is subject to a monthly cycle which affects her emotional stability to a greater or lesser extent. Inevitably, she is therefore more aware of ('in touch with') her feelings and those of others around her. This enables her to be more intuitive, and the man who ignores or dismisses this female expertise is a fool. While she may be more prone to irrational fears (1 Peter 3:6), this vulnerability is the inevitable downside to a sharpened emotional sensitivity.

Straying even further under the guns of the feminists, I would suggest that the 'weakness' of woman extends to her spiritual nature. Spiritual truth comes through the mind and a whole mass of recent research has again thrown wide open the old debate on the differences in the way men and women think. The development of a systematic theology may well be considered a task better suited to the male brain. But this is not the place to get into that debate. [9]

One of the several reasons the Apostle Paul gives for not allowing a woman to teach or have spiritual authority over a man is that 'Adam was not the one deceived; it was the woman who was deceived...' (1 Timothy 2:14). In fact, Paul uses an intensive form of the verb when applying it to Eve. Unlike Adam, she was ' **thoroughly** deceived'. Various unsatisfactory explanations are offered in the commentaries for Paul's deliberate contrast. The simplest explanation, however, is that the apostle is drawing attention to a vulnerability. The Lord did not design the woman to be the first line of defence when it came to spiritual discernment. That is why Satan, in the form of a serpent, 'more crafty than any of the wild animals the LORD God had made' (Genesis 3:1), decided to get to Adam through Eve. Satan's exploitation of essential male/female differences lay behind that original, disastrous reversal of leadership roles.

A Universal Imprint

Christians need to be aware of these inbuilt distinctions if they are adequately to defend the scriptural roles of men and women in both church and family from charges of mere cultural determinism. In this brief survey, we have seen that the strong/weak axis is fundamental to a biblical understanding of male/female differences. Properly understood, this axis explains the essence of masculine and feminine traits.

Ultimately, we do not need to concern ourselves overmuch whether it is nature or nurture that has the greater influence in establishing gender differences. No doubt, biologists, psychologists, sociologists and historians will continue both to throw light and to cast darkness in turn on the question. But if this differentiation is imprinted on the soul as part of the image of God that men and women bear (Genesis 1:26,27), and if it is part of the law of God 'written on their hearts' (Romans 2:15), then all that matters is that we believe it and conduct ourselves accordingly. Of course, scientific research into the way gender differences are introduced into our lives is perfectly legitimate. Such investigations will not make much progress however if they are driven by a political agenda committed to the principle of androgyny. Despite numerous attempts to reinterpret the ethnographical data, the evidence is overwhelming that all human cultures and societies are built on the premise of male leadership. Sociologist Steven Goldberg writes: 'All anthropologists agree that there has never been a society which failed to associate hierarchical authority and leadership in these areas with men.' [10] More recently, David Gilmore has attempted to collate the findings of numerous anthropologists worldwide in an ambitious attempt to answer the questions: 'Is there a deep structure of manhood?

Is there a global archetype of manliness?' Again, the answer from this agnostic researcher is affirmative. [11] Even arch feminists are bound to agree: 'All contemporary societies are to some extent male-dominated'. [12]

While this has resulted, in almost all cases, in the sinful subjugation of women as a consequence of the Fall (Genesis 3:16), the existence of a universal patriarchy is as mystifying to humanistic anthropology as the existence of a universal morality.

The fact is that male leadership is the product of God's creation and not of male chauvinism. It is a vital part of the design plan for humanity. We are at present suffering the effects of a sociopolitical experiment in degendering that threatens the fabric of our society. There is no gender confusion in the Bible and that means there need be none in us. Certainly, in the light of these abiding scriptural principles, we should re-examine the rigid roles sometimes laid down for men and women by traditional evangelicalism. But we should not be intimidated into throwing the baby out with the bathwater.

Notes
1. As an example of how vindictive the backlash against feminism could get, see Goldberg, H. *The Inner Male: Overcoming Roadblocks to Intimacy.* New York: Signet, 1988.
2. In 1979, 55% of churchgoers in England were female. This figure had risen to 58% in 1989. The percentages hold across the age ranges. Source: Brierley, P. *'Christian' England.* London: Marc Europe, 1991.
3. Rotundo, E. Anthony. *American Manhood: Transformations of Masculinity from the Revolution to the Modern Era.* New York: Basic Books, 1993.
4. For an interesting discussion on the development of what was a new social arrangement, see Seccombe, W. *Patriarchy stabilised: the construction of the male breadwinner wage norm in nineteenth century Britain.* Social History 2:53-75, 1986.
5. Connell, R.W. *Masculinities.* Cambridge: Polity Press, 1995, p. 43.
6. Much of the present information on Promise Keepers was gleaned from an article in *Christianity Today, 6/2/95.*

7. Foxe, J. *Actes and Monuments,* 1570. There are numerous modern versions of Foxe's *Book of Martyrs!*

8. Other Septuagint references where *andrizo* is used to translate *hazaq* include: Joshua 10:25 Samuel 13:28; 2 Chronicles 32:7; Psalm 31:24; Nahum 2:1.

9. See the next chapter for a fuller discussion of brain and other biological sex differences.

10. Goldberg, S. *The Inevitability of Patriarchy.* New York: William Morrow & Co, 1973/74, pp. 26,27. The objectivity of Goldberg's findings at this point is actually reinforced by his overt atheism.

11. Gilmore, D.D. *Manhood in the Making: Cultural Concepts of Masculinity.* New Haven: Yale University Press, 1990.

12. Rosaldo, M. Z. and Lamphere, L. eds. *Women, Culture and Society* Stanford, California: Stanford University Press, 1974, p. 3.

Women are different!

Sheila Stephen

Sheila has a degree in biblical studies and social theory from the University of Wales and is a trained counsellor with considerable experience in speaking on gender-related issues. She currently lectures for the Prepared for Service training course and is involved locally and nationally in the work of the Cleft-Lip and Palate Association. Sheila is married to Jonathan Stephen, the pastor of Carey Baptist Church, Reading, and they have one son.

Women are Different!

M any people are anxious about gender and the implications of wrong views for both individuals and society. One Christian group may distinguish very precisely areas of church and life in general which are primarily 'woman's work' and discourage men from those areas, lest they become insecure about their manhood. Others, from careful reading of the Scriptures would see gender roles as being interchangeable. In the secular realm Freud and his followers maintained that masculine and feminine identities are formed very differently and divergence from the norm will result in pathology in the adult. Gender confusion is a hallmark of our postmodern society.

Gender is inherent in the way in which all societies are organised. The basic divisions of labour in all known human societies from time immemorial have been based on it. Even in societies like China, which hold to an ideology of minimising male-female differences, there are many ways of expressing gender distinctions.

Society seems to be confused about the meaning of 'masculine' and 'feminine'. Elaine Storkey, along with many others, rightly complains about the huge generalisations which are frequently made about sex and sexuality. However, it is interesting to note that there does seem to be a common body of these assumptions. It is said that men are the initiators, active and masterful. Women are passive, dependent, intuitive and responsive. Many would see these as being only the product of stereotyping, reinforced by language, the media, psychology and the education system.

What contribution can the evangelical Christian bring to this anxious state of affairs? Are gender stereotypes God-given to every human society or an aberration of the Fall?

In every culture there have always been criteria for boys to know how to be men and girls to know how to be women. The Bible is not silent on the subject of such societal norms. In these uncertain days, men and women are unsure as to how they should relate. Gender anxiety produces fear, uncertainty, tension, isolation and insecurity. Confronted with the modern woman, seeking to replace patriarchy with matriarchy, the man responds with aggressive chauvinism and women fight back.

Secular Backlash

The secular world now states that it has been merely 'fashionable' to minimise male/female differences. Scholars in various disciplines are publishing studies to demonstrate that men and women differ in many more ways than just the physical. This may be a backlash to the dogma of radical feminism.

Among these scholars are Anne Moir and David Jessel who say: 'Some will find what we have written a justification for conservatism and the sexual status quo, and they will be wrong. We do not consecrate the natural, just because it is biologically true; men for instance, have a natural disposition to homicide and promiscuity, which is not a recipe for the happy survival of society. If this book is a prescription for anything - and it isn't intended to be - it's for a radical rethink of the relationship between the sexes, a relationship we can at least base on fact rather than on theory. With the knowledge of who we are and why, we can clear the landscape of the clutter of prejudicial nonsense. There is no point, for instance, in laws and educational theories which both deny the differences between men and women, and then seek to eradicate them.' [1]

Today's unisex mentality is not based on a Christian worldview. The Bible asserts that being male and female reflect the image of God (Genesis 1:27).

A Digest of Differences

Many secular researchers are publishing data that does not support a unisex model. Space does not permit a full survey of recent material, nor is it totally within the remit of this book. Interested readers are directed to the studies mentioned in the notes at the end of this chapter. Empirical data gathered can be summarised as follows:

Though cultures develop gender roles differently, the anthropological evidence reveals significant underlying patterns in all human societies. This is particularly evident in the sexual division of labour and the societal division of roles, especially noticeable in subsistence economies. [2]

Doreen Kimura, a Professor of Psychology and Honorary Lecturer in Clinical Neurological Science in Canada has taken a different line, studying the neural and hormonal basis of human intellectual functioning. She stated that: 'Women and men differ not only in physical attributes and reproductive function but also in the way they solve intellectual problems.' [3]

Doreen Kimura feels that the bulk of evidence suggests that the effects of sex hormones occur so early in life that from the start the environment is acting on 'differently wired brains' in girls and boys. Many differences emerged in performance of spatial tasks and mathematical reasoning, where men performed better. While women excelled in tasks such as verbal fluency, arithmetical calculation and recall.

Kimura, detailing research on brain symmetry and brain organisation, concludes that men's and women's brains are organised along different lines from very early in life. During development, sex hormones direct this differentiation. Kimura states also that the findings of consistent, and, in some cases, quite substantial sex differences suggests that men and women may have different occupational capabilities and interests, independent of societal influences. [4]

In noting many functional differences, for example in vision, taste and smell, many neuroscientists and researchers are prepared to conclude: 'It seems unrealistic to deny any longer the existence of male and female brain differences. Just as there are physical dissimilarities between males and females... there are equally dramatic differences in brain functioning.' [5]

It is fascinating to see that some scientists suggest that the difference in emotional response in men and women can be explained by their differing brain structure and organisation. For men, the emotions are kept in place in the right side of the brain, while the power to express feelings in speech is located on the left side. The flow of information from one side of the brain to the other is more difficult since the two halves of a man's brain are connected by a smaller number of fibres than a woman's.

The woman may be less able to separate emotion from reason due to the way the female brain is organised. The female brain has emotional capacities on both sides of the brain with more information exchanged between the two. Also the verbal side of the brain is more integrated with the emotional, thus enabling her to express her emotions in words. [6] This difference is demonstrated in the interesting interplay of decision-making and perception. With a greater innate sensitivity to personal and moral aspects and a greater capacity to take in more information and factors than a man, a woman's deductive process is more complex.

In endocrinology, studies have shown a strong correlation between testosterone (the male hormone) and certain behaviours (eg dominance, assertion, aggression, confrontation and drive for power.) [7] After puberty, a man has twenty times more of this hormone in his body than a woman.

In the field of sociolinguistics, Deborah Tannen's bestseller, *You Just Don't Understand - Men and Women in Conversation,* began as a research project dealing with how friends talk to one another. In analysing the material, the author was struck by the overwhelming differences that separated males and females at each age studied. She also noted the striking similarities that linked the females on the one hand and the males on the other right across the ages. [8]

Differences in body language were evident. In physical alignment and in verbally expressing personal concerns, it was noted that men tend to be more indirect than women.

In this research, Tannen asserts that there are gender differences in ways of speaking. Comparing boys and girls of the same age, Tannen noted that girls were more inclined to talk to one another and boys more inclined to do things together and make jibes at each other. Boys would challenge the existing hierarchy but girls would defer to it.

Tannen proclaims: 'Denying real differences can only compound the confusion that is already widespread in this era of shifting and re-forming relationships between men and women. Pretending that women and men are the same hurts women, because the ways they are treated are based on the norms for men. It also hurts men who, with good intentions, speak to women as they would to men, and are nonplussed when their words don't work as they expected, or even spark resentment and anger'. [9]

Many more detailed examples could be cited of recent research that supports the assertion 'male and female, he created them' (Genesis 1:27). It is only in this century that it has been necessary to prove the point, and to do it from so many disciplines.

It is in recognising and accepting gender differences that we can answer questions about who we are and why we are and so find out how we are to be.

It seems to be very clear that the different qualities that are God's unique gifts to men and women correspond so well to the roles that God has prescribed and that have served mankind in every race and culture since the beginning of time.

Roles are being challenged and re-negotiated as we approach the millennium, and so are definitions of masculinity and femininity. Is there a need to define what it means to be essentially female? Is it linked with the modern preoccupation with fulfilment?

Defining the Terms: Secular Attempts at the Definition of 'Femininity'

For centuries there seems to have been a common, unspoken, unwritten agreement about what it means to be a woman, about the essential ingredients of what it is to be 'feminine'. Is it part of what is written indelibly on women's hearts? Has it been there since creation. Today these issues are under the microscope. Can manhood and womanhood be defined in terms of certain invariable distinctives?

Margaret Mead, in her classic book *Male and Female, a Study of the Sexes in a Changing World*, examined perceptions of sexuality among seven ethnic groups in the South Pacific and the USA. What emerged was a tremendous diversity of masculine and feminine traits, varying from culture to culture. She did, however, discern some regularities, which she felt stemmed from basic physiological distinctions and related to the tension between activity and passivity, initiative and response, potency and receptivity. [10]

In a study of six modern cultures, men and women were asked to describe the 'kind of person I would most like to be'. Cross-culturally, women were more likely to describe their ideal selves as loving, affectionate, impulsive, sympathetic and generous. In another survey, assessing the value placed on different interests and pursuits, girls gave higher ratings to social, aesthetic and religious values. Women valued 'having interesting experiences' or 'being of service to society'. [11]

Androgyny

With the importance of political correctness the concepts of 'persons' and 'personhood' have taken on new and powerful meanings. Some students of personality theory who have studied masculinity and femininity have concluded that socially desirable traits which characterise the 'healthy' individual are common to humanity rather than related to sexual identity. They are related to 'persons'. Such traits are *androgynous* in that they characterise the healthy human regardless of gender. Thus a male and female might be both assertive and yielding, forceful and compassionate, ambitious and sensitive to the needs of others.

An early study by Abraham Maslow (1942) suggested that an androgynous model of personality might be manifested in healthy women. He found that women with high levels of self-esteem were also tolerant, assertive, initiatory, decisive, self-reliant, independent and ambitious. However, these characteristics, so valued in our modern society, do not preclude the traditional feminine qualities of empathy and concern for others. [12]

Liberation is seen as a pilgrimage towards 'humanity' rather than towards femininity. Just as men, in responding to the women's movement, are getting 'in touch' with the feminine within them, so might women be free to draw on virtues and strengths that are considered 'masculine'. [13]

To what extent this movement towards androgyny is reactive and is bound up in the collapse of traditional societal and family values is an open question. Is it a reaction to fear and threat; the fear and threat women have of divorce and abandonment? In coming forward to secure the economic future of their family, women have had to take initiatives, decisions and assert themselves to survive.

The Princess Myth

If there is one thing that characterises the 90's it is the obsession with image. It's powerful, it's postmodern and it attracts money! An analysis of the images and messages young women are getting today from popular culture seem to deny the influence of the androgyny model.

Body consciousness for women, has, if anything, intensified and the desirable images of femininity are of bodies thinner and curvier than ever before. What the women's magazines call 'biologically impossible women' are held up to be the norm. [14] Alongside this, the instances of anorexia and bulimia have increased dramatically in the last twenty-five years.

American thinker and writer Naomi Wolf views the 'beauty myth' as a political weapon in the backlash against feminism. [15] She calls for a redefinition of beauty which is 'non-competitive, non-hierarchical and non-violent' [16] and allows for self-expression rather than a homage to the beauty industry.

No one seems to have embodied the image of femininity in the 90's more than the Princess of Wales. Between engagement and marriage 28 pounds of weight were shed and the accolade was 'beautiful'. She was the personification of femininity in her purity, beauty, and goodness, and numerous dress designers, beauty shops, therapists and charities have profited from her image.

The Goddess Myth

This is an ancient concept given modern significance by a group of women who want to define distinctives and yet not lose the power that feminism seems to give to the modern woman. Allied to the former myth and yet moving forward into the spiritual realm, is a 'collective force rising up on earth today, an energy of the reborn feminine' (Marianne Williamson). [17]

Here is an emphasis on the inner life, on a quest to a place where what is feminine is sacred. It is about power and goodness and about rebirth into an enchanted kingdom of the Goddess within. When the Goddess is ready to re-emerge 'like the energy of Christ, of which she is a part' [18] she does so and finds her way into the hearts and minds of individual women. And they change. This myth is also seen as a reaction to patriarchy, and to the denial of the feminine principles of nonviolence and surrender and of the values of intuition, nurturing and healing. Inner beauty and sensitivity are praised and the spiritual life encouraged.

Interestingly, Marianne Williamson is convinced that women have adopted a masculine psychological mode, that of doing to feel worthy rather than focussing on the internal. The imprisoned Goddess is the invalidation of feminine, non-linear modes of thinking and being and the repudiation of feeling and love. She will be released, either sweetly or angrily.

Why bother?

Why are secular writers seeking to define femininity in an era when it would be the last thing one would expect? It is all part of the changing face of feminism. Even Germaine Greer, author of bestseller *The Female Eunuch,* argues in her later book *Sex and Destiny* for women's traditional role as mothers. In so doing she is surely supporting the feminine quality of nurturing.

Betty Frieden, much quoted in feminist literature, warns women in her book *The Second Stage* not to be influenced by a 'feminist mystique' and so miss the joys of a family. [19]

Defining the Terms: 'Femininity' - Some contributions from Christian writers

Mary Kassian

Mary Kassian, author of *The Feminist Gospel* [20] embodies the gender-stereotype debate in images of Barbie Dolls and GI Joe (Action Man). As a lecturer in Women's Ministries she has reason to be close to the subject. It is her opinion that toys, books, clothing etc. often portray images of men and women that unfairly stereotype, yet she asks an interesting and perceptive question : 'But are the images that Barbie and GI Joe portray totally unfounded? Or are they shadows of reality which are distorted by carrying them to an extreme?' [21]

Kassian is critical of the idea that since society has foisted gender differences on us, all that needs to happen is a correction so that each of us possess a gender blend of what is good in both masculinity and femininity.

She goes on to say that this is not consistent with the image of man and woman presented in the Bible and therefore cannot fully restore the unity of male and female that existed in the beginning. Scripture portrays male and female as being equal in value, yet fundamentally different in nature.

The Godhead together purposed to create humans in their own image and likeness. While scholars generally agree that God's image is reflected morally, intellectually and spiritually in mankind, Kassian sees it in a relational sense and believes that the distinction between man and woman is also a manifestation of the image of God.

She observes that there are distinct patterns of conduct which characterise the interaction of the persons of the Godhead : the authority of the Father over the Son (John 14:28; 1 Corinthians 15:27-28; Hebrews 5:7-8); the Father being the source of the Son's authority (John 8:54; 17:1-3,24; Hebrews 1:3) the Son, though equal with the Father, submitting himself (John 6:38; 14:31; Philippians 2:6-8). The Father initiates and the Son responds, and this pattern is never violated. It is this aspect that God has imprinted onto humans. Although both male and female exhibit both traits, Kassian states that psychologically and physically man is principally characterised by initiation, woman by responsiveness.

Kassian asserts that 'The Bible presents a picture of gender roles that holds the concepts of equality and hierarchy in tandem. According to Genesis, who we are as male and female is nothing less than a picture which wondrously and mysteriously reflects the character of God'. [22]

Kassian's major contribution to our debate is in exploring the question of whether femininity is a quality written on the hearts of women. We are reminded too that equality and difference are not mutually exclusive and that the authority relationships of male/female mirror those in the Godhead.

Stephen B. Clark

In *Man and Woman in Christ* Stephen Clark tackles the subject extensively, beginning from the conviction that the modern discussion about men and women normally misses the crucial perspective of social roles. [23] He points out that three types of women have a problem with 'Christian womanliness': the insecure woman, the 'masculinized' woman and the woman influenced by the feminist movement.

Clark is surely right when he emphasises responsibility. This is not often discussed in all the books and articles written on this subject, yet when God created male and female he delineated their responsibilities at the outset. He helpfully points out that Christian women could well learn to be more assertive, selectively, especially in situations where their responsibilities call for it.

A crucial area for character formation for women is seen by Clark as trust, in a society where many women are fundamentally characterised by anxiety.

Clark sees the restoration of a Christian social structure as one of the main factors in the formation of womanly Christian character. Congruent to that is the respect afforded to women's social roles. Women should aspire to strong and supportive relationships with other women in the community.

Clark would want women to be free from excessive emotional dependency upon men. This is interesting, particularly as some Christians seek to define femininity only in relation to men, and rightly, women who are single or widowed challenge this contention. Surely a woman is not only a woman when she has a man at the centre of her life. 'If women are to grow into confident, responsible, Christian womanhood, they need a certain emotional freedom from men.' [24]

Stephen Clark has much to offer on the subject. His emphasis on the responsibilities of women and their social roles in the community as well as in the family are a helpful reminder that the subject of a woman's influence should not be limited only to the question of leadership within the church.

Susan T. Foh

Susan Foh, in her book *Women And the Word of God*, looks at this subject under the title of 'The Metaphysics of Sex.' [25] In this careful chapter she consigns most attempts to identify existential distinctions between masculine and feminine to the realms of metaphysics. She makes an interesting and provocative point about the possibility of God's law being written on human hearts via hormones in a long note on Steven Goldberg's *The Inevitability of Patriarchy.*

When it comes to the Bible, Foh does not think that it tells us who man or woman is. She concedes that the Bible does make distinctions between men and women, both ceremonially and in relation to marriage but sees the only real gender distinction in Scripture as being functional distinctions. She emphasises the similarities of men and women and she feels that personhood is more important than sexuality.

Foh is highly critical of Betty Frieden who defines a person's identity in terms of his or her work. If the work is unimportant, Frieden maintains, then the person is unimportant. One's work has to be valued by society if one is to feel worthwhile, and housework does not meet this standard; it cannot give one identity. Frieden is addressing an elite, whose jobs or careers could be evaluated as 'meaningful'. Foh reminds women that recognising that satisfaction comes from God should free them from preoccupation with finding fulfilment and value in their occupations.

Foh makes the suggestion, albeit in a tentative footnote, that femininity may be written on our hearts.

John Piper

John Piper and Wayne Grudem's *Recovering Biblical Manhood and Womanhood* is bursting full of contributions from various disciplines on the whole issue of gender, the church and society.

In the foreword, Piper is anxious to reassure single men and women that this book is for them too. His persuasion is that masculinity and femininity are rooted in who we are by nature; they are not simply reflexes of the marriage relationship. A woman does not become a woman by getting married. [26]

When defining femininity Piper views as important the response of the woman to the pattern of initiative established by mature masculinity. His definition of femininity is: 'At the heart of mature femininity is a freeing disposition to affirm, receive and nurture strength and leadership from worthy men in ways appropriate to a woman's differing relationships.' [27] For him, this includes all that is meant in Genesis 2:18 by 'helper suitable for him'.

Piper's concentration on disposition is his attempt not to limit his definition of femininity to a set of roles or behaviours. Mature femininity is a question of attitude. The mature woman has an inclination to yield and to follow. She is subject to Christ. She does not want to usurp the role of the male head, but rather seeks to nurture and strengthen. She is the helper.

Piper becomes less dogmatic when he tries to prescribe how a woman might relate in different relationships, particularly those of authority structures. He attempts to define how women may influence men, in keeping with mature femininity. He maintains that to the degree that a woman's influence over a man is personal and directive it will controvert God's created order. If a woman gives directives to men it will need to be non-personal. (For example, she may design the traffic pattern of a city's streets, but she will not direct the all-male Traffic Warden Team.)

Piper again highlights the fact that femininity is rooted in nature. He sees it being expressed in responsiveness, nurturing and strengthening in the context of male leadership.

George A. Rekers

George Rekers, also contributing to *Recovering Biblical Manhood and Womanhood,* writes as Professor of Neuropsychiatry and Behavioural Sciences and Adjunct Professor of Counselling. He looks at the rearing of masculine boys and feminine girls.

He sees the modern unisex approach being rooted in humanistic relativism. His extensive research into children with problems in sex-role adjustments would make sober reading. Clinical records showed that in the families of disturbed boys the mothers held the balance of power. The male role model was absent or inadequate.

Rekers also highlights the importance of the role of the father in the normal heterosexual role and sexual identity of his children. He sees the father more than the mother as being most involved in preparing children for their roles in society, particularly masculine and feminine roles. The affection and leadership of the father are crucial factors.

He also highlights the importance of the role-model example. He says that the girl who is encouraged to act in a feminine way will develop a firm female identity. He regards true female sexual identity involving the whole person in her biological, social and spiritual life. [28] True femininity involves sexual purity and fidelity, conceiving and caring for a child only within marriage and protecting the child in utero and beyond. Rekers quotes 1 Timothy 5:14; 2:9-10 and Titus 2:3-5 to support his comments. His table of Examples of Sex Role Distinctions gives an insight into the practical outworking of his views. [29]

Rekers' contribution shows that male leadership and affection play a vital part in shaping femininity as does the female role model.

Elizabeth Elliot

Dealing with 'The Essence of Femininity' in Piper & Grudem, Elizabeth Elliot tries to verbalise the unfathomable and indefinable qualities of femininity. For her the essence of femininity is in receiving.

Elliot points out that gender differences have been understood for millennia. [30] Drawing on her years of experience living in a stone-age culture in S. America, she observed that femininity was deeply-rooted in a woman's very being. She equates femininity with a mystery, equal to that of the relationship between Christ and the church. She quotes C.S. Lewis as saying that we are dealing with the 'live and awful shadows of realities utterly beyond our control and largely beyond our direct knowledge'. [31]

Elliot emphasises that femininity is rooted in human consciousness and that it is a mystery.

Defining the Terms: Some Biblical Distinctives

Mary Stewart van Leeuwen makes an amusing point in her book *Gender And Grace.* She contends that a large body of literature on gender role stereotypes reveals that most of the feminine qualities expected of marriageable women are also those that are considered socially undesirable and clinically immature. [32]

These qualities are: unambitious, dependent, emotional, submissive, naive, indecisive, illogical, passive, unselfconfident and homebound. With this in mind, it is interesting to look at some biblical texts which make specific comments about the character of the godly woman.

Her Adornment

Some key texts on this subject are 1 Timothy 2:9-10 and 1 Peter 3:3-4.

The Bible is not silent on the subject of image. It gives it some importance. Nor does the Bible denigrate beauty and encourage frumpiness as the dress of some modern Christian women might suggest! Skimming through the verses of the Song of Solomon, one cannot avoid noticing the delight the lover has in the physical beauty of his beloved. Isaiah 3:18-23 gives a list of the jewellery of the day. Jewellery was prized by God's people (Jeremiah 2:32).

Cosmetics and perfumes were used by the bride in the Song of Solomon and by Esther. Peter is criticising the wearing of clothes and jewellery for show. In ancient times and perhaps until recently wealthy women could dress in ways that a poorer person could not match.

Their very dress would make a social comment, that they originated from a higher social class. These were distinctions that New Testament writers were at pains to discourage, emphasising that since believers were one in Christ Jesus there were no class distinctions.

The adornment of the Christian woman is to reflect modesty. She is not to attempt to be ostentatious or alluring. Her dress is to be suitable for the occasion. Melody Green, in *Uncovering the Truth About Modesty* (Last Days Ministries, 1982), makes the point that many Christian women are oblivious about the effect they have on others. Some who are really zealous for the Lord dress in ways that send out a totally different message.

What is needed is a balance, based on careful consideration of scriptural principles. A drab appearance is not a requirement for godliness. Christian women should dress according to the custom of the culture and country where God has placed them, with a sense of decency and wisdom. [33] It does matter. It is part of what it means to be a woman.

Her Attitudes

A key text on this subject is 1 Peter 3:3-6.

Injunctions to cultivate the 'inner self' are legion today: the requirement here is for the Christian woman to cultivate that part of her nature that will last. The word 'gentle' is also used of Christ in Matthew 21:5. Gentleness, or meekness (KJV), is the opposite of self-assertiveness and self-interest. Christ had all the power of the Godhead and yet he was meek.

Lest Peter be accused of advocating the female doormat approach, it is interesting to observe that he commends the example of Sarah. In Genesis 21:9-13 we see Sarah's assertiveness and it is approved by God. But her assertiveness was Godward not selfish.

The word 'quiet' refers to an inner disposition of tranquillity. We have referred earlier to the fact that anxiety characterises the modern woman and suggested that this is related to the breakdown of traditional society. Quietness is linked to a holy trust and hope in God.

Her Responsibilities

The most comprehensive text to illustrate this point is Proverbs 31:10-31.

The woman commended as an example to others in Proverbs 31 is described as 'noble' or 'excellent'. The Hebrew word means 'force' or 'strength'. This woman needs to be strong physically, emotionally, intellectually and spiritually to cope with the demands of the many responsibilities she has.

The noble woman is capable of great responsibilities: management of and leadership in the home, economic activity, provision for the whole household and interior design. In addition to her responsibilities for her home and family, she extends her gifts to serve others in the community. She has a teaching role and has a reputation for being wise. She is appreciated and valued, not only by her husband and children but by the community.

What women certainly lack today is a sense of being valued. Feminists are rightly criticised for devaluing women who are home-based: for denigrating the option of motherhood as a career. But women who go out to work and manage their homes are criticised for working long hours to cope with both and for doing neither well. Women certainly can't win!

The Respect She Deserves

Our main text is again 1 Peter 3:7.

A discussion of the meaning of 'weaker partner' appears in the previous chapter. The point being made here is that a woman is worthy of respect and honour because of how God has made her, and particularly because of her vulnerability.

This verse attacks the 'Superwoman' model. Accepting certain limitations does not mean devaluing self. A woman should not be expected to do everything, nor should she expect it of herself. This verse makes it clear that it is up to the men to realise this.

Jesus' attitude to women was a radical break with the negative attitudes of his time. What is needed today is to recapture something of the dignity and value that he placed on the persons and service of women.

Concluding Remarks

God has dignified and honoured women above measure in the incarnation (Genesis 3:15). Any modern preoccupation with what a woman may not do in the church rather than what she may do as God's servant (Luke 1:38) is devaluing what God has honoured.

Men and women are different by design. Debate on this goes on but, as we have seen, the differences are evident in nature, as well as in function. Nowhere in Scripture does functional subordination negate spiritual equality, any more than it does in the operation of the three persons of the Trinity.

Men and women are different in essence and these essentials are fashioned in the image of God (Genesis 1:27). The determinants of male and female are written in our hearts (Romans 2:15) and worked out in the different but complementary roles that are laid out in the Scriptures. These have characterised every stable human society since the beginning of time.

Our western society is not stable. Like Hamlet we can say 'the time is out of joint'. Is evangelicalism taking up the gauntlet thrown down by the feminist movement to restore God's balance and so restore the foundations of society (1 Timothy 3:15)?

This can only be done as we wrestle with the theological and hermeneutical issues while maintaining the positive and vibrant role models of what it means to be a Christian man and a Christian woman.

In the nineteenth century, Catherine Beecher, whose sister Harriet wrote that provocative novel *Uncle Tom's Cabin*, founded a seminary to train women in the roles given to them in Titus 2:4-5. One of the aims of setting up this establishment was to honour such duties.

Is the content of our Bible College courses and our sermons on this issue only confined to the doctrinal challenge posed by feminism? Where distinctives are preached, are they preached positively? And who is engaged in the challenge of pursuing biblical femininity and its practical outworking in our postmodern culture? If there is a war to be won more thought and work needs to be directed to these areas.

Notes
1. Moir, A. and Jessel, D. Brain Sex: *The Real Difference Between Men And Women.* Mandarin, 1989, p. 190.
2. Clark, S. B. *Man And Woman In Christ.* Servant Books, 1980.
3. Kimura, D. *Sex Differences In The Brain* Scientific American 267:80-87, September 1992.
4. Ibid.
5. Restak, R., in Moir and Jessel, op. cit., p. 20.
6. Ibid.
7. Johnson, G. 'The Biological Basis For Gender-Specific Behaviour', in Piper, J. and Grudem, W. eds. *Recovering Biblical Manhood And Womanhood.* Crossway, 1991.
8. Tannen, D. *You Just Don't Understand - Men and Women In Conversation.* Virago Press, 1992.
9. Ibid.
10. Quoted in Stott, J. *Issues Facing Christianity Today.* Marshall Pickering, 1990, p. 272.
11. Moir and Jessel, op.cit.
12. Williams, J. H. *Psychology of Women.* 3rd Edition. Norton, 1987.
13. McCloughry, R. *Men And Masculinity.* Hodder & Stoughton, 1992.
14. Innes, S. *Making It Work.* Chatto & Windus, 1995.
15. Wolf, N. *The Beauty Myth.* Vintage, 1991
16. Ibid.
17. Williamson, M. *A Woman's Worth.* Rider, 1993.
18. Ibid.
19. Quoted in Harper, M. *Equal And Different.* Hodder and Stoughton, 1994, p. 126.
20. Kassian, M. *The Feminist Gospel.* Crossway, 1992.
21. Kassian, M. 'Barbie, GI Joe and Genesis', special issue of *The Gospel Witness,* Vol 73. No2 (2848), 5/5/1994.
22. Ibid.
23. Clark, S. B., op.cit.
24. Ibid.

25. Foh, S. T. *Women And The Word of God*. Presbyterian and Reformed, 1979.

26. Piper and Grudem, op.cit., Foreword, xxvi.

27. Ibid. p. 50.

28. Ibid. p. 306.

29. Ibid. p. 307.

30. Ibid. p. 394.

31. Lewis, C. S. in Hooper, W. ed. *Essays on Theology and Ethics*. Eerdmans, 1970.

32. van Leeuwen, M. S. *Gender And Grace*. IVP, 1990.

33. Woodrow, R. *Women's Adornment*. Ralph Woodrow Evangelistic Association Inc., 1991.

Chapter 12

Roles without relegation

Sharon James

Sharon has a Master's degree in history from Cambridge University and is a Master of Divinity graduate of Toronto Baptist Seminary. She has taught in secondary schools in the United Kingdom and Malawi and has written articles for a number of publications. Sharon is a mother of two children and is actively involved in Emmanuel Evangelical Church, Leamington Spa, England, where her husband Bill is pastor.

Roles without relegation

1. The contemporary challenge

For about nineteen hundred years a broad consensus in the Christian church accepted the biblical teaching of male headship in the family and in the church. In the twentieth century this has been challenged. It seems unreasonable that women should be relegated to positions of submission while leadership roles are reserved exclusively for men. In Christian circles a revolution has been taking place seeking to remedy the apparent injustice of gender distinctions.

Concerns about male domination and exploitation of women are understandable. Ever since the Fall the sinfulness of the human heart has distorted role relationships, and male headship has too often been expressed in sinful oppression (Genesis 3:16). Such injustice has been one of the main causes of the feminist movement.[1] The church has now been made to question whether differentiated roles inevitably lead to the relegation of women to second-class status.

Very broadly modern feminist thought has filtered down into popular thinking as follows:

i. Equality means sameness. Talk of different roles is discriminatory. Women should be able to do everything men can do. Men and women are essentially the same[2]; only the most basic biological differences divide them. Sexist stereotypes must be opposed.

ii. Difference in role relates directly to personal worth. Submission or subordination equals relegation.

iii. Women will only be 'empowered' when they have become the same as men: when they have filled the same jobs and reached the same status.

These assumptions are so much a part of our culture that they permeate the church also. Evangelical feminists have performed exegetical gymnastics to rewrite the biblical texts regarding headship and submission. Marriage must now be an equal partnership where each submits to the other. Women and men are equal in spiritual worth (true) and are therefore equally qualified to fulfill every ministry in the church (false).

It is a tragedy that such creative energy has been consumed in transforming the plain sense of the biblical evidence in order to conform to the world's demands. The church should have been standing firm to the realities of the situation, obvious to commonsense and clear in Scripture: men and women are fundamentally different. [3] They were created for different roles. The Equal Opportunities Commission spends three million pounds of taxpayers money each year primarily on promoting the idea that 'Apart from a few trifling differences of shape, males and females are essentially identical.'[4] An effective demolition job has been provided by the recent work *Brain Sex* by Anne Moir and David Jessel. Of this book one newspaper said, 'For the past 30 years we have been told that men and women are interchangeable in every way. Now a sensational book explodes the myth of sexual sameness.' This book is a celebration of difference. 'Many women have been brought up to believe that they should be "as good as the next man" and in the process they have endured acute and unnecessary pain, frustration and disappointment...some women feel that they have failed. But they have only failed to be like men.'[5] Deborah Tannen's work on the differences between the genders[6] has hit the best-selling lists because on a personal level relationships suffer when the assumption is made that men and women are the same and communicate and relate in the same way.

The failure of whole sections of the church seems all the more tragic when now we hear non-christian commentators saying what we should have been declaring all along: modern feminism is based on a lie. It has caused untold damage. The real victims of feminism are women.[7] Women have been told that they should be able to succeed at career and motherhood at the same time, and all too often have been burned out in the process. *A Lesser Life* by Sylvia Ann Hewlett is a powerful testimony of how a leading feminist felt utterly cheated when motherhood did not fit so easily into a highflying career as she had assumed.[8] Actually there has been a real backlash against feminism during the 1980s (a whole book by Susan Faludi has been devoted to this phenomenon)[9] yet the church continues to leap on the bandwaggon even as the wheels fall off.

2. The Biblical Vision of Complementarity

The term 'complementarity' expresses the truth that men and women while equal in status (Genesis 1:27; Galatians 3:28), have been created for different roles (Genesis 2:18; 1 Corinthians 11:3; Ephesians 5:22-24). Their differences complement each other. 'Picture the so-called weaknesses and strengths of men and women listed in two columns. If you could give numerical value to each one, the sum at the bottom of both columns is going to be the same. Whatever different minuses and pluses are on each side of masculinity and femininity [they] are going to balance out...God intends them to be the perfect complement of each other, so that...the weaknesses of manhood are not weaknesses and the weaknesses of womanhood are not weaknesses. They are the complements that draw forth different strengths in each other.'[10]

Different roles do not mean relegation, or loss of dignity, either in the Holy Trinity in the family or in the church. Rather our highest joy and dignity is in fulfilling the roles laid down for us by our Maker.

The biblical language of headship (eg. 1 Corinthians 11:3) and submission (eg. Colossians 3:18) is not accidental. It reflects a relationship between the sexes which was part of the original design for creation. In a massive work, Man and Woman in Christ, Stephen Clark develops the concept of complementarity. He shows that different roles for women and men in the church are not arbitrary, but they originate in 'God's purposes for the human race as expressed in his original creation.'[11]

The New Testament picture of the church is that of a body. 'Every member ministry' will mean all of the men and all of the women serving: a minority of men serving as elders, and the majority of men and the women serving in other capacities. An unbiblical exaltation of the 'clergy' (or 'professional' ministry) has sometimes led to the relegation of the 'laity' (men as well as women). So, in some churches, women have been denied the opportunity to engage in all manner of ministries which are in keeping with Scripture. This has rightly frustrated many Christian women. But throwing out role distinctions is not the answer: biblical complementarity is.

3. Homemaking and childrearing: a genuine ministry

The New Testament does not portray a situation in which the 'ministry' only takes place in the context of church 'programmes.' The great bulk of its exhortations concern everyday life; this is where real service occurs.

All Christians, both men and women, are to regard their employment as a 'calling' to be done as unto Christ. Women have been liberated from the assumption that 'all' they could do in life would be to stay at home and they are free to enter virtually all occupations. There are many areas of employment in which Christian women make an outstanding contribution. Women today spend a far shorter proportion of their life in childrearing, due to increased life expectancy and the availability of contraception. It is unrealistic to expect women to plan to make homemaking their lifelong career. Christian women (and men) in employment should be supported as they fulfil their callings and act as salt and light in society. But those who are not formally employed and who work in the home should also be supported. Increasingly women are losing the freedom to choose to spend part of their lives as fulltime mothers and to see that as their role with a respected status of its own. There is enormous pressure to be economically productive, for in our society status is measured by the pay cheque. In contrast, the Scripture accords great respect to the role of wife and mother.

Christian women with homemaking responsibilities have as high a calling as any other church member. What the New Testament says about this could not stand in sharper contrast with the propaganda of some in the feminist movement. 'The fundamental fact that...doomed women to domestic work and prevented her from taking part in the shaping of the world was her enslavement to the generative function...'[12] wrote Simone de Beauvoir. She believed that women should be liberated, forcibly if necessary from the subservient roles of wifehood and motherhood. For Betty Friedan, home was the 'comfortable concentration camp' in which women suffered a slow death of mind and spirit, housewives being by necessity 'nameless, depersonalised, manipulated...'[13] For Germaine Greer, the wife was a slave: 'If women are to effect a significant amelioration in their condition, it seems obvious that they must refuse to marry. No worker can be required to sign on for life...'[14] Despite later recantations by Friedan and Greer,[15] they and their like utterly discredited the idea that a woman could find her main fulfilment in life as a wife and mother. So pervasive has that message been that even Christian women find it necessary to apologise for staying at home. 'I'm only a housewife' is after all the ultimate admission of defeat. Or is it?

Titus is instructed to encourage the older women in the church to train the younger women 'to love their husbands and children, to be self-controlled and pure, to be busy at home, to be kind, and to be subject to their husbands, so that no-one will malign the word of God' (Titus 2:5). This being busy at home is nothing to do with being frantically houseproud. We glimpse something of how the Christian woman was to be 'busy at home' in 1 Timothy 5 'No widow can be put on the list of widows unless she...is well known for her good deeds, such as bringing up children, showing hospitality, washing the feet of the saints, helping those in trouble, and devoting herself to all kinds of good deeds...I counsel younger widows to marry, to have children, to manage their homes...'(1 Timothy 5:9-10,14).

In the Jewish culture of the day this would have been unsurprising. John MacArthur points out: 'The Jewish laws were clear: the woman's priority was in the home. She was to take care of the needs of her home, her children, her husband, strangers, the poor and needy, and guests. The wife who faithfully discharged her responsibilities was held in high regard in her family, in the synagogue and in the community.'[16]

Christians have a great opportunity to prove that homemaking and motherhood need not be the boring, mindless drudgery portrayed by many feminists. Mothers do not have to escape into another (often boring) paid job in order to find fulfilment and purpose. 76% of British Social Attitudes Survey respondents (1988) said they thought it best for mothers of under-fives to be at home all the time,[17] but over the past twenty or so years many mothers have been pushed out to paid work by economic pressure. The burden of taxation has increasingly been shifted onto married parents to the benefit of the single and the childless; the most heavily penalised are one-earner families with children.[18] Betty Friedan drew a picture of the bored and frustrated housewife of the 1950s but in the 1990s, we see stressed and exhausted women, rushing from job to creche to school to home. In a recent survey, 86% of British women in work complained that they 'never have enough time to get things done'[19] In an article tellingly entitled "Go Home, your job is wrecking you", it was stated: 'employers are realising that women cannot balance family and long hours at work...jobs were designed for full-time working men with full-time wives at home.'[20] Of course it is not just economic pressure which denies women the freedom to choose to be full-time mothers, it is also peer pressure to keep up a career. Moir and Jessel call it a tragedy that 'just at the moment when women are freest to enjoy and exploit their natural, superior, skills in motherhood, a stern sisterhood tells them that this is an unnecessary, low-value, and socially regressive role...'[21] With an increasing number of non-Christian writers advocating at least the choice of a return to fulltime motherhood, surely Christian women should be demonstrating that this can indeed be a high calling. Above all, there is the great privilege of bringing up the next generation with spiritual values. (Paul recognised the significant contribution of Lois and Eunice to the ministry of Timothy, 2 Timothy 1:5). As a calling, the aim is to glorify Christ. Yes, the home and family can become an idol and this should be resisted. The energetic compassion of the ideal wife of Proverbs 31 and of the godly women of 1 Timothy 5 point away from self-absorption.

Women who are not married may well be able to use their homes as a base for good works in keeping with the above passages. Indeed the

New Testament regards singleness as an opportunity for greater devotion to the Lord (1 Corinthians 7:32-35). A similar perspective may be brought to bear on childlessness (cf. Isaiah 56:3-4).

4. Evangelistic Ministries

When Paul speaks of his fellow labourers in Romans 16, and of his co-workers in the gospel in Philippians 4 (Euodia and Syntyche) he is speaking of women who worked alongside him in the task of spreading the gospel.[22] The New Testament assumption is that women and men work together in evangelistic ministries. There are suggestions that women in the early church were particularly concerned to reach other women. For example, Clement of Alexandria (c.150-215AD) comments: 'The Apostles, giving themselves without respite to the work of evangelism...took with them women, not as wives but as sisters, to share in their ministry to women living at home: by their agency the teaching of the Lord reached to the women's quarters without raising suspicion.'[23] The apocryphal work, The Acts of Paul, confirms this pattern: 'So Thecla went in with her and rested in her house for eight days, instructing her in the word of God, so that the majority of the maidservants also believed; and there was great joy in the house.'[24]

In the New Testament women were converted, served, witnessed and were persecuted alongside the men, but there were some who were especially gifted at the work of evangelism. Similarly today, all Christian women are to be involved in the work of evangelism in a general way while some will be particularly suited for specific ministries.

In the broad sense Christian women evangelise as they live as salt and light in the world. Women who are joyful, contented and fulfilled rather than complaining, covetous, and dissatisfied; women who are willing to serve, actively looking out for the needs of neighbours and the needy in the community; women who are 'focused' in the true sense of having purpose in life; women who refuse to waste time on the all-too-often poisonous trivia of TV or women's magazines; women who refrain from gossiping or backbiting; wives who are loyal to their husbands rather than running them down as part of a perpetual power struggle; mothers who are committed to their children but not so family-orientated that they are insensitive to the needs of others; employees who work cheerfully as for Christ: surely all such women are a shining testimony to the power of the gospel. Such lives mean that words of witness when spoken, tracts when given, books if lent, invitations when extended, may by the grace of God be effective as non-Christians see that 'it works!'

In the more specific sense, some women are particularly suitable for evangelistic ministries. There are numerous ways in which this gift can be used.

Door to door work is an essential means of presenting a friendly invitation to hear the gospel and visit the church. People often respond better to women than to men on the doors. At the very least a man-woman team is less threatening than two men knocking on the door and for safety reasons a man-woman team may be preferable to a two woman team. Alongside a friendly invitation and offer of literature, if there is any interest in spiritual things a one-to one Bible study can be suggested. If it is a woman who is interested it should be a woman who conducts these studies.

One-to-one Bible studies for seekers are an important way of answering questions and going through the basics of the gospel. This is increasingly necessary as many are ignorant of the very fundamentals of the Christian faith. Ideally there should be several women in the church who are competent and confident to do this important work with women seekers. Similarly these women should be able to conduct discipleship studies with new converts and lead one-to-one studies to prepare women for baptism. Such studies can take place in the context of a prayer-partnership; a valuable means of discipling young believers.

Many churches have found parent and toddler groups to serve a vital need, and numerous opportunities for evangelism can arise from these meetings such as morning Bible studies or evangelistic supper parties. Women can host evangelistic coffee mornings in the home and lead evangelistic Bible studies. Ideally there should be women gifted at speaking who can share the gospel on such occasions; it is a sad reflection of the lack of training, opportunities and encouragement for such women that men are very often called on to minister at such women's meetings for lack of practised and accomplished women speakers.

There are many other opportunities for evangelistic outreach: to seniors; to young people; children; hospitality to overseas students; outreach to ethnic minorities (here more than anywhere it will be women who must reach women).

The whole field of cross-cultural mission (in this country or overseas) opens up a vast range of possibilities. The opportunities are numerous and diverse: from directly evangelistic work, to translation, marking correspondence courses, support ministries such as medicine or administration etc. But female involvement in cross-cultural mission should take place in such a manner as to preserve the biblical principle of male headship in the family and the church. If, as has been argued in this symposium, women are excluded from authoritative leadership positions in the worshipping community, this must be applied whether at home or abroad.

Honesty demands that we admit that there is often a double standard, and that evangelical churches sometimes encourage women to engage in ministries abroad which they would prohibit at home. On the one hand this reflects the failure of conservative evangelical churches in this country to involve women in the variety of ministries which the New Testament demonstrates. There are few opportunities for women in recognised or full time Christian ministry in conservative evangelical churches 'at home.' There are many areas of diaconal and mission work which could well occupy numerous full time women workers in our churches, but many devoted and godly women have to go abroad to serve in a way which should be possible here. On the other hand the double standard also reflects the failure of conservative evangelical churches to be consistent. If a woman is performing authoritative eldership functions, as long as it is a few thousand miles away, few if any questions are asked. As in so many areas of modern evangelicalism, pragmatism rules. If women missionaries have been successful, then debate is disallowed. But surely there should be one, biblical standard for ministry. The office of elder (or its functional equivalent) is not open to a woman, but all other serving, witnessing, and evangelising ministries are open to both men and women, and this should apply at home and overseas.

5. Prayer Ministries

The truly great Christian women have been women of prayer. The glorious prayers of Hannah and Mary, for example, demonstrate an overwhelming concern for the glory of God, and the whole life of Anna was spent in prayer and fasting (1 Samuel 2:1-10; Luke 1:46-55; 2:36-38). The work of God is only spiritually effective when advanced by the Holy Spirit himself and we acknowledge this in prayer. The greatest ministry any of us can engage in is labouring in prayer for the gospel, and any fruitful activity will only flow from that. Certainly women are to engage in prayer in the church prayer meetings[25] and other occasions when there is open prayer. But a diligent private prayer ministry may be extended into the practice of praying together with other women on a regular basis, either in a prayer partnership or in a small group. In the past women's groups for support of missions (in prayer and practical ways) have been a feature of church life. Their decline may be indicative of a decline of enthusiasm for missions; revival of missionary passion may result in renewal of such groups. If there are Christian women with a similar concern to yours, whether it be a concern for the local school, concern to reach out to ethnic minorities in your area or concern for the homeless, why not meet regularly to pray specifically for that concern? The Lord may well then use you as part of the answer to those prayers by opening up some practical field of service.

An ever more fruitful ministry in prayer can be a positive accompaniment to increased physical weakness or immobility. The greatest in the Kingdom are not the most vigorous, energetic, active or vociforous. How much that is of lasting value has been achieved in answer to the secret prayers of godly women.

6. Teaching Ministries

There is a distinction between the authoritative teaching ministry to be exercised by elders only and the teaching of 'one another' that characterises an 'every member ministry' church (Colossians 3:16). Stephen Clark draws an enlightening contrast between the modern concept of teaching (transfer of information) with the Jewish/Early Christian concept which 'saw teaching as an activity involving personal direction and an exercise of authority. The teacher did not just give his views. He laid out what he expected the student to accept...teaching took place within a relationship in which the teacher had authority over the student...In other words, Scripture views teaching primarily as a governing function...'[26] Given this understanding, the authoritative teaching of the Word is entrusted to elders (1 Thessalonians 5:12; Hebrews 13:7,17; 1 Timothy 3:1-7; Titus 1:5-9).

Women were expected to participate in the worship of the early church, in that they could pray and prophesy (I Corinthians 11:5). The issue of prophecy cannot be explored here. There are strong arguments for the cessation of prophecy.[27] If these arguments are accepted then the closest equivalent of NT prophecy would be the reading of inspired Scripture, which non-elders (women and men) can do.

We do see women in the New Testament exercising teaching gifts. Priscilla and Aquila together explained the way of God more clearly to Apollos (Acts 18:26). This instruction took place in their home. There are many situations in which such teaching can take place, ranging from informal discussions in the context of hospitality to Bible study groups, marriage preparation sessions, and evangelistic studies. Often it will be appropriate for a husband-wife team to conduct such studies. Titus was commanded to teach the older women so that they would be qualified to teach the younger women. The content of such teaching is specified (Titus 2:5). This teaching will be by example and by informal encouragement. But it may also take place in the context of women's meetings or women's retreats. Today more than ever with the assault on the womanly virtues set out by Titus, it is imperative for churches to take on board the necessity of biblical teaching vis a vis manhood and womanhood.[28]

Some women are particularly gifted at teaching children and young people. Their gifts are used in Sunday Schools, Bible Clubs and other ministries. By real love, prayer, and concern for children, by God's grace they may be saved and used wonderfully in the Kingdom (2 Timothy 1:5). Christ's teaching and example (for example Matthew 18:5) forbids us to regard children's work as of secondary importance, or to take the teaching of children less seriously than any other teaching.

Mature women should be qualified and trained to engage in pastoral visiting where counselling is required for other women. If this is not possible then a husband-wife team visit is called for. Women do have a different capacity than men for empathy, sensitivity and understanding; such God-given qualities are sorely needed in a deeply hurting world.

For all of these ministries to take place more effectively there must be a serious effort to train those women who are gifted at teaching. In North America it is more common than here for Christian women to have at least one year of formal Bible schooling. There the responsibility of teaching Sunday School (often in the context of an all-age Bible school) is taken more seriously. Ideally there should be several women in the church with such training; a good grasp of doctrine is necessary to lead one-to-one or group studies. Even if full-time training is not an option, correspondence courses (or even better, study groups within the church context to provide encouragement and accountability) can be utilised to prepare both women and men to teach others. Any form of teaching from the Scripture should be regarded with the utmost seriousness. The Bible is abused when a passage is simply taken as a springboard for pious thoughts; it is abused if a group study degenerates into a sharing session of 'what this passage meant to me.' Women (and men) involved in teaching or leading studies should have at least some training in how to find out what a passage is actually saying and then how to open it up and apply it.

Women can also exercise their gifts through writing; many of the best loved hymns and songs are written by women, and so are many helpful Christian books. On a less formal level, a real ministry of encouragement can be pursued through letterwriting.

7. Serving Ministries

All Christians are called to a life of service, following in the footsteps of the Lord Jesus Christ who did not come to be served but to serve. The home is to be a focus of active and outgoing service and Christian women can be engaged in service as they go about their everyday duties. The Lord clearly lays out the criteria for acceptance into the Kingdom on the last day (Matthew 25:31-46). The qualifications are: feeding the hungry and providing drink for the thirsty; welcoming strangers and clothing the naked; visiting those who are sick and in prison.

The New Testament gives practical examples of ministries of mercy that are particularly appropriate for women. Jesus was accompanied by a group of women who supported him and his apostles out of their own means and cared for their needs (Luke 8:1-3; Mark 15:41). Tabitha (or Dorcas) was engaged in the good work of providing clothing for the poor (Acts 9:36-43). The characteristic lifestyle of the godly women described in 1 Timothy 5:10 involved being 'well known for good deeds, such as bringing up children, showing hospitality, washing the feet of the saints, helping those in trouble and devoting herself to all kinds of good deeds.' There is ample scope for women to engage in all manner of service ministries based from home, the local church, or in a para-church or mission organisation. Equally it is the case that women with particular gifts in the area of service to others may find that these gifts are utilised in certain areas of paid employment.

Such a myriad of opportunities are open that only a few may be listed: visiting and helping the elderly, lonely, or handicapped; hospital visitation; helping new mothers; counselling opportunities with an organisation like LIFE; involvement with CARE (eg. campaigning against pornography; writing to MPs and others on ethical/social issues; extending hospitality to the needy; getting involved with the local school); supporting an organisation such as Jubilee or Christian Solidarity International by writing letters on behalf of persecuted Christians, and publicising the plight of the oppressed for prayer and action. Setting up small prayer groups for specific needs or ministries can be a preliminary and an essential support in such action.

There are other areas of service within the local church too numerous to list exhaustively, but women may be used in music ministries, administration or church hospitality and their creativity may be exploited in ensuring tasteful and comfortable surroundings for the various activities of the church.

8. Should we reinstate a recognised Female Diaconate?

Comparatively few conservative evangelical churches recognise women deacons today. Why?[29]

In the New Testament there is an expectation that all Christians will serve others, yet there were those who were formally set aside for this practical and compassionate ministry. It is widely accepted that we see a foreshadowing of the diaconal role in Acts 6:1-6 where seven men were set aside to administer food distribution. The qualifications for deacons are set out in 1 Timothy 3:8-10; 12-14. There is no evidence that deacons were involved in 'governing' the church. The elders/overseers/bishops were those to whom the Christians were to submit (Hebrews 13:17).

The ministry carried out by men deacons involved the collection of money, food and other supplies, and the organisation of distribution. But the practicalities of this distribution seems to have been carried out by women, such as Tabitha and her circle of widows (Acts 9:39), and the widows of 1 Timothy 5:3-16.

The passage on the appointment of deacons contains the sentence: 'Likewise the women are to be worthy of respect, not malicious talkers, but temperate and trustworthy in everything' (1 Timothy 3:11 - author's translation). It makes most sense to take this as referring to women deacons; the qualifications are parallel to those for the men deacons.[30] The reference to Phoebe as a 'servant' or 'deacon' (same word) in Romans 16:1, though not in itself conclusive, points in the same direction.[31] So Haldane comments: 'As deacons were appointed to attend to the poor, so deaconesses were specially set apart in the churches in order to attend to the wants of their own sex.'[32]

There is very clear evidence that the early church did appoint female deacons and widows for practical ministries and intercession.[33] To summarise this evidence: during the New Testament period women appear to have fulfilled the function of deacons, and many believe it to be significant that Phoebe was named as a deacon. At Ephesus there was a list of widows who not only received alms but were expected to practice prayer and good deeds (1 Timothy 5:5,10).

During the second century there is ecclesiastical evidence for positive duties performed by appointed widows (Polycarp, Bishop of Smyrna) and secular evidence for a group of women called deaconesses (Pliny, Governor of Bithynia). During the third century there was a formalising of the functions of widows and deaconesses. The church at Carthage followed detailed instructions for the appointment of widows, while the church at Rome formally named them for a ministry of prayer. At Alexandria the widows were listed as a distinct category with other clergy; their function was visiting the sick, prayer, and good works. Widows performed similar functions in the church in Syria.

By the mid third century in Syria the deaconesses were a distinct and honoured group with a pastoral and practical ministry to other women. In the following century there are many more references to deaconesses in the Eastern churches. However, the growing emphasis on a formal liturgy and on the authority of 'bishops' meant a shift in the function of the diaconate. Instead of being a service ministry devoted to ministries of mercy, the deacon was seen as a 'priest in training' and was involved more and more in liturgical functions. The New Testament emphasis was forgotten and so the appointment of deaconesses and widows died out. This quickly led to the situation, which still pertains in the modern Anglican church, where being a deacon is simply a stepping stone to becoming a 'priest'.

The Reformation saw something of a revival of the true concept of diaconal service. Calvin defined the diaconate as 'a permanent ecclesiastical ministry of care for the poor and sick, the ministry of the church as a body to the physical suffering of human beings.'[34] He envisaged a two-tier diaconal system, of men deacons collecting benevolence and women deacons (such as the widows of 1 Timothy 5:9-10) distributing benevolence.[35] Since then there have been a few notable examples of a diaconate devoted to good works. Chalmers in Scotland was famous for his comprehensive diaconal coverage of his parish. More recently the Lutherans and the American

Methodists have had outstanding female diaconates.[36]

In non-conformist churches today it seems rare to find a diaconate functioning primarily for the relief of the poor and needy. In many churches the diaconate functions as part of the church government. Even where there is the more biblical situation of a plurality of elders fulfilling the functions of church government, the diaconate functions primarily for the upkeep of church building and other non-benevolent, albeit practical, tasks. Often elders and deacons together are regarded as being part of the church government and that sits uneasily with the appointment of women deacons.

If there were to be a revival of the true concept of diaconia, and a corresponding reformation in practice, then it seems likely that there would be a return to the New Testament and early church practice of actively involving women in such a diaconate. This is a matter of urgency. It is urgent that we open our eyes and our hearts to the poor and needy of our contemporary society: the socially estranged, alcoholics, drug abusers, prostitutes, abused children and women, homeless teenagers, prisoners. At a personal level we may, like the Samaritan, be presented with individual cases of immediate need. But surely as evangelical churches we should be more proactive than that and be going out to those who are suffering. A well-functioning male and female diaconate may be used by God to give leadership in this fundamental area.

9. Conclusion
The teaching of Paul concerning the body could not be clearer. Each member is to play its part without grumbling and comparing itself with others. The Bible has a most high and exalted view of woman, but her dignity does not lie in grasping the role of headship. If she truly desires to glorify God, she will not listen to those who equate submission with relegation but will go back to Scripture. There we see women joyfully, energetically, willingly serving Christ to the utmost. They are labourers for the gospel, servants of the gospel, martyrs for the gospel. Then as now the fields are white to harvest. There is no shortage of avenues of service for Christian women; there is more than enough work to be

done. As the Danvers Statement so eloquently expresses it: 'With half the world's population outside the reach of indigenous evangelism; with countless other lost people in those societies that have heard the gospel; with the stresses and miseries of sickness, malnutrition, homelessness, illiteracy, ignorance, aging, addiction, crime, incarceration, neuroses, and loneliness, no man or woman who feels a passion from God to make His grace known in word and deed need ever live without a fulfilling ministry for the glory of Christ and the good of this fallen world.'[37] But God's work is to be done in God's way. God himself has designed us for different roles and set out these roles in his word. There is no relegation in obeying our Lord.

Notes

1. Since the 1960s one can trace a number of different streams within feminism, eg. liberal feminism, marxist feminism etc., the latest trend being 'power' feminism as opposed to 'victim' feminism (cf. Naomi Wolf, *Fire with Fire*). Perhaps the most telling divergence is between the 'sameness' feminism of the 1960s and the 'difference' feminism emerging from the emphases of women's studies courses from the 1970s onwards. However despite all the inner contradictions and tensions within the movement there is a broad consensus that women need to be liberated from patriarchy and all its implications. I would argue that modern feminism is incompatible with biblical Christianity and is to be strongly opposed. For an excellent critique of feminism see Mary A. Kassian, *The Feminist Gospel*, Crossway Books, 1992.

2. This was the thrust of feminist writing in the sixties, cf. Germaine Greer, *The Female Eunuch*, or Kate Millet, *Sexual Politics*. Feminist thought in the 1970s to 1980s acknowledged the differences between male and female, and exalted the feminine characteristics of non-aggression etc, cf. Elizabeth Gould Davis, *The First Sex*. But it is the (academically discredited) dogmas of the earlier stage which are being pushed, eg. by the Equal Opportunities Commission. These assumptions lie behind the UN Convention on the elimination of discrimination against Women, ratified by our Government without debate in 1986.

3. Arianna Stassinopoulos, *The Female Woman,* is a sustained attack on feminism on common sense grounds. David Poynter, 1973.

4. Joanna Bogle, 'The Equal Opportunities Commission', in *Feminism v. Mankind,* Family Publications, 1990, p.25.

5. Anne Moir and David Jessel, *BrainSex,* Mandarin Paperbacks, 1991, p.4.

6. Deborah Tannen, *You Just Don't Understand: Men and Women in Conversation,* Virago Press, 1992.

7. For example see three books published by the IEA Health and Welfare Unit.

Ed. Caroline Quest, *Equal Opportunities: A Feminist Fallacy,* 1992.

Ed. Caroline Quest, *Liberating Women . . . From Modern Feminism,* 1994.

Patricia Morgan, *Farewell to the Family,* 1995.

There have been a number of effective 'secular' critiques of feminism, eg. Arianna Stassinopoulos, *The Female Woman,* Davis Poynter, 1973: Nicholas Davidson, *The Failure of Feminism,* Prometheus Books, 1988. See also a symposium *Feminism v. Mankind,* Family Publications, 1990.

8. Sylvia Ann Hewlett, *A Lesser Life: The Myth of Women's Liberation in America.* Warner Books, 1986.

9. Susan Faludi, *Backlash: The Undeclared War against Women,* Vintage, 1992.

10. J. Piper and W. Grudem ed. *Recovering Biblical Manhood and Womanhood: A Response to Evangelical Feminism,* Crossway Books, 1991, p.49.

11. Stephen Clark, *Man and Woman in Christ,* Servant Books, 1980, p.211.

10. J. Piper and W. Grudem ed. *Recovering Biblical Manhood and Womanhood: A Response to Evangelical Feminism,* Crossway Books, 1991, p.49.

11. Stephen Clark, *Man and Woman in Christ,* Servant Books, 1980, p.211.

12. Simone De Beauvoir, *The Second Sex,* Picador, 1988, p.148.

13. Betty Friedan, *The Feminist Mystique,* Penguin, 1992, p.268.

14. Germaine Greer, *The Female Eunuch*, Paladin, 1973, p.319.

15. Betty Friedan, *The Second Stage*, Michael Joseph, 1982.
Germaine Greer, *Sex as Destiny*, Secker & Warburg, 1984.

16. John MacArthur, jr., *Different by Design*, Victor Books, 1994, p.71.

17. Patricia Morgan, *Farewell to the Family*, IEA Health and Welfare Unit, 1995, p.67.

18. Patricia Morgan, *Farewell to the Family*, IEA Health and Welfare Unit, 1995.

19. *The Time Squeeze* a report by Demos, the independent research group. The Times, 6 June, 1995.

20. Mary Ann Sieghart, The Times 28 September 1995.

21. A. Moir and D. Jessel, *BrainSex*, Mandarin, 1991, p.147.

22. He was not speaking of the office of the Evangelist (Ephesians 4:11). We only have one man in the N.T. named as an evangelist: Philip (Acts 21:8).

23. quoted in S. Clark, *Man and Woman In Christ*, Servant Books, 1980, p.116.

24. quoted in S. Clark, *Man and Woman In Christ*, Servant Books, 1980, p.116.

25. 1 Timothy 2:8 is an indication that public prayer in the worship services is to be led by the male leaders of the church, most probably the elders. See J. MacArthur jr., *Different By Design*, p.112.

26. Stephen Clark, *Man and Woman in Christ*, Servant Books, p.196.

27. For example, O. Palmer Robertson, *The Final Word*, Banner of Truth, 1993, and Richard B. Gaffin, *Perspectives on Pentecost*, P&R, 1979.

28. For example, men's and women's meetings could conduct a series of studies on the key Biblical texts, using MacArthur's *Different By Design* as the recommended text with Piper/Grudem and Clark as the main resources for the leaders.

29. K. Walker, "A Diaconal Role for Women", in *The Ministry of Women*, BEC Study Conference 1995. This is a good discussion of this issue, and points out that there is no rigid distinction between practical and pastoral ministry. For example a visit to a sick person may involve

practical aid but it will also include encouragement and prayer.

30. The NIV translates 'γυναικας' as 'their wives', but if Paul had meant their wives the way to make this clear would have been to include 'αὐτων.' The word 'ὡσαυτως' is used in Greek to introduce the second or third in a series, the series here being church officials. *(The Expositor's Greek New Testament, ed. W. Robertson Nicoll, Eerdmans, IV, p.116).* This word 'would support the contention that a new class is introduced analogous to the preceding order of deacons.' (Donald Guthrie, *The Pastoral Epistles*, IVP, 1957, p.85). Those who favour the translation 'likewise women' (ie. who performed the function of deaconesses) include Chrystosom, Theodoret, Theodore of Mopuestia, Clement of Alexandria, and more recently, Meyer, Danielou, Gryson, Bruce, Lock and Lenski. Those who interpret this verse as referring to some women who performed deaconing functions, yet who hesitate to allow that women would have been given the title deacon, include Ryrie, Guthrie, and Fairbairn.

31. Those who argue that Phoebe served as a deacon in the official sense (as in 1 Timothy 3:8-13) include Lightfoot, Haldane, Hodge, Morris, Lenski, Cranfield, Gryson, Bruce, Hendriksen, and in earlier times Chrysotom, Origen, and Theodoret of Cyprus.

32. R. Haldane, *An Exposition of the Epistle to the Romans,* Evangelical Press, 1958, p.633.

33. J. Danielou, *The Ministry of Women in the Early Church,* Faith Press, 1961.

J.G.Davies, "Deacons, Deaconesses and the Minor Orders in the Patristic Period", Journal of Ecclesiastical History, XIV, 1963.

C.C. Ryrie, *The Role of Women in the Church,* Moody Press, 1958.

These writers document the evidence from such as Polycarp, Ignatius of Antioch, Pliny the Younger, Tertullian, Cyprian, Hippolytus, Clement of Alexandria, Origen and the Didascalia Apostolorum (a Syrian church order dating from the mid 3rd century).

34. E.A. McKee, *Diakonia in the Classical Reformed Tradition and Today,* Eerdmans, 1989, p.64.

35. J. Calvin, *Institutes of the Christian Religion,* ed. J.T. McNeill, tr.

F.L. Battles, Westminster, 1960, vol. 2, p.1061.

36. C. De Swarte Gifford, *The American Deaconess Movement*, Garland Publishing, 1987.

37. J. Piper and W. Grudem, *Recovering Biblical Manhood and Womanhood*, Crossway Books, p.59.

General Index

General Index

Scripture Index